Vineyard
Gazette

Reader

Vineyard Gazette

Reader

❧

An Anthology of the Best of
The Island Newspaper
1970-1995

Edited by Richard Reston and Tom Dunlop

Vineyard Gazette, Inc.
Post Office Box 66
34 South Summer Street
Edgartown, MA 02539

Library of Congress Catalog Card Number: 96-60129

Vineyard Gazette Reader
An Anthology of the Best of the Island Newspaper 1970-1995
Editors: Richard Reston and Tom Dunlop

ISBN 0-9651023-0-0

Manufactured in the United States of America

First Edition

10 9 8 7 6 5 4 3 2 1

❧

Illustrations by Steve Durkee

In memory of James "Scotty" Reston
1909-1995

For the staff of the Vineyard Gazette
Past, present and future

Contents

SEA AND SKY

LAND

INHABITANTS

NATURE

FAME

ISLAND

Foreword

THE CONVERSATION GOING ON in the back of the old newsroom of the Vineyard Gazette was about Shakespeare and newspapers, small towns and country journalism, big cities and bogus headlines. A columnist, long retired from mainland dailies but still writing for the Gazette, was talking to a couple of young reporters about style and the importance of a good community newspaper. I remember thinking how unusual, how different this conversation was from any in my experience in some of the world's big city newsrooms. I don't remember where Shakespeare fit in on that afternoon. But I'm sure the playwright was used for good purpose in that talk about the craft of journalism. Somehow it seemed comfortable and appropriate and not at all out of place for the little newsroom at the Vineyard Gazette.

The moment lingers in memory, perhaps because it was my first day at the newspaper. I had come to Martha's Vineyard to take over as editor of the Gazette, to begin a new career in community journalism after many years on The Los Angeles Times, a time spent wandering the world on tours of duty in Washington and abroad. Jody, my wife and fellow newspaper publisher, and I were asked often in those early years if we intended to stay on the Vineyard and on the Gazette for any length of time. I don't think even we knew the answer then, and we sometimes wondered if the lure of great news events, international capitals and daily journalism would draw us back to the world we lived and worked in before our arrival in this extraordinary Island community.

Now the Vineyard Gazette celebrates its 150th anniversary, a century and a half of unbroken publication since the weekly was founded as the Island newspaper of record in 1846. The publishing of this book, Vineyard Gazette Reader, an anthology of some of the best of the Gazette over the past quarter century, is a part of the anniversary celebration. The last and only other Gazette Reader came out roughly 25 years ago. Looking back I suddenly realize I have been editing the Vineyard Gazette for more than 20 of the 25 years covered in this book; it was nearly 30 years ago that my family bought the newspaper.

It's been a long time since that first newsroom brush with Shakespeare. And those early thoughts about returning to the hurried and impersonal life of daily newspapers seem so distant now. It soon became apparent that the running of this remarkable old community newspaper and the recording of the character and special quality of Island life would take all our attention and energy.

Nothing has been more rewarding in the past two decades or more than the privilege of working with so many wonderful and talented friends and colleagues, young reporters in early stages of their careers, editors, columnists, town correspondents, outside contributors, photographers and all the others who print, produce and help support the business side of a small community newspaper. It is their work that makes this new Vineyard Gazette Reader possible.

The staffs of the Gazette may have changed through the years but their commitment to journalistic excellence did not. They work hard to capture the spirit and identity of the Island. It is this strong sense of place that sets the Gazette coverage apart from most other mainland community newspapers. Over the quarter century framed by this book the Vineyard has grown as has the newspaper. In 1970 the average yearly circulation of the Vineyard Gazette was less than 7,000; today that figure approaches 14,000.

The new Vineyard Gazette Reader is not meant to provide a history of the last 25 years, a time of rapid growth and great change on the Island. Instead the book speaks to the rhythms of Vineyard life, to those qualities that make an Island community distinctly different from life on the mainland. All the news stories, features, profiles, columns and editorials that appear in these chapters have been published in the Gazette. The newspaper material has been edited for purposes of book publication.

Readers will find in chapters to come an effort to touch certain themes and influences central to Island life. The Gazette is but a reflection of the Vineyard community, from the beauty of its physical landscape to the diversity of its human environment.

The book plays across the majesty of the sea around us, along the ocean boundary that forms the never-ending shoreline unique to islands. We will take readers to the Vineyard countryside, to the land and the environmental battles to protect this place against outside development pressures that would turn the Island into just one more ordinary stop along the way. The voice of Island inhabitants past and present is heard and the importance of the natural world so precious to the quality of Vineyard life is recognized. The price of fame is of growing concern to Martha's Vineyard and, finally, the book addresses the theme of why the life of this Island seems so different to so many.

Readers of the book also will learn much about the voice of the Vineyard Gazette, about the newspaper's deep commitment to the Island community it has served without interruption for the last 150 years.

Lastly, I wish to acknowledge and thank certain people on the newspaper staff for their key roles in the publishing of the new Vineyard Gazette Reader. Without them the idea of another Gazette Reader would have been unthinkable.

Eulalie Regan directed the main research effort. She assembled the newspaper record of the last 25 years and assisted with thoughtful editorial advice and judgment about final selections in the book. Mrs. Regan, for years the newspaper's librarian and historical columnist, is responsible for creation of the modern Gazette library, now a resource of supreme importance not only to the paper but to the Island public at large. The foundation for this book rests on that library and her work as the valued keeper of the Vineyard public record.

To Tom Dunlop, my friend, colleague and co-editor on the book, I extend gratitude for a job well done. His wise counsel and commitment to this project were crucial to the shape of the book, to the final selecting and editing of the anthology. Mr. Dunlop wrote the introductions to each chapter.

Jody Reston, co-publisher and general manager of the Vineyard Gazette, coordinated the entire book project. It was her leadership and belief in the book that from the start kept everything and everyone together.

Appreciation goes to Steve Durkee for illustrations and Steven Burton for typesetting the Gazette Reader.

And finally I thank Alison Shaw, my longtime friend and colleague on the Gazette, for lending her many talents to the graphic layout of the Vineyard Gazette Reader and to the photographic art and design of its cover.

Richard Reston
Editor and Publisher
Vineyard Gazette
May 1996

SEA AND SKY

❧

I N THE FIRST ISSUE of the Vineyard Gazette on May 14, 1846, Edgar Marchant, the publisher, introduced the paper to his readers, and defined its purpose, without using the word Island once.

This was not conceit. He made no mention of the water either. To Marchant and the men and women of his time, Martha's Vineyard was an entity whose borders ranged out as far as the farthest whaler or boldest fisherman sailed. The Vineyard reached up and away from where they stood, an admixture of earth and ocean and atmosphere, of harvests and fishing stocks and weather that each year boiled down either to bounty or deprivation.

It was a continent sufficient unto itself, an Island only if you looked at it from the mainland. Vineyarders rarely did. They assumed that the way they toiled and what they saw when they looked beyond the shore would simply always be.

And so throughout the length of his two separate terms as editor, and of several editorships that followed his, the Gazette never recorded what life was like aboard a schooner out fishing on Georges Bank. No writer was there when the Splendid tied up at Osborn's Wharf in Edgartown and the whaling men came down the plank after an odyssey of three years to the far side of the world. No witness described the blackness of the sky, the gray sizzling murk of snow and ice, or the wail of wind and humanity when a winter hurricane drove brigs and packets onto the beaches of the North Shore or clean through Steamboat Wharf in Vineyard Haven.

The Gazette only began to acquire a recognizable sense of its Island spirit with the editorship of Elizabeth Bowie and Henry Beetle Hough, mainlanders both, who set out after 1920 to tell their readers week by week something of the sea and sky around them. Hough, a devotee of Thoreau, wrote of the taste in the air when a spring wind blew down from the hilltops, of the gurgle and muck on the flats when the tide was at lowest ebb, of the soaring blue overhead as one hiked the plains of Katama, picnic basket on the arm. This sort of writing entranced a mainland readership, increasingly large, that knew and loved the Vineyard as an Island first and last, and wanted to know what it was like when they were not here.

More fancifully, but with the same attention to detail, Joseph Chase Allen, a Chilmarker whose forefathers were all Island men, began to tell the stories of fishermen who were venturing out to Nantucket Shoals, Georges Bank and beyond. He wrote how in hot spells the fish sometimes fell from the nets pre-cooked, how the wild wind often tore the whiskers from a codfisher's face and left him with a permanent larboard list. The whaling masters and the gaff-riggers of his youth were vanishing when his column, With the Fishermen, got underway in the spring of 1925. For 50 years Mr. Allen preserved the old stories, idioms and know-how in prose and poetry that so often began, "If this was sixty years ago...."

Today the Gazette remains dedicated to the preservation of the coastal traditions. Here you will find selections from the modern era about topsail schooners and scallopers battling a northeast storm for their livelihood, about the bold but whimsical way the elements sometimes decide to rearrange a couple of million tons of sand on a beach or ocean floor.

But the modern era finds, too, that a third of Georges Bank and a huge area beyond Nantucket Shoals once thick with yellowtail are closed to commercial fishing, unthinkable even in the first few years covered by this book. Pollution remains a threat above and beyond the endless shoreline. These new tempests advance upon the Island from every point on the compass, and the Gazette records them all. We may no longer assume that the way we toil and what we see when we look beyond the shore will simply always be.

– T.D.

     ❧   ❧   ❧

When the Sun Rises and Cockerel Crows Things Begin to Happen
By William A. Caldwell

THIS HAPPENED ONLY AN HOUR OR SO AGO, and at first I decided no use trying to tell anybody about it and brewed myself a pot of tea, but now I sense a compulsion to write it all down before the memory of the only witness leaches out.

It is something like the compulsion that made Luke sit down

and gnaw his pen and begin, "Forasmuch…" and it is why Hamlet came back muttering, "My tablet — meet it is I set it down."

At any rate, in the hour or so between dawn and sunrise this morning I was wandering around in the yard doing chores — running the flag up the pole, picking long stiff basil blossoms for a vinegar we're inventing, sponging the dew off the chaises on the deck, and suchlike boondoggling when I noticed a ghostly shadow behind me. It was my shadow. This must have been a little after 6 a.m., half an hour or so before there'd be any Sun in the sky, and the Moon was, of course, away off on the other side of the house.

Well, a long bar of cloud was lying just above the eastern horizon, and the Sun, still below the rim of the Earth, was shining on the cloud's underside, and the reflection was what threw that vague shadow. End explanation, but now I'm afraid I shall have to afflict you with more information about the next five minutes than you really need.

Just then a rooster crowed, in a farmyard I know is some two miles deep across the Chappaquiddick outwash and, as happens in Peer Gynt and Coq d' Or and somewhere I think in Homer, when the cockerel crows things begin to happen.

To the east our horizon ranges unbroken from pole to pole — those toy dunes and scrub forests and moors on Chappaquiddick rise only a matter of feet or inches above the edge of the sea — and suddenly this whole immense sky was ablaze. I tried to take down a catalogue of the colors, but it was a disappointment, even as I did it; they were, as you'd expect, old rose and purple, gold, Williamsburg green, azure, gray with a streak of brown fog out beyond Nantucket, black, white, pink, deep fireplace-ember, orange-red, ice-blue, ivory, scarlet.… But it doesn't convey any more than taking down the notation conveys what happens in the B Minor Mass or the gigantic discord in Don Giovanni when the statue comes to life. The overwhelming size of the thing, the terrifying extravagance of the totality — and then abruptly gigantic shafts of dead-black shadow radiated across the whole sky from the point at which the Sun was just about to rise. Like the spokes of a wheel I'd say, except that the metaphor would diminish the reality, as if you were to say Niagara Falls is like a splash of soda in your bourbon only, you know, man, um, well, like bigger.

I was about to get Dorothy out of bed and run across the road to the Webers' and haul them out, but suddenly there was with the angels a heavenly host, first nine great white swans, then a multitude of Canada geese, flying in single file low over their reflection in the pewter water of the slack tide and praising God in their own Scottie-dog tongue. There is something so damned gallant about these birds in flight, and about the herons I now saw standing on the clam flats as austere and patient as an ibis on an obelisk, that I stood paralyzed for a moment too long.

In the next instant the Sun had risen, or the Earth had turned, rather, enough so that the bar of cloud came between it and the atmosphere on which all this melodrama had been screened. All the lights went out except a wash of watery magenta on the southeast quadrant, and I was glad I hadn't gone to summon witnesses, because now they'd look at the sky then back at me, and they'd grunt, as grandma Caldwell did to Pa when he called her attention to a like miracle, "Yup, yup, Sun's comin' up." I have no proof, but I saw it, and again I think I know how those poor stammering Christians felt after the light had gone out and they tried to tell how it was and people said yup, yup.

Now I guess I'll go downstairs and brew me another pot of tea. In all the excitement of testifying I seem to have forgotten the first one, and by this time it must be cold and bitter enough to melt the teeth out of an iron dog. Nothing else new except canning jellies and jams and relishes and hunting the last of the beach plums, which are so scarce this year the Moms running the roadstands are getting $1.25 per small glass of jelly.

– October 13, 1972

Shenandoah: A Living Symbol
Of Our Seagoing Heritage

By George W. Adams

WHO DOES NOT THRILL TO SEE SHENANDOAH come clear of West Chop, a smoky sou'wester behind her and a flood tide beneath?

At the can she hardens up for the passage into the harbor, her yards braced tight against the leeward shrouds. Her flags straighten out in the West Chop williwaw; she heels a few more degrees, like a runner crouching at the start, then accelerates in the flat water till the spray fairly flies from her stem.

A figure scrambles up the starboard shrouds to the futtocks, up and over to the topmast shrouds, then disappears 85 feet aloft in the tangle of rigging alongside the topmast. The weather leech of the 'gansa'l goes soft; the sail flogs for a few moments as the yard drops into its lifts, then quiets as invisible buntlines and leechlines gather it into a still mass at the center of the yard.

The billowing foretopsail is tamed in the same manner, and the entranced eye is freed to look aft where the corners of the gaff topsail are giving two last wild shakes before being subdued behind the mainmast doubling.

The schooner stands up a little, and imperceptibly slows. The taut luff of the outer jib turns to scallops and the sail tumbles down to the jib boom; then the inner, then staysail. She heads up, almost bare now, but still coasting so fast the crowd of little craft trying to catch a closer view are left in her bubbling wake. The foresail, then the mainsail, drop slowly onto their booms. Majestically, the queen passes the breakwater and takes her throne in the inner harbor.

If modern-day scepticism has frozen the adult heart, is there any man who is not at least reminded of childhood dreams — call them foolish — of a scene like that? Shenandoah is in part a dream, but she is more than that. To her passengers she is a Wellsian machine which expands the present moment to include a hundred years of history. To her crew she is mother and child, home, job, way of life, and glory.

To the Island, she is decoration for sign, bank note, and the dominant living room wall; the refined essence of our nautical past and a simple tourist attraction; a paradigm of the seamen's skills and a symbol of Quixotic folly. And a dream.

Those who cry "quixotic" have blinded themselves to the facts. Shenandoah is no windmill monster. Since 1964 when she was built, not a summer week has passed with her idle. She has but 10 or 12 weeks of the year in which to earn her keep, but she does it, carrying her load of 29 passengers from Monday morning to Saturday afternoon, plying the waters bounded on the east by Nantucket, and on the west by Long Island Sound.

By day in a stiff quartering breeze she may be sifting at 12.5 knots with everything set, or she may be making a meager two knots or so with her yawl boat shoving on a flat day. But every night as dusk settles her passengers gather on deck under the kerosene lamps, happy after a handsomely spread dinner, ready to explore another port which to them, usually, is another mysterious name: Nantucket, Tarpaulin Cove, Padanaram, Newport, or Mystic.

She is owned by Capt. Robert S. Douglas of Vineyard Haven. He designed her, he oversaw her building at the Harvey Gamage yard in Maine, and he sails as captain every day she is underway.

As he explains it, she took her form in a logical way. The only economic base for a sailing vessel nowadays is the passenger business. The economics of the trade pretty largely define her size: under 100 gross tons, but big enough to carry about 30 passengers. The details, says Captain Douglas, wind up being "something pretty close to a picture you have had in the back of your mind for a long time."

He started sketching in 1957, while he served the last year

of a hitch in the Air Force as an all-weather interceptor pilot. During the next couple of years, he gradually settled on a hull form similar to that of an old revenue cutter named the Joe Lane. The topsail schooner rig is easy to handle, adequately weatherly, and offers the advantages of square sails that fore-and-aft-only sailors haven't dreamed of.

Her grace of form is no more describable than the question, "Why a sailing vessel?" is answerable. You can speak of the proportions of her rig, the sweep of her sheer, the balance of her rounded counter and her clipper bow. But then you can speak, as Captain Douglas does (when pressed), of giving today's youth something he wished he had when he was young, of keeping alive skills and tradition and knowledge that were close to starvation by lack of interest or a hundred other reasons.

– August 6, 1976

✄   ✄   ✄

Skiff's Island Performs Its Appearing Act

By George W. Adams

SKIFF'S ISLAND, the Vineyard's irresolute Atlantis, appears to be making an effort toward reestablishing its proper claim to the "island" in its name.

For the past two weeks, the capricious spit of sand has been standing boldly above the highest tides, plainly visible from Wasque even in breaking seas. But interpretation of its reappearance should be cautious — just three years ago it rose from the surrounding shoals for a few weeks, just long enough to stir speculation that it might offer a solution to increased crowding here, only to quickly dampen those new hopes as it descended once more.

The on-again-off-again island has made itself so scarce of late that in 1966 the government revoked its rights to a place on nautical charts, giving rise to a yacht club protest filed by William G. Saltonstall against several boats for "having gone around a nonexistent island on the wrong side." The Edgartown Yacht Club ocean race circular then required yachts to leave Skiff's Island to starboard.

Some 40 years ago the island rose so substantially above the sea that beach grass took root and the state department of conservation was tempted to take a census of the tern population there. Shortly afterwards it again subsided. It has reappeared several times for short periods. In early February 1940, Phil Demarias of Oak Bluffs landed a light plane there with his passenger, Rep. Joseph A. Sylvia. They were attracted by the large numbers of seals there. Landing was easy, but the two men discovered to their dismay that the airplane's wheels sank so deep into the soft sand that takeoff was impossible.

As darkness came on, their situation appeared desperate. Finally, they made good their escape by rolling the plane to the edge of the water where the winter's broken ice proved substantial enough to support the plane for its takeoff roll.

During the past century, the island took on such proportions, it is said, that some enterprising capitalists settled on the spot as a site for a hotel. Tradition says they somehow acquired firm legal title to the spot, but their title proved more firm than their property which had disappeared when they returned from their lawyers' offices to start construction.

During this century the island formed a crescent-shaped harbor on one side, but local fishermen never dared anchor there lest the whimsical pile of sand suddenly choose to close its two arms around their vessels.

– April 9, 1976

Color Christmas Black Out at Fishing Rip

By Richard Reston

BELOW, THE SILENT GLIDE OF A LONE GULL ended in a sharp dip toward the water.

Behind, the shores of the Vineyard faded. To the left, the coastline of Nantucket loomed.

Ahead, the twisted and broken hulk of the Argo Merchant lay black and soiled, a grim reminder that all was not well in this area on Christmas Eve, 1976.

Her oil slick reached out as far as the eye could see. It was, even in the final death throes of the tanker, licking at Georges Bank, the world's richest fishing ground.

From the Vineyard by air, the scene of the disaster, perhaps the worst ecological tragedy in the history of American waters, is only a short hop. The plane heads 135 degrees east southeast and 20 minutes later — 50 nautical miles away — the disaster unfolds for all those who wish to observe.

As the saga of this already accident-prone tanker wore on deep into Christmas week, the story only grew sadder. Periodic flights into the area showed that the end was at hand even at the beginning of the crisis.

On Sunday, the plane carrying Gazette reporters and photographers dropped from 1,800 feet to 250 feet for a closer look at the tanker which was still intact. More than a million and a half gallons of oil already had spilled into the sea but the rest of the cargo still remained aboard.

Seas were dark blue and restless. A single, helpless Coast Guard cutter stood by and radioed the plane to use its own discretion while overflying the area.

Coast Guard helicopters began to land personnel and equipment. "Have a Merry" was scrawled across the vessel's oil-splattered bridge. A commercial tug, the Sheila Moran, meandered aimlessly a few hundred yards away.

A mile or two to the stern of the Argo Merchant several fishing boats continued to work as if nothing had happened. They had all disappeared as Christmas Eve approached and the oil slick spread.

From the crippled tanker a thin finger of filmy oil reached out like a knife point directed at the nearby fishing grounds. Looking like giant, dirty pancakes, huge globules of oil floated just beneath the water's surface.

Still, there was hope last weekend that something could be salvaged from the mess and that the worst of the pollution fears would not materialize. But that hope and all the brave words about preparations to save the oil were not to come true as the week wore on.

A second storm, carrying angry seas and high winds, moved into the area. The Argo Merchant tore apart into three pieces and spilled its entire cargo of 7.6 million gallons of oil into the sea.

By the time the plane, piloted by John Pratt of Martha's Vineyard Aviation, headed into the area again, late in the week, there was little left to be seen.

One piece of the bow had disappeared completely. The other piece was pointed crazily at the sky like a missile launching pad. The after cabin section was almost submerged. The bow was pointed northeast and the stern west.

The seas by Thursday had moderated and turned a cold, wintry green. Waves washed at the shattered sections of the vessel as if to cleanse the last few gallons of oil from her battered tanks.

The Coast Guard cutter Vigilant continued her patrol of the area. She could do nothing but help direct a few news photographers attempting to take pictures of what little was left of the disaster. A commercial tug also stood by.

Three black buoys stood like sentinels at a graveside, the only evidence of earlier preparatory work to salvage the Argo Merchant and her cargo. Everywhere around her the water was discolored, as if bruised and infected by illness. The water in the slick area also was calmer than the uninfected parts of the sea. But, as one expert noted with sadness, the calmer water will only attract wildlife and thus add even new dimensions to the catastrophe.

As the plane climbed out of the area and headed for home, the shoreline of first Nantucket and then the Vineyard sparkled in patchy sunlight. From nearly 2,000 feet the Islands lay open and vulnerable. By Christmas Eve there was little anyone could do but hope that the ruinous cargo from the Argo Merchant will not spread through the Georges Bank fishing grounds and ultimately come to rest along the New England shoreline.

– December 24, 1976

❧   ❧   ❧

90-Mile Winds Hammer Island; Sea Bursts into Katama Bay

By William A. Caldwell

A WINDSTORM THAT WHIPPED shrieking ghosts of snow and squalls of driven sand horizontally on gusts ranging up to 90 knots lashed Martha's Vineyard this week through a day that felt like a season in Antarctica. Or hell. Then, having reestablished who's in charge around here, Nature next morning blandly invited Islanders to forget it.

They won't.

For decades to come grandchildren yet unborn will have to listen to ancients' retelling the day of the tempest of '76.

Great trees came thundering down. The old ferryboat City of Chappaquiddick sank at her mooring in Edgartown harbor.

In clattering sheets windows blew out of the lee side, the vacuum side, of shops and homes and greenhouses. The 34-year-old tetrahedron wind vane at the Martha's Vineyard Airport was crumpled and carried away. Brick chimneys and television masts toppled into backyards. The lights went out. The barometer plummeted to 28.4. Scallopers' boats were swamped or torn from their moorings, to drift until they lodged on ice floe or frozen shore. Shingles and clapboard sidings fluttered down the wind. For hour after frantic hour children existed in a world without TV, their elders in a world without access to mainland.

There was no accountancy that could estimate the damage in dollars. Eventually, as the summer's tens of thousands return to their Island homes and repair mischiefs now unsuspected, the cost might total hundreds of thousands. But some of the losses were intangible — what is the worth of a tall old cedar? — and at least one was incalculable.

The most spectacular effect of the storm was the sea's broaching an opening through county-owned South Beach into Mattakesett Bay.

At the height of the fury Monday morning the Atlantic had clawed away some 300 or 400 yards of the barrier beach and its grassy dunes just to the Wasque-ward east of the Katama Road opening, and authentic surf was breaking on the shallow little bay at the head of Katama Bay. The condominium complex at the intersection of Katama and Pond Lot Roads was ocean-front property.

For the last 10 years or so Chappaquiddick and the main Island have been joined, twinned, by a narrow isthmus of sand. As of Monday morning, Chappaquiddick was an island again, severed from the Vineyard not only by the sea's invasion of Mattakesett but by a torrential outflow to the sea from the salt pond at Wasque.

Wind and high water in Katama Bay, of which the pond is an arm, had raised the pond level five feet or so above sea level, and its pent waters were streaming over the easternmost neck of the beach at a businesslike four miles an hour.

By dawn Monday the wind was robust enough to prune weak branches from trees and raise a chop that swamped a few small boats at their moorings in Vineyard ponds and harbors, but a routine check at the utility offices, the Coast Guard station at Menemsha and the Martha's Vineyard Shipyard produced no evidence of damage. The highest wind velocity recorded at Menemsha during the night was 36 knots.

Then things started coming apart.

By 9:30 o'clock anemometers at the shipyard and the airport were recording velocity from 60 to 90 knots, the barometer reading at Woods Hole was 28.27, the lights were going out all over Martha's Vineyard, and the tide was over the docks at Menemsha and over the beach at Katama and rising.

Groundhog Day had come. The tradition dictates that if the groundhog is feebleminded enough to emerge from its burrow that day and sees its shadow, it proceeds to go back to the sack on the theory that winter has six weeks yet to go. The groundhog would have seen its shadow Monday; periodically, patches of clear sky reminiscent of the eye of a hurricane would throw a slant of sunlight across tortured woods and whitecapped waters.

After the Nantucket's first round trip from Vineyard Haven, ferries to the Islands did not venture out of their slips that day. At Woods Hole the tide was high, surf was breaking over the wharves, and spray was sifting into the village. The temperature, which had been near 50 here at daybreak, was dropping sharply. It was snowing on Nantucket by 9 o'clock. The snow would begin on the Vineyard within the hour.

After rising to abnormal highs on Monday the tides were running uncommonly low and, it seemed to attentive tide watchers, as much as six hours off schedule.

Everett H. Poole, the Chilmark selectman who runs the Menemsha fish market bearing the family name, said that when the tide went out of the Menemsha Basin Monday, three and a half hours before it was entitled to do so by the tide tables, the pipes through which normally sea water is pumped from the basin into his lobster tanks gasped and went dry. They were sucking air. "There wasn't any water left in the basin to pump," he said, and he had to work through the small hours to keep the tanks habitable for lobsters, a bucketful at a time. In the 10 years he has been pumping water mechanically no tide so low had occurred before.

Along with a little colony of skiff- or Whaler-sized scalloping boats and the Grant & Carbon Marine pile-driver barge, the old Edgartown-Chappaquiddick ferryboat City of Chappaquiddick sank at about 8:50 a.m. Monday at her mooring in the inner Edgartown harbor. Like the small boats that had strayed from their moorings in Menemsha Pond and drifted into the basin, the scallopers' craft were duly retrieved at Edgartown. What became of the City of Chappaquiddick was, pro tem at any rate, one of the mysteries of the sea.

Trees went down by the hundreds, in due time, sawed and split to fireplace size, to replenish householders' winter-shrunken stacks of cordwood. In West Tisbury four stately cedars collapsed in a long shattering crash. In Vineyard Haven a tall pine took an oak alongside with it in its fall. Trees blew down on Church street, and near the Winifred House in Oak Bluffs, behind the Captain Fisher House in Edgartown, deep in the state forest, high in the up-Island hills. On Chappaquiddick the moors' cover of wind-dwarfed oaks was barbered. Throughout the Island, pines up to a foot or more in girth died, fighting.

Trees irregular in shape were split lengthwise by the torsion of the twisting winds, then taken down a vertical slab at a time. Some lost their footing in the mud below — the temperature was still about 40 above zero when the worst of the blow began — and just slipped and fell the way people were doing, or acquired a permanent lean to the north or northeast. One fine old spruce passed away into a long hereafter. Its owner, Margaret Hufstader, said she would have it reduced to studs and boards and would use it in the structure of a cottage.

The little ferry On Time brought a consignment of school-children from Chappaquiddick to Edgartown at about 8 a.m and returned them to their home island at 2:30 o'clock or so. That was the extent of traffic across the harbor that day.

What else?

The storm warning flag, a square red flag with a black square centered on it, crackled on the copper codfish-topped pole at Machine & Marine Service on Beach Road, Vineyard Haven. Its appearance was one signal that something extraordinary was going on; another signal was the fact that the flagstaff was bent nearly in two.

– February 6, 1976

❧   ❧   ❧

With Island Fishermen On the High Seas

By Mark Alan Lovewell

IT IS THE FIRST TOW of the morning on the third day of fishing when the 75-foot fishing boat Unicorn encounters trouble.

The boat is 30 miles south of Nantucket. The sky is blue, the ocean blue-green, the morning air cold. At 6:30 a.m. the fishing boat moves smoothly over large Atlantic rollers. Moments later the Unicorn is stuck. The captain calls his mate, Dominique Penicaud, with alarm.

"We're snagged," shouts Capt. Gregory Mayhew.

Captain Mayhew rushes from the deck, grabs the handle on the watertight steel door, opens it, enters, slams the door shut and runs up the narrow corridor to the pilot house.

He eases the Unicorn's throttle and looks anxiously through

the window to the stern, where straining cables vibrate, spraying water.

Mr. Penicaud is already at the winch, its wheels spinning as the cable rises from the water.

The 80-foot wide net has hung up on something, 64 feet down. Captain Mayhew stares at the electronic fishfinder screen, seeking a clue of what lies below. It is blank except for a school of fish. Under the boat are 14 fathoms of water. "I don't understand it," he complains. "I've fished here many times and never gotten caught up."

The bottom is supposed to be sandy here. Captain Mayhew watches out the stern window and waits, worrying about damage to the net, hoping he won't have to back the Unicorn up and risk catching the net in her five-foot propeller. That would end the trip. But moving forward too fast, he knows, could also tear the net badly.

Mr. Penicaud leans over the stern, his eyes on the surface of the shining water. His hand grasps the hydraulic throttle. The net is inched up slowly, haltingly. Something is badly stuck.

The captain watches his fishing partner of 11 years struggle alone with the incoming net. Tied as she is to the bottom, the Unicorn falls into a disturbingly different rhythm with the seas. Mr. Penicaud braces his legs against the bulkhead, riding the stern as it pitches and rolls.

Soon Mr. Penicaud waves his free arm at the captain. All of the net is safely aboard. Captain Mayhew, relieved, turns the Unicorn and heads her northwest.

On the navigation chart, the captain marks the snag. It's new, perhaps a recently sunk boat, he says. In any case the Unicorn won't fish here again.

Repairing the net takes two hard hours. The two fishermen sit among hundreds of feet of wet net, seaweed and flapping fish. Their cold fingers take turns tying.

"We were very lucky. It wasn't too bad because the net was hanging on the side," Mr. Penicaud says. With bare hands pink and raw from the cold, he yanks a large plastic needle, drawing new line through the broken mesh.

Only an eight-foot section of net is torn, says Mr. Penicaud. "We've seen worse." Both fishermen know that when a net hangs up, it can be lost altogether, and can even capsize a boat.

Breakfast is late this morning. The two fishermen don't eat until the net is back in the water.

The meal is the catch of the morning — yellowtail fillets fried slowly in butter. The mate serves the meal in the warm pilot house at 11 o'clock. The two eat slowly, their fingers still stiff from the cold.

"There is nothing like fresh yellowtail for breakfast. It is the most delicious," the captain says, between bites.

The Unicorn's luck turns in the afternoon. Captain Mayhew and Mr. Penicaud work hard sorting thousands of pounds of sand dabs and hundreds of pounds of codfish that are brought aboard with each tow.

With the automatic pilot, the captain steers the boat back and forth over the most productive grounds.

The work is hardest when there are fish to catch. Each tow lasts two and a half hours, about the time it takes the fishermen to sort the catch of the tow before. Baskets are filled with fish, four baskets of sand dabs to every one of cod. The fish, by the hundreds of pounds, are dumped below.

Both men take off their jackets and bend to their work, sweating in the light southwest wind.

The captain sees a strange fish in a pile of several hundred pounds of trash fish and sand dabs.

"You see this fish? It's called the lucky fish," Captain Mayhew says, and he carries the preposterously ugly creature over to display on the mid-deck in full sunlight. The face of the 15-inch-long fish looks like the dragon in a Chinese New Year's parade. The belly is bloated like a puffer's.

"For as long as I can remember we've called this a lucky fish," Captain Mayhew says. "You know why it is lucky? Because no

one in their right mind would ever eat a fish this ugly."
The fish opens its huge mouth and reveals a row of sharp teeth.
With a flip of the wrist the captain throws the fish overboard,
where it floats upside down in the water.
Another interesting character from the deep is the ocean pout,
also called ling. Its eyes are on top of its frog-like head. Its mouth
is like a sea robin's, and it has the meaty tail of an eel.
Skate is the most common fish on the deck. The flat bottom
fish ranges from 10 to 30 inches in length. Its mouth looks almost human. Mr. Penicaud, a Frenchman who was raised in Paris,
says in Europe skate are considered a good eating fish.
Sometimes the fishermen are knee deep in skates. They are
pushed over the side with brooms and a hose that runs sea water.
Moving so much fish on this day makes both men tired. For
hours they have been bent over, picking the sand dabs from the
deck, filling baskets with 80 pounds each.
"That is why they call this dragging," says the weary mate.
"It is a drag."
"I always wondered whether someone could invent a device
like what young children have," the captain says. "Have you
ever seen a Jolly Jumper?" An infant is suspended in a basket.
The basket hangs from a spring and the child bounces around.
"I wouldn't mind being able to bounce around like that on
deck," the captain says.
Mr. Penicaud laughs.
The captain jumps on the deck, spring-loaded, a cartoon swing-
ing his arms and his fish pick in the air. More laughter.
Today, despite the break in the net, the fishermen have put
more than 3,000 pounds of fish on ice below. Even in their fa-
tigue, they are cheered at this success.
Late in the afternoon, the captain spots a small songbird resting at the end of the 40-foot outrigger, the steel boom that extends out over the water.
"We are a little like Noah's Ark," Captain Mayhew says. Out
at sea with land nowhere in sight, a fishing boat can be the first

place a migrating bird stops to rest.

"It happens. The birds fly east instead of west and get lost. I've tried to feed them," he says. "Sometimes a bird is so exhausted that it falls on the deck and just dies."

A few hundred feet away, a flock of herring and greater black-backed gulls follows the slow progress of the Unicorn.

The sea birds await the next catch. Hundreds of birds take flight and drop into the water just ahead of the boat on the port side. They float in the water until the fishing boat is a quarter mile ahead. Then they take flight again, flying ahead of the fishing boat to start the cycle over.

When the heavy net is brought aboard, another bird arrives. This one is no stranger. It is a large northern gannet which circles the boat effortlessly and with grace. The bird is ivory-white like the gulls, but its wings are longer and narrower, its wingtips jet-black.

The gannet has followed the Unicorn now for two days. The bird dives into the stern wake of the boat, disappearing for a moment underwater, and then reappears with a herring in its beak.

It is near dusk when the captain notices that the lone songbird has disappeared.

Late at night, when the mate has gone to sleep, Capt. Gregory Mayhew sits in the pilot house. In his notebook he records the catch of this very good day: 4,000 pounds of fish.

– May 12, 1989

Autumn Sun

She waves the world a wild goodbye
By whipping scarves across the sky
Which sail the stratospheric gales
Like tattered, dying comets' tails.

D.A.W.

Operation Scallop Saves Thousands

By Michael F. Bamberger

MONDAY AFTERNOON AT ONE O'CLOCK, the wind blew raw and cold from the harbor across the parking lot between the Edgartown Yacht Club and the Dock Street Coffee Shop. Cheeks red, noses dripping, hair wet, a small group of men stood in foul-weather gear patched with duct tape, by a pickup truck. The air smelled of storm and of salt, and the high tide nearly swept over the town docks.

"Damn," said one of the men, looking to the harbor where wooden mooring stakes swayed and bobbed maniacally, driven by the wind and rough water. These six men standing in the March rain were colleagues. They were all scallopers.

"We're going to lose a lot more," said another. He was a scalloper, and the subject was his living.

"Least the tide's going down now." It was Monday afternoon at one o'clock, and the tide charts said the tide was falling.

"The full moon, the storm, three days of blowing northeast, it had to happen," said another.

"Tide's going down, at least. We'll meet at Fuller street at three," said one of the men, the group's leader. It was Joe Sutton, the Edgartown shellfish constable.

Monday afternoon, three o'clock. There are 203 commercial scallopers in Edgartown, and six of them met at the end of Fuller street. Six pickup trucks with over-sand vehicle permits were parked at the end of Fuller street and pointed at Nantucket Sound.

The seas were very rough and not at all blue; they were gray with churning sand and white with foam. Wearing waders and carrying bushel baskets, the men hiked through stiff winds half a mile, up to the cut where Nantucket Sound meets Eel Pond. The walk was over cold, soft sand, through flocks of sea gulls and always through the wind, whipping now, biting against their skin. At the entrance cut, and a hundred yards before it, small mountains of green fleece piled up, the rubbery seaweed children throw playfully in summer. But the green fleece seemed hardly friendly now. In a sense, it was the enemy.

For in the seaweed were bushels and bushels of scallops washed ashore by an unusual confluence of tides and winds. The scallopers, with thick rubber gloves, set themselves among the green fleece, and scallop by scallop, picked through the seaweed. The scallops were thrown into burlap bags, bushel baskets and milk crates, and carried to a boat.

Peter Paltrinari brought his boat from Edgartown harbor to Eel Pond Monday for the salvage effort. The journey brought water over the bow and freeboard, for the seas were truly fierce. The scallopers kneeled in the green fleece, digging little craters in their search for scallops. Mr. Paltrinari waded through the icy water, threw the scallops up on the bow, and headed out to Eel Pond. There they were released.

The work continued nearly till dusk. Wading through the seaweed, collecting scallops, carrying them to the boat. Nearly to dusk in a bone-chilling wind, nine men, trying to protect their living.

Tuesday afternoon at four o'clock, Mr. Sutton, as shellfish constable, appeared before the Edgartown selectmen to explain Monday afternoon's procedure.

"We've saved about 115 bushels of seed. We're going to lose another 200 to 300 bushels," Mr. Sutton said.

"I started putting the word out Sunday afternoon. Made calls. Put it on the radio. Saw people in the street. We probably lost $90,000 worth of scallops.

"For every bushel of seed you're saving probably five times as much of scallop, because of the growth of the scallop in the next year," Mr. Sutton said.

"I'm very disappointed in the low turnout. I expected more from the scallopers in the town of Edgartown," said Fred B.

Morgan Jr. of the selectmen.

"It's their livelihood," said Mr. Sutton.

The scallopers who did work are David Berube, Joe Smith, Scott Castro, Paul Jackson, Rick Willoughby, Bruce Lundeen, Mr. Paltrinari and Earl Depinkowski. The town constables also worked: Mr. Sutton, Jimmy Goodwin and Warren Gaines.

Wednesday morning at seven o'clock, a small group of scallopers headed out to Cape Pogue in four-wheel drives, because at the entrance to the gut thousands and thousands of seed scallops had washed up. This was an effort to save them, for by next year they'll be a cash crop.

– March 23, 1984

❦ ❦ ❦

Alongshore We Submit to Winter's Icy Grip

By George W. Adams

ICE. Afloat and ashore, winter locks the Islands in its steel gauntlet: now crystal, now shining alabaster, now muddy brown. Piled into cliffs, lying in flat sheets, wrapped around pilings, crawling through pipes. But always, a steel grasp.

"For the most part, it's worse than I've ever seen it, and I've been here since 1964," Master Chief Jeremiah O'Neill of Coast Guard Group Woods Hole said yesterday.

People love records. The ice is making some.

From Nantucket, in expectation of a shipment of gasoline: "We're in bad shape, Mobil is considering it an emergency, and so are we."

On the other hand: When a Coast Guard helicopter landed this week on Pasque Island to inquire how keeper Fred Gaskill is making out, the crew got the answer before they asked the question. "What's the commotion all about?" Mr. Gaskill asked in surprise.

Commotion? Yesterday the Uncatena turned back from Nantucket after an unsuccessful struggle with the ice. The day before, the 100-foot icebreaking tug Yankton freed her from a raft just inside the jetties. The day before that, she couldn't make the run. And so on.

The Cape Cod Canal was shut down Saturday by the ice, and it has stayed shut ever since. The canal is clear now, but the eastern end of Buzzards Bay is filled with ice up to two feet thick, crisscrossed by seven- and eight-foot high pressure ridges. The Yankton and the 180-foot buoy tender Bittersweet, at work there yesterday, were slowed to a crawl of a tenth of a mile an hour. "And as fast as we break a track, it closes in behind us," they report.

The necessary supplies are getting through, even to the outposts. Alan Wilder, keeper of Nashawena Island, put his outboard motorboat on a cart and hauled it to the western end of his island for a run through the ice-free waters of Canapitsit Channel to Cuttyhunk early in the week.

With one respectable expanse of warm weather it will all vanish. But damage will be left behind.

Along the Vineyard's shores where piers reach into salt water, the ice has been playing one of its queerest tricks, turning wharves into broken bridges to the sky, standing on bandy legs. On the low tide, the ice grabs solid around the pilings. With the rising tide it pulls them upward a foot or more. Then, perversely, it lets go to descend for another tug. Upward, ever upward. Excelsior.

In the fields, ice from another source is working damage that will last for a year or more. Stretches of ice lying on the grass where no pond ever existed are suffocating the vegetation beneath; when thaw comes, the land will be barren.

The two great bottlenecks in the marine world are the Nantucket jetties and the entrance to the Cape Cod Canal. Both jams are caused by the prolonged and unbroken freezing weather, and by the continuous northwesterly winds. "We've had worse cold, but we've almost never gone so long without a winter northeaster in the middle of it," said one observer. As ice forms to the west, the winds pile it into the waiting arms of Nantucket's crescent, and into the corner pocket of Buzzards Bay. Cuttyhunk freezes up in an easterly, and these winds have kept it free. But still the Alert, Cuttyhunk's ferry and supply boat, has been unable to make runs because of the ice in New Bedford, and, if it could get clear of that, the slush ice in the bay.

"We're doing fine," Cuttyhunk selectman Bruce Borges said Tuesday. "Packer had an oil barge in here about a week ago, so we're fine on that score. We all live out of freezers in the wintertime, so we're all right there. As far as food goes, well, you might run out of milk, but somebody else has some you can borrow. But if I could get out of here for a week or two, I would. Over there where you people are, you can get a change of scene...."

Winter made it, and only winter — or maybe spring — can take it away. But it's of no great mind yet, as the Gazette saw Wednesday on an aerial tour provided by Jon Ahlbum.

Against the blue sea to the south, the Island lies delicately fringed in white. Great icy skirts have grown around the legs of piers. Jetties are thickly coated white. Shorelines exposed to the northwest are piled with icy cakes. Instead of azure holes in the land, ponds and harbors have become prominent treeless extensions of the snowy shore, filling every indentation along the Island's edge.

Vineyard Sound is clear. But along its undefined border with Nantucket Sound patches of slush appear, like a milky oil on the water surface. They hurry eastward in the wind, merging into streams, coalescing into tiny cakes which look like curdled cream. One wisp curls from the tip of Cape Pogue down Muskeget Channel to land on Skiff's Island. Others entwine the shoals off Tuckernuck and Muskeget islands.

But most of it seems bent on joining the Nantucket Block-ade. The streams merge into ponds, then into lakes, still fluid enough to be rippled by the waves passing underneath. Then it becomes a solid wasteland.

Scale vanishes. Pressure ridges, crisscrossing the expanse this way and that could be tiny veins on an insect's white wing. Open spots could be microscopic imperfections. A spot of dust appears, creeping toward somnolent Nantucket. It grows to be a vessel, backing and filling, twisting and turning to free itself from win-ter's grasp.

– February 4, 1977

❦   ❦   ❦

Camouflage to Cover the Hurt

A GREAT STURGEON MOON floated full over the Vineyard Sunday night; it trailed silver light across Island harbors and in and out of shadows and silhouettes all along the shoreline. Nightfall arrived on sea breezes blowing fresh and cool.

And then Monday, yesterday's opening to the week after Hurricane Bob, the beginning of a renewed push toward recovery, to the day ahead when the Island community will again find balance in a normal rhythm of life. One week ago the violence of the worst storm to hit the Vineyard in 37 years tore the Vineyard apart. Yesterday unfolded on gentle winds, as full of the warmth of August summer as was the moon of precious glitter the night before. It was one of those noble Island days when the deep blue sea glitters with flecks of gold and the high blue sky extends forever, out and beyond the Vineyard's battered South Shore, perhaps toward Spain.

What a difference a week makes. It is almost as if nature is offering apologies for her ravages and anger of a week ago Monday afternoon. First the full moon when sturgeon and blues and stripers run plentiful in warm Vineyard waters, and then the best of summer, these bright, calm days when bathers return to beaches and the business of tans along this Island's never-ending shoreline.

In spite of all that has happened since Hurricane Bob, in spite of all the wounds and damage, the Vineyard still holds, more than in most places, a beauty to camouflage the hurt. Even if summer now looks and smells like autumn, it makes no difference, for this is an Island for all seasons and it matters not whether hurricane time marches out of seasonal sequence.

The sights and sounds of recovery are never far off these days. But that is not cause for despair; it is a sign of life, of an Island community grappling well in the aftermath of storm, of people rising on all fronts to clear the debris that Bob left. We shall live for some time yet with the shriek of chain saws, the piles of wood stacked along country roadsides, the line crews in swaying crow's nests and the rumble of dump trucks on their way to landfills.

But the real point is this; the moon is near full — with sturgeon running beneath it — and the Vineyard landscape is too lovely to linger long beside the scars of Hurricane Bob.

– Editorial, August 27, 1991

🌂 🌂 🌂

Spite

We watched the rain without remorse,
Because we had to work, of course;
We chuckled as the raindrops fell:
Another beach day shot to hell!

D.A.W.

A View Toward Aquaculture

By Joseph Chase Allen

If this was sixty years ago —
    The Island fisher found it paid,
To take some thought to things ashore,
    And maybe learn a landsman's trade.

And so, when breezed the autumn gales,
    And fish schools left; then there were men,
Who shingled barns, chopped firewood,
    And kept a porker in the pen.

Then in the early spring some plowed,
    And planted cabbages and beans,
They got ashore at times to hoe,
    To pick their peas and turnip greens.

And now some wise men have proposed,
    That fish and clams be raised like hens.
In pools and puddles, ringed with fence,
    Just like the garden plots and pens.

If this was sixty years ago —
    Those oldsters might know what to do.
But to the fishers of today,
    A farmer's life is something new.

It's going to take some time to learn,
    Of planting oysters in a row.
The instincts of the land have failed,
    Since men farmed, sixty years ago.

—July 9, 1971

Larsen Family Sells Fishing Boat;
Sale Ends an Era in Menemsha

By Mark Alan Lovewell

A COMMERCIAL FISHING BOAT will leave Menemsha harbor Monday and will not return, ending an era for one Chilmark fishing family. Louis S. Larsen, 68, who has spent his career as a fisherman on the high seas from the waters off Newfoundland to the Caribbean Sea and the waters off the Yucatan, has sold his 70-foot steel-hulled western rig fishing boat, the Mary Elizabeth.

Mr. Larsen said he had no choice. The commercial fishing industry is at the brink. The boat has been sold to a Long Island fisherman for an undisclosed amount.

The Mary Elizabeth is one of three working steel-hulled draggers that fish out of Menemsha. The other two are owned by brothers Gregory and Jonathan Mayhew. The sale of the vessel reflects a serious fishing crisis that exists in the waters around Martha's Vineyard. Fish stocks are at record lows.

"It is too rough," Mr. Larsen told the Gazette on Wednesday. "The storms ashore are far worse than they are out there. Every time you turn around there is a new regulation. It is just not worth it at my age to continue on."

Regulators and scientists in recent years have reported fish stocks at the lowest levels ever on Georges Bank and Nantucket Shoals. Scientists are now calling on fisheries regulators to impose a closure so fish stocks can recover. The status of the fishing industry is being described as worse than a depression, according to fisheries analysts, because until groundfish stocks recover (which will take years) the industry cannot recover.

On the Vineyard the commercial fishing industry has been in decline going back almost 20 years. If the Vineyard fishing industry does recover, the boats of the future will be smaller than the Mary Elizabeth and they'll be less efficient.

But Mr. Larsen sees the fishing closures and regulations differently. The way he sees it, he is being denied an income. Regulators have imposed draconian fisheries restrictions that limit the number of days a fisherman can go to sea. "Last year they [fisheries regulators] gave me 136 days to fish on Georges Bank for groundfish, flounders and yellowtail. This year they gave me 117 days at sea. Next year it will go down to 90 days. Add to that another requirement that for every two days we are out we have to stay in a day. And we have to take a 20-day layup period."

Mr. Larsen said: "It is terrible. If they close Georges Bank, what are the Gloucester fishermen going to do? They will all come here [to fish Vineyard and Nantucket Sound]."

The Mary Elizabeth was built in 1981 in Westport at a cost of $383,000. She had the finest equipment and was built for deep sea fishing. Below deck there was plenty of room for ice and fish so that the vessel could go great distances and stay offshore for days at a time. "They don't build boats there anymore," Mr. Larsen said.

The vessel was named after Mr. Larsen's youngest daughter Mary Elizabeth — everyone calls her Betsy and she runs Larsen's Fish Market in Menemsha.

Mr. Larsen said he sold the Mary Elizabeth to Melvin Moss of Shinnecock, N.Y. "I sold it for a hell of a lot less than I should have gotten." he said. "He is going to keep the same name. His grandmother's name is Mary and his daughter's name is Elizabeth." But from now on the transom will have the words New York, New York.

Mr. Larsen had tried for some time to sell the vessel before. "This was the best deal I could get. In New Bedford the docks are loaded with fishing boats. If you have $10,000 you can buy a boat and the banks will give you any mortgage you want. They will let you have the boat if you just take over the payments. They are good boats."

With the sale of the fishing boat, Mr. Larsen reflected back on his career as a fisherman. "Fishing was something that I enjoyed. I enjoyed harpooning for swordfish. That went. I knew then that it was a downhill slide. If I had my life to live over again I wouldn't do it. I would have stayed close to the shore."

During the height of his fishing career, Mr. Larsen spent upwards of three months at a time away from home. In the 1970s, Mr. Larsen said, he would go to the Gulf of Mexico in January and fish for months. "The only way my wife Mary would see me was if I had her fly down."

Mr. Larsen's children have all been deeply affected by the life of a fisherman. All of them remain in the fishing industry in different ways. They all run fish markets on the Island and stay close to shore. In the family there are three fish markets: Larsen's Fish Market, the Net Result and Edgartown Seafood.

Mr. Larsen said he will probably purchase a small lobster boat to keep his feet wet. "I just can't see where fishing is going to be any better for a while."

Louis S. Larsen Jr., owner of the Net Result, said of his father: "I feel sad for him." It is an end of a livelihood derived from the sea. "I feel the fishermen have done it to themselves. If anyone is the least guilty it is my father. But as an industry, the fishermen did it to themselves."

The younger Mr. Larsen said he saw the writing on the wall years ago and that is why he runs a fish market. "I saw the fishing would end before the selling of fish would end."

Sgt. William L. Searle, state environmental police officer for the Island, has known the Larsen family for years. The sergeant was himself a commercial fisherman for a time. He said: "The selling of the Mary Elizabeth marks the end of an era, the last line on a page of an American history book. The Larsen family was world renowned like the Mayhews. As swordfishermen they were internationally known among fishermen. It is really too bad. It speaks of problems not only for Martha's Vineyard but the whole North Atlantic."

– September 23, 1994

37

Roberto Germani Fishes for Life

By Mark Alan Lovewell

ROBERTO GERMANI LOVES AND LIVES TO FISH. And he believes that fishing has helped keep him alive.

Since being diagnosed with lung cancer in 1979, Mr. Germani has lived at the edge of life.

"I was told that if you can make it to five years you'll be okay. I beat the odds," he says. And for the last 12 years he has spent much of his time fishing the waters of the Vineyard, catching the biggest fish and introducing many would-be fishermen to the fine art of flyrod fishing. He believes the fishing extended his life.

But this summer, his disease came back.

To Vineyard fishermen, this 56-year-old man with the salt-and-pepper beard is a sort of guru. Over and over again, fishermen tell of the time they were out with Roberto, when the fish appeared from nowhere. And they speak of Roberto's deep relationship with the fish and the art of fishing.

He fishes off the Oak Bluffs wharf, off Menemsha jetties and in the waters of Chappaquiddick.

"No matter where I go, I seem to find Roberto fishing," marveled one fisherman this week. "He is everywhere."

There is a mystical quality about this fisherman that even he admits borders on the edge of religion.

Mr. Germani fishes every chance he gets. And with all the fish that he catches, he has not kept a single one.

"A man is made up of two personalities. There is the one that wants to survive, to keep going. Then on the other side there is the man that wants to quit, that wants to throw in the towel and die," says Mr. Germani this week.

Since coming down with lung cancer in 1979, Mr. Germani says, the disease has coalesced his love around the pleasure of fishing. Every spring he is one of the first fishermen to take his fishing rod down from the rack and make a few casts into the water. And in the fall, long after most fishermen have gone home, he is the last to call it quits.

"Fishing is part of the salvation. No, it is not a religion." He laughs. "Fishing keeps me out there breathing the freshest air you can breathe. It is not like fishing in Flatbush," he says.

Since moving to the Vineyard in 1979 from Providence, he has had many jobs. He has been a school bus driver and pumped gas. Mr. Germani admits that his vocation is of little importance compared to his avocation. One's job puts food on the table, but it is the fishing that feeds his spirit.

On Oct. 31, 1981 he caught two 31-pound striped bass. "Those were the last striped bass I kept," he says. With striped bass being considered a threatened species, Roberto was one of the first Vineyard fishermen to catch and release his bass.

And Mr. Germani was one of the first fishermen to popularize the use of a canoe. In his kitchen there are plaques from the 1985 Martha's Vineyard Striped Bass and Bluefish Derby which marked the year that he perfected bonito fishing on this unlikely boat.

The decision to fish from a canoe came in 1983. "I wanted to extend my range. A canoe is cheap. There is no pollution and you can carry it to the water," he says.

Canoes are unstable in open coastal waters, so Roberto designed outriggers, plastic soda bottles extended from the center of the boat outwards on sticks. "I wrapped them in tape," he says.

"I was in Edgartown harbor when I caught my first canoe bonito."

During that 1985 fishing derby, Roberto admits, "I made a lot of boat owners upset. Here they were fishing for bonito with their 50-grand motorboats. I had an advantage. I had no fumes. There was no petroleum product. I had no motor to spook the fish."

In that year Roberto cleaned up with derby prizes. He got a first, second and third prize in the category of boat bonito. As funny as he looked out in the harbor, Mr. Germani came in with the fish.

There is a definite disadvantage to a canoe too. "I did capsize," he says, "three times. But then that is when you are messing with the edge. You know the edge when you capsize." Mr. Germani was one of a small number of fishermen to go fishing with a flyrod instead of a spinning reel. "I bought my first flyrod in the fall of 1983 and haven't picked up a spinning rod since," he says. In that year you could count the number of Island flyrod fishermen on one hand. Today there are hundreds of flyfishermen fishing the Vineyard.

The technique of fly-fishing is more competitive and the sport is more of an art. On top of Roberto's living room cabinet are 50 yet-unused flies that he made himself using special threads and tiny hooks.

In 1989 Roberto came down with lung cancer again. In the operating room doctors reduced Mr. Germani's lungs to less than one.

"You do mind games," Roberto says. "You get involved in visualization. I'd imagine myself inside my lungs going around with a dustpan and cleaning it up, getting rid of these black beads," he says.

"The funny part about it is that visualization works."

Despite the advanced stage of the disease, Mr. Germani continued to focus his life on fishing. That fall Mr. Germani decided not to join the derby. His philosophy about fishing had gone through another change.

When you live to fish, the fish themselves gain in importance. Mr. Germani would catch and release every fish he caught.

Something unexpected happened when Mr. Germani stopped fishing competitively in the derby. "People became nicer. They knew I wasn't a threat," he says. A fellowship arose that had not existed before. Roberto became every fisherman's friend.

Many of the fishermen he fished silently with in the years before came up to Mr. Germani for advice. "More people know me than I'll ever know," he says.

Mr. Germani says he couldn't fish to win the grand prize at the derby.

"The reward of fishing is fishing. It is not a grand prize.

"I've been to the Grand Canyon and seen beauty everywhere in the world. But it is nothing compared to here. The marine environment is wonderful. It is all subject to change. In minutes the sea can change colors from slate gray to pea green and to purple."

Mr. Germani earned fame beyond Vineyard shores when he was featured in the book Reading the Water, by Robert Post. This year he has been used as a consultant by a fishing tackle firm.

But this summer getting to the water to go fishing has taken on a greater challenge. The hardest part about this stage of the disease, he says, is the shortness of breath. "I notice it getting worse on a weekly basis.

"There is nothing left for the surgeons to cut out. I don't think I can take more radiation treatment," he says.

Instead of visualizing that he can win over the disease, his thoughts have changed. "You tend to appreciate the world here and now. You adjust your concepts. My thoughts now are more of the immediate. And I speculate less and less on what will happen next year."

This fall Mr. Germani plans on being out among the best of fishermen in the fall derby, which starts in two weeks. He may need a little help getting his canoe in the water, but there will be plenty of fishermen ready to help him with that task and to keep him close to the edge.

– August 30, 1991

To Each His Own

IN HIS RECENTLY PUBLISHED MEMOIRS, Between Thee and Me, Dr. Elden H. Mills of Chilmark recalls the woman who came from Kansas for a visit. Looking out at the ocean off Horseneck Beach, she tartly remarked that she had never seen so much of anything she couldn't use.

For Midwesterners, lacking sea, it is the sky that is important — that, stretching to infinity as it seems to, makes one mindful of infinity. For coastal peoples, the sea serves the same purpose. It extends, too, to infinity. On its way there, like the sky, it does such wondrous things. Sometimes it dances. It sweeps, it thrashes. Its waves roll and they toss, and, reaching distant shores, they thunder and roar, or gaily splash and laugh. The sea is tumultuous, evocative, provocative. It is alluring, hypnotic, seductive, raging and stern.

So, of course, is the sky to which the Kansan was accustomed — gentle, hazy-blue and solicitous, comforting with fluffy clouds. Then the wind comes and the rain and the blue turns to black. The sky scowls and chastens in anger. The sea, like the sky, is predominantly blue because of the scattering of short blue wavelengths of the sun in the water. But then, too, the sea's colors reflect the moods of the sky.

The sea can be aqua, turquoise, blue-black, lavender, green, pink salmon. It can be platinum, silver, gold, lead gray and velvet black. And its shades are even more varied than those of the sky because of its yellow and red and brown microscopic plants and because of the sand and the rocks of the sea's bottom.

It is understandable that miles of ocean seemed a mite useless to one who valued land because it could be planted and the sky because it nurtured the land (and was lovely to look at, too). But the sea useless? Far from it. Surely they are both marvelous, sea and sky. And we coastal peoples are the more fortunate, having both.

– Editorial, March 7, 1986

L A N D

&

I N THE WINTER OF 1973, as part of a study, the Vineyard
Open Land Foundation took a look at how the people of
Martha's Vineyard saw and valued the land on which they
lived. It revealed an interesting thing. When asked to sketch
a map of the Vineyard, Islanders from six fundamentally different towns, who worked at different jobs and believed different
things about how the Island should grow, drew all the same features — South Beach, the Great Ponds and the triangular points
of Gay Head, Vineyard Haven and Chappaquiddick.

But oddly enough, they sometimes left out more common
things, like roads — just the reverse, said the report, of the mainland, where people usually drew the roads first and often ne-

glected "major natural features such as coastlines."

Perfectly understandable. The morainal hills, the windy green openness of the plains, the misty recesses of a cove — these had forged a physical devotion to the land so strong that folks actually forgot to include the streets when asked to draw a map of the place where they lived.

Why, then, did the land lie so completely unprotected in the first year of that decade?

The rudimentary tool by which villages begin to plan — zoning — had only just been adopted in Edgartown in 1970. Tisbury had set up a few building regulations in the summer colony of West Chop in 1959, but had done nothing more. West Tisbury, Chilmark and Gay Head lacked even planning boards. On Sengekontacket Pond in the far-sighted township of Oak Bluffs, where zoning was first established in 1948, a developer was about to propose a plausible plan to build 867 houses on 507 acres — more homes on one shoreline than in all of Gay Head and Chilmark combined, and on a fraction of the acreage.

Islanders didn't want to be told how to use the land that had been worked by the family for hundreds of years. Summer residents feared charges of meddling and snobbery if they spoke out for conservation. And the allure of the Vineyard only grew.

Between 1970 and 1990 the population of Dukes County doubled to 12,000. Passenger traffic carried by the Steamship Authority to and from the Vineyard more than doubled between 1970 and 1995, reaching nearly 2,140,000. Automobile traffic tripled, to 369,000.

Speculation outraced reason for long periods, even as the towns tried, fitfully and at first individually, to preserve their size, their character, their neighborliness. Yet Martha's Vineyard did not go the way of Florida, or southern California, or even Cape Cod. The question is, why not?

First, the Vineyard discovered that an insular devotion to the land begets an insular determination to fight for its preservation. Though the separateness of the towns and the people prolongs and often muddies argument, the separateness of the Vineyard from the mainland finally contains and clarifies it. Vineyarders see that debate matters. They feel that what they say at town meeting or in the editorial pages makes a difference.

Second, they have come to realize that each result affecting a piece of Martha's Vineyard invariably affects the whole. South Beach cannot be saved for the public if West Chop won't contribute. The West Chop Woods cannot be saved from exploitation if Edgartown stands aside. The forces of change are too great. Vineyarders understand that they are separate from the main, but they are connected to each other. Everyone has a stake in everywhere.

Will Vineyarders of the next millennium continue to draw the Vineyard as an Island, or will it become just another road map?

To no other question has the Vineyard Gazette paid closer attention in the last 25 years. The stories that follow suggest the breadth and depth of the conflict, the size of the gains and losses. The Gazette argues that the fate and prosperity of the Vineyard depends on the conservation of land and character, and considers it a sign of hope that there remain large areas of the land, breathtakingly beautiful, worth arguing about.

– T.D.

❧   ❧   ❧

To Save Rural Land on Martha's Vineyard: The Challenge of the Seventies

By Edward Logue

I N THE SPRING OF 1970, the Vineyard seems as beautiful as it has ever been. The long quiet roads, the broad fields and farms, the rolling moors and still ponds, the great wild stretches of beach — the pleasantly separated small towns and villages

— the scattered old houses and the not so scattered new houses. It is lovely indeed and very special. Could we not just enjoy it as it is. Would it not be wonderful to accept it as it is and assume that for a long time to come it will stay the way it is, more or less. After all, it has survived the post World War II surge of affluence better than most places we know. Even the most striving summer people come to enjoy the Island, not to change it.

But the Vineyard is part of the seventies. It will share in the great growth and development which seem, unavoidably, to confront those of us who live and work in the northeast megalopolis.

There are no reliable projections about the Vineyard's share of the coming growth. There are just trends that we must try to analyze.

Much of the shoreline of New Jersey, Long Island, Connecticut, Rhode Island and Cape Cod has lost the charm it had 25 years ago. Nearest at hand is the strident example of the south shore of Cape Cod. Not so long ago quite comparable to the Vineyard, it has become a summer slurb. Route 28 runs along the south warm water shore of the Cape. It is now dominated by the hard sell of the quick-buck summer entrepreneur pushing McDonald hamburger joints, leaning pizza parlors, fried clam emporia and neon garish motels with their backyard-size swimming pools.

Until quite recently there have been ample mainland resort areas in the northeast megalopolis. However as the megalopolis has increased in size and affluence many former resort areas have become year-round living areas. In addition the number of vacation homes has substantially increased. Once quite remote places like Vermont are feeling the pressure. So is the Vineyard. There is no way to turn it away. It can only be controlled and then only if there is the will to do so.

The Vineyard shares with Nantucket the distinction of being virtually the only warm ocean water summer resort area in the Northeast which is unspoiled, unpolluted and underdeveloped. (Happily some people don't care about swimming, and others enjoy fresh water or the development pressures would be much greater.)

The Island has done very little through local government to protect itself. It could do much more. How likely that is is a subject for speculation.

There has been an absolute minimum of Island planning and most of that has been a kind of rote planning by off-Island consultants with little to show for the money spent. (Consultants can be very useful but they are no substitute for a competent full-time planning director.)

The tool of zoning has been for the most part rejected outside the more built-up areas. The great open sparsely settled areas where most of the recent development has taken place are unprotected by any public policy.

Such zoning as has been adopted or proposed seems more aimed at protection of existing business areas from competition than in regulating the development of rural land.

The rural character of the Vineyard has thus far been maintained by a web of informal conventions, entirely without the force of law.

Assessment policies have been the most strikingly effective. Large landholdings are decidedly under assessed and, comparatively, summer houses are over assessed. Nobody seems to mind too much, although the custom is of questionable legality.

The force of public opinion in the still small year-round communities has preserved this and conventions that have done much to preserve the quality of the environment. So far one would have to say that the old ways have been strikingly effective.

There is reason to believe that this old system is not strong enough to withstand the pressures of the seventies. The year-round residents' economic well-being is increasingly tied to the summer season as farming and fishing decline in relative profitability. Speculation in land has greatly increased.

The Island once had a balanced economy. Thousands of acres were actively farmed. Fishing, often in combination with farming, provided a livelihood. Although there have been summer resorts on the Island for more than a century, the summer visitor was not the dominant force in the economy.

Today farming has all but disappeared. Fishing has declined. No new sources of employment have taken their place or are likely to.

Whether any of us likes it or not, providing for summer visitors in one way or another is going to become an even more dominant factor in the Island's economy.

Inevitably development will become the preoccupation of more and more of the Island's year-round residents.

Speculation in land has increased and will continue to. The dream of getting rich through land speculation goes back to George Washington's time. It has become the latest rage on the Island.

Large scale development has begun and will continue. Many Islanders will profit from land speculation and from development. However, it is in the nature of things that as large scale development does take place it is likely to be financed, managed and owned by off-Island interests. Planned growth is more likely to be financed, managed and owned by Island interests.

A major change for the worse in the character of the Island is clearly possible. If present trends were to continue it is in fact inevitable.

Just what do we mean by major change for the worse? Increased commercialization with no aesthetic controls (Route 28). Small lot, single family development filling up the roadside and obliterating the sense of tranquility. (This is already happening.) Billboards, big buses. Unplanned residential sprawl. Pollution of the water and the necessity to spend huge sums for sewage disposal facilities that could have been avoided.

However, Vineyarders, both year-rounders and summer people alike, have a passion for the Island. They like its special quality and increasingly they are determined to try to preserve it.

Citizen concern has greatly increased in the last few years. Local and all-Island conservation groups have been formed and are increasingly active. Ad hoc committees have sprung up to deal with particular crises, the jet airport proposal being the most exciting example.

There have been several noteworthy dedications of land to the public interest. Some have been individual acts of philanthropy and others have involved a quite broadly based fundraising effort such as the Wasque and Cedar Tree Neck properties. These efforts have not only been highly commendable in themselves but they have had an enormous educational value as well. We hope they continue. However, it would not be prudent to rely entirely on this approach alone.

One can reasonably doubt whether informal conventions, enlightened private enterprise, aroused citizen concern or the present rate of dedication of land for conservation are enough. Though each is useful, few seem confident that enough is being done. Concern about the future of the Island is growing rapidly.

In all of this ad hoc ferment there has generally been a recognition that a more comprehensive, less crisis-oriented approach would be more desirable. However, one must say in all candor that the elected local governments seem unable or unwilling to do what is clearly within their legal power to do.

We are especially concerned with those rather special large rural tracts of land which are very much in the public view, which have ready access to main roads and which by their beauty add particularly to the quality of life on the Vineyard. The habit of the past has been to take for granted that these lands will remain undeveloped except for the old farmhouse and outbuildings. There is increasingly less reason to be comfortable about that prospect.

– April 17, 1970

Up and Up and Up

THE PURCHASE PRICE of the 230-acre tract bought last week in West Tisbury by Benjamin J. Boldt from William H. Brine of Weston and Edgartown and John Black of Edgartown was $232,000. Less than a year ago, the property, as reported earlier, was bought by Mr. Brine for $20,000 from Arthur Leslie Tawell.

– March 10, 1972

❧ ❧ ❧

Sound Land Plan and a Profit Besides: Success at Sweetened Water

By Henry Beetle Hough

WITH ONLY FOUR LOTS UNSOLD, the Vineyard Open Land Foundation's planned community at Edgartown, Sweetened Water, has become an accomplished reality, plainly attaining the foundation's aim "that the structures and activities of man be humbly combined with the land so that man's presence is a mild enhancement of the dominant natural and agricultural features of the property."

One house has been occupied, two are under construction, and construction plans have been approved for three more on a beautifully contoured tract on the West Tisbury Road, embodying most of what for many years was the Clement Norton farm and later the W.W. Pinney farm, named for the historic Sweetened Water Pond beside the road, a familiar accent of the farmland, mostly open but with copses of tupelo trees and thicket-bordered swamp.

As to the financial aspect of the enterprise, the purchase price in 1972 was $150,000. Total gross sales so far come to $184,000. Since the foundation is a charitable trust organized under Massachusetts law, the financial side is also an assured success. The aim here has been to clear 10 per cent of the gross to make possible a revolving fund out of which other significant land acquisitions can be made, as well as providing for unforeseen and extraordinary expenses.

The marketing is handled through Vineyard Land Use Inc., an entity set up for the purpose. The planning, which in this case was done with unusually close attention to all the characteristics of the land, was by Kevin Lynch and Bob Komives. Responsible for the success of the sales effort are Tom Counter, executive director, and Rob Kendall, his assistant.

The plan contemplates 15 home sites, as against a possible 110 which would have been allowed on this property under Edgartown zoning regulations.

Common wetlands, to be held under a conservation restriction by the Sweetened Water Association Inc., embrace 11.8 acres; common pastures include 12.5 acres; and common recreation grounds, 4 acres. The conservation restrictions allow no construction other than for agricultural purposes, and of course no dwellings. Development rights are to be conveyed to the town with the approval of the Department of Natural Resources.

It is emphasized by Robert G. Lawrence, chairman of the Vineyard Open Land Foundation, that Sweetened Water has served a need principally for Island residents, including the group of sites designed particularly to make it possible for resident Islanders including the young and those of moderate incomes to acquire land for homes. These sites are in a range of somewhat more than an acre each.

Eight sites have been bought by year-round residents, one by a summer resident of long standing, and two by summer visitors to Edgartown in recent years.

The Sweetened Water Association is a property-owners' association in which all owners have equal rights to the common lands and barn. The home sites designed for all-year residents carry a forgivable mortgage of $12,000, should the residence be maintained for 10 years.

No one can say with authority how the name Sweetened Water originated. An elderly inhabitant speculated more than 50 years ago that a sweet flag growth may have, either in reality or imagination, given rise to the boyhood notion that the pond water was sweetened. This patriarch recalled that the name had been current in his childhood.

– December 12, 1975

❧ ❧ ❧

They Came to Rest; They Stayed to Fight

By Andrew J. Shanley

SUSAN AND PETER GRILLI came to the Vineyard to tune out. They came to their place on Lake Tashmoo to get refreshed, to leave their careers behind for a moment. They sought neither causes, nor social events.

"We always assumed nature was first, and we needed to get absorbed by it," Susan says.

This summer it's different. Everything seems to be happening to them and around them; specifically the Grillis are suddenly awash in the politics of the Vineyard.

Susan and Peter Grilli have been in the news. On the front page. The phone in the little house under the trees at the end of a long dirt road has been ringing endlessly.

"The last two weeks we've met more people and I've learned more about the Island than I knew in coming here my whole life," Susan says.

Their retreat by the lake is now a command headquarters.

The Grillis' story has been played out many times and in many ways around Martha's Vineyard. A developer comes to town, as they often come to town, but this time he sets up shop next door. This time he plans to cut down the trees outside the back window. This time it's not a philosophical issue. It's a time to act and act fast.

The SMI company of Delaware wants to build 99 condominiums in the woods across the lake from the Grillis. SMI wants to sell living space to at least 200 people who will use the lake, use the woods, drive cars, flush toilets, confuse the ospreys and change the quality of life on Lake Tashmoo.

The plans came to the Tisbury Planning Board earlier this summer. A hearing was held. The developers said 50 of their 107 acres off Franklin street will be left wild and free, that the 99 units were designed to have the least possible impact on the lake and the town. The Grillis were horrified.

From the moment the hearing ended they set to work, along with their neighbors and others, to block, if possible, the construction of the 99 units. They think 99 is too much.

The Grillis and their friends joined in what is now the Committee to Save Lake Tashmoo for Martha's Vineyard. They sent a letter out to all the town residents alerting them to the dangers inherent in the development. They talked to lawyers, environmental experts. They helped arrange meetings and a letter-writing campaign.

They stopped looking at the Vineyard as a place for rest and contemplation.

Susan and Peter Grilli were scheduled to be in New York Friday afternoon. Any other year that schedule would have remained unchanged.

Susan directs a Suzuki preschool in New York. She teaches children aged two, three and four to play the violin, basing her teaching on the musical education precepts of Shinichi Suzuki, an approach that attests that music instruction can become as natural a part of a child's early learning experience as math, science, art and language.

Susan should and would have been back in New York Friday afternoon preparing the curriculum, practicing the violin.

Peter Grilli is director of education and communications at the Japan Film Center of the Japan Society Inc. in New York. He would have been back in New York, too. But Susan couldn't do it all herself.

And neither of the two would have been able to concentrate on their New York work anyway, even if they had gone back.

The planning board begins deliberations tomorrow night on SMI's application to build the 99 units, but the board is expected to take two months to reach a decision.

Susan has been coming to the Vineyard summers since she was a little girl. She worked here summers as a teenager. She and Peter were married on the banks of Lake Tashmoo behind their little house. Her parents bought the place years ago.

"They always cherished this above all the places they lived and I do too," Susan says. "I just cherish it so much."

Peter came to know the Vineyard through Susan's deep attachment. He feels the same way.

"We feel that we're honored to be a part of this beautiful, natural place," he says.

The land across the lake from the Grillis has been a subject of argument for more than a decade in Vineyard Haven. Joseph Chira, a summer resident of the town, first proposed building 200 units on the property 10 years ago. But after a long battle, and even after roads and tennis courts were built on the property, Mr. Chira went bankrupt. SMI bought the property and offered plans, but the planning board said they were inappropriate. The issue went to court. For a few years there was no public discussion about building on the property.

"I guess I had some unrealistic hope that it wouldn't be developed," Susan says. "I should have known that it would rear its ugly head."

The June hearing on the new SMI plan in the Katharine Cornell Theatre in Vineyard Haven lasted about two hours. Susan says she didn't breathe.

"You just know, you just know that the land can't support what they want to do," she says.

"And that it's just a business venture."

So she and Peter have made it their business to learn as much as they can about how such battles are fought and won. They've had a crash course in the political ways of the Vineyard. More than ever, they want to resolve whatever issues divide the summer people and people born on the Vineyard. They see a much larger issue.

"We've been summer people," Peter says.

"And I guess we've just fallen into the pattern of us and them. That's not how we feel about it. We don't really understand it, but that's just the way it was. But, obviously, this is not an us and them situation."

The Grillis have found many new allies, new friends, people born here, year-rounders and summer people.

"I always felt that we could never qualify as natives," Susan says. "That we should keep our distance. But both groups have come together here."

They share a feeling about the land.

"I would really do anything I could to see that this land is developed sensibly," she says.

"For SMI, this is a business thing. But that land is really a nature sanctuary now. It can accommodate more people, but only if it's done thoughtfully and carefully."

So the plans for school, the house in New York, the quiet summer vacation, and the professional lives of two people have receded into the background while Susan and Peter Grilli think about, worry over and fight for the land across the lake.

– July 26, 1983

Norton Family Heritage Sold To Pay Price of Government

By Michael F. Bamberger

ALLEN W. NORTON carries on his general contracting business in the same shop his father and grandfather did, off
Pease's Point Way in Edgartown. He wakes up at six in the morning and is asleep by nine. In between he smokes plenty of cigarettes and does plenty of hard work. On weekends he hunts
and fishes on land that his father hunted and fished on, as did
his grandfather and his great-grandfather and his great-great-
grandfather.

And now, for the first time in the very long history of Nor-
tons owning this land, Mr. Norton is selling pieces, parting with
land he loves dearly. He is the victim of inheritance taxes and
capital gains taxes, legal fees and brokerage fees, mortgage payments and interest fines.

So, Mr. Norton, a man plainly made of native intelligence and
muscle, is selling family land. He needs to, for the money he
owes is great.

He recently sold a 20-acre parcel with a farmhouse built by
a Norton in 1847 to a man named Richard L. Friedman of Boston
for $472,000. The land is part of the 228-acre Norton Farm on
Oyster Pond. It is land of Indian tepee holes and Norton family stories, of sheep grazing on large cleared fields and wood lots,
dense and lush. It is land of majestic sunsets. It is as historic as
it is beautiful.

The sale will not make Mr. Norton rich. It will not even bring
him close to eliminating his debts.

"Thank God for Mr. Friedman," he says. "He is a fine gentleman and he loves the property as much as I do."

Mr. Norton talks in his small office crowded with family pho-
tographs and stuffed deer heads. The conversation is of family

history, of capital gains taxes and of catching white perch in Oyster Pond.

"The neck of land is called Nonamesset, an ancient Indian name. The farm was bought in 1834 by my great-great-grandfather, William A., who bought it from Benjamin Norton, not a relative. Benjamin got it from Solomon Norton. Solomon got it from Bayes Norton. That brings us to 1743.

"William A. gave it to Allen, my great-grandfather, and Allen gave it to Frank L., my grandfather. Frank L. gave it to Winthrop B., my father."

When Winthrop B. Norton died Jan. 22, 1981, he left three children and 228 acres of land. Allen Norton, who was given 90 acres, was designated trustee of the estate.

The 228 acres of the farm were appraised at $1.4 million, a low figure explained by the land's agricultural use. "The federal government wanted $329,000 six months after death. The state wanted $121,000. That was a year and a half ago," says Mr. Norton.

Not having $450,000 handy, Mr. Norton decided to sell parts of the land to pay the taxes. To make matters worse, the federal and state government assessed an interest charge of 20 per cent annually.

"I worked out the numbers. The state interest came to $49 a day. The federal interest came to $201 a day. Just in interest it was $250 a day," Mr. Norton says. "That includes Sundays and holidays."

Another $130,000 owed.

"I had to do something, before the federal government did a public sale of my land for me."

Thus the $472,000 sale to Mr. Friedman.

Capital gains tax on the sale came to $100,000. Mr. Norton is paying the taxes by giving a 16-acre tract to Sheriff's Meadow Foundation. The tax credits will allow him more than the $100,000 owed.

"It's to save soul, to save face," says Mr. Norton.

Mr. Norton is still trying to sell four 12-acre lots. "This baseball game isn't over yet. We've still got an inning or two left. But I'm hoping we'll have the estate settled by Jan. 1, 1984."

That would be three years after Winthrop Norton's death.

"My father was an intelligent man, a traditional man.

"If the land was set up as a trust, with my father as life tenant, a lot of this could have been avoided. If he would have deeded some of the land to conservation interests, this could have been avoided. But he was of the old impression that you had to die before you could give anything away," says Mr. Norton.

Mr. Norton keeps about 15 sheep on the property and says Mr. Friedman plans to raise more.

"It's one of the most beautiful pieces of land on the Vineyard, or anywhere in the world. It's rural, it's wonderful," Mr. Friedman says. "It's a beautiful piece of land, and that's the way it is going to stay." Mr. Friedman is president of Carpenter and Company, developers of commercial properties in Boston and Cambridge.

To Mr. Norton it is terribly important that traditions be maintained. And he says Mr. Friedman is a man who respects the land and understands its history.

"In my business, I am trying to uphold the traditions started by my grandfather, Frank L., when he started it in 1910."

He shows a photograph of his grandfather's work crew.

"They built the Edgartown Yacht Club, and the original hospital. They made a lot of money. After the construction, they gave a $10,000 gift. In those days they employed 28 people.

"Look at this photo. That's Elmer Burnham and Ken Galley. That's a Model T Ford behind them. And that Buick, I learned to drive in that Buick. Years later we cut off the top and used it as a work truck."

Mr. Norton is 48. He was born in Edgartown and grew up there. By his own admission he was a difficult child, and his parents sent him to Tabor Academy in Marion for high school, which he attended from 1952 to 1954. He was expelled for drinking, and returned to the Edgartown School, from which he was graduated in 1954. He joined the Navy and served four years of active duty, four in the reserves.

In 1958 he married Judith Lapham of Carlisle and they have since adopted three children, Rachel, Melissa and Mark. The family names are painted on Mr. Norton's truck.

Mr. Norton says his children do not love the land as much as he does. "That's to be expected. You have to be older to appreciate the beauty of a piece of land. When I was growing up I took it for granted. Now I appreciate it."

The business that once employed 28 people is now a one-man operation, and the one man does only renovations. "There are enough houses already.

"The Island is going to hell, I'm afraid. Thank God for George Flynn and others who have land and who have been willing to sacrifice to keep the land from being developed.

"We started off with a planned community. Then we got the zoning. So now we've got the zoning, but not the planning."

But Mr. Norton prefers talk about the character, the beauty and the meaning of land, not about development and capital gains taxes, or the pain associated with the parting of his family land. This becomes evident while wandering the Norton Farm with him.

"Look over there. It's an osprey with a fish in its mouth. That's quite a sight, isn't it?"

Mr. Norton, his face full of dark creases, squints into the late afternoon sun. He looks out across the sweep of fields, some still his, others not. "You come down here and you can really breathe, I mean really breathe," he says.

– August 9, 1983

Changes in Scale

W<small>E CANNOT UNDERSTAND</small> the meaning of growth and development in the life of the Vineyard if we persist in thinking that growth simply means more of the same. It is easy to think of growth in terms of more houses with families like ours inside, more children like ours in the schools, more shops and services like those we already know. But growth is not simply more of the same, because it brings changes in scale which profoundly affect our social relationships, and the relationship of our society to the local environment. Examples of these changes are all around us.

Each summer the Island population balloons, and no one with fresh memories of the season just past will argue that the Vineyard in the summer is just like the Vineyard in winter, only with more people. The Island's resident population has also been steadily growing, and bringing dramatic changes in community scale. All across the Vineyard, growth is changing the way we know each other, and are known in return. It places new strains on government, on services, on the very connective tissue that binds us together as neighbors.

It is becoming possible to be anonymous on the Vineyard today, unknown in the sense that one can be unknown on the streets of a city. This change most directly challenges those institutions whose work is helping people, for the first task in this work is identifying those in need. And citizens feel increasingly alienated from the institutions — including government — which serve the Island. Our population grows each year, but fewer people are willing to serve. The Vineyard's small pool of public servants is under increasing pressure, and reinforcements in their battle for the quality of our Island life are urgently needed.

The environment is the area in which growth is changing life on the Vineyard most dramatically. The Island environment has a certain scale and set of natural limits which define its carrying capacity: Its single aquifer can supply only so many million gallons of water per day, and its soil can absorb only so much waste before it is poisoned.

We are witnessing the buildout of the Vineyard, an era in which yesterday's junk acreage is today's prime buildable land, if only you can afford it. We are running out of land and out of landfills. We are expanding our schools and town halls and are studying our town charters to figure out why local government isn't working like it used to any longer. The scale is all wrong.

No builder of another house or business wanted to change the Vineyard — the idea was to pack more into the same beloved place, but somehow the equation isn't balancing in the same way now. For while we build and build, the Vineyard itself — the field on which this game of increments is being played out — is not growing at all.

– Editorial, October 10, 1986

❧ ❧ ❧

Dunkirk at South Beach

OUTRAGE IS THE WORD most often heard in public reaction to the private pillage of South Beach on the Vineyard. The shredding of South Beach for personal profit amounts to a declaration of war against the Vineyard — all the Vineyard. And the message of what historians will call plunder at South Beach is this: The Island is for sale and nothing is safe or sacred.

Not even South Beach, this most cherished public symbol of what the Vineyard is all about. We are witnessing the rape of Island treasure, the defiling of the Vineyard's Atlantic face. It is as if someone shattered precious stained glass, leaving only shards and wreckage inside the Island church. Or worse. In the case of South Beach the sanctuary was sold — sold out from beneath the congregation that is the community of Vineyard people.

And if this onslaught of development, this ransacking march of the developer, is not halted at the South Beach barrier, then the Island community will face nothing less than a sense of despair about the future. South Beach, now bleeding in this battle for the future of the Vineyard, is only the latest target of developers in pursuit of huge profits and narrow interest.

It is time for the Vineyard to wake up and act. There is a war going on here. The barricades are up and they stand at South Beach, a barrier beach. In another war, at another time, Winston Churchill, then the British prime minister, said this about another island, his island, his nation: "We shall defend our island, whatever the cost may be, we shall fight on the beaches...we shall fight in the hills; we shall never surrender." The Vineyard would do well to hear his words if it is to avoid further retreat and its own Dunkirk at South Beach.

– Editorial, July 14, 1987

✼ ✼ ✼

Lost in the Rubbish of War

By Julia Wells

IT WAS ONE OF THE TOUGHEST subdivision battles in the history of the town of Edgartown.

It raged on for years and resulted in lawsuits complicated by title claims complicated by layers and layers of mortgages, and finally foreclosures.

It was Vineyard Acres II, a subdivision whose name became synonymous with Rhode Island developers Louis Giuliano and Patricia Lett in the early 1980s. Mr. Giuliano and Miss Lett quickly became familiar figures in town offices, where more often than not their presence at planning board meetings was marked by heated arguments and ominous threats. It was a heady time for development on Martha's Vineyard.

In 1982, after a long and acrimonious struggle, the Edgartown Planning Board granted approval for Vineyard Acres II — 148 lots on 245 acres off the West Tisbury Road.

Today, more than eight years later, there is not one completed house in the subdivision. There are three starts: one foundation, one house which burned to the ground while under construction two years ago (arson is suspected) and one unfinished house. The empty shell sits amid quiet acres of scrub oak, its plywood weathered by the elements, holes that should have been windows boarded up. All around is evidence of vandalism and illegal dumping. Down cul-de-sacs once planned for houses lie old mattresses, piles of construction rubbish, discarded washing machines and dead automobiles. Some have been used for target practice. Everywhere the woods are strewn with trash.

Whatever happened to Vineyard Acres II?

At this writing ownership of a vast portion of the subdivision is unclear, and as for the future no one will speculate, given the state of the economy and the real estate market on the Island. It is known that Sheriff's Meadow Foundation owns 39.1 acres in the center of the subdivision; the foundation won a land court ruling in 1986 upholding its claim to the land. Developers Lett and Giuliano appealed the court decision, and in December of 1987 the state supreme court upheld the land court decision. The case involved a complex title claim, but in the end the high court found sufficient evidence to rule that Sheriff's Meadow had established title.

The successful title claim raised questions about the status of the special permit for the subdivision; the developers later became involved in numerous transfers of portions of the property. There were stacks of mortgages, including more than one construction loan. But little construction ever took place at Vineyard Acres II (part of the subdivision was known as Bay Courte because it was transfered to a new owner — he soon went bankrupt).

This year in early August a foreclosure auction was held on a portion of the property; at the auction the Title USA insurance company purchased a substantial number of lots — the exact number is not known, although 62 were offered for sale. Late this summer the title company paid to have the main entrance to the subdivision blocked by piling up a lot of the old cars and trash. The Edgartown Board of Health has been monitoring the illegal dumping on the property; the board has written to both the title company and Sheriff's Meadow citing the dumping. No one has been able to trace the source of the dumping.

In the meantime Louis Giuliano and Patricia Lett have been making headlines elsewhere, first in central Massachusetts and more recently in Rhode Island, where they were promoting plans to build a $15 million harness track in Burrillville, R.I. (the track proposal was killed by Rhode Island voters in early November). A story published in the Providence Journal in early October reported that Mr. Giuliano and Miss Lett have had business ties with organized crime figures extending over the last two decades. Among other things, the story revealed that one of the early backers of the Vineyard Acres II subdivision was Eugene Carlino, a convicted felon who is reportedly a close friend of Raymond J. "Junior" Patriarca, son of and successor to organized crime boss Raymond L. S. Patriarca.

The story also reported that the Ocean Heights home used by Mr. Giuliano and Miss Lett as a home base when they came to the Vineyard for planning board meetings in the early 1980s had a curious ownership history. Miss Lett sold the house to convicted New Bedford gambler Horacio "Babe" Ferreira for $10 in 1978, and then bought it back from him three years later for $1. The Journal reported that the dollar transaction occured one month after the FBI raided Mr. Ferreira's Acushnet home and 22 other locations in an interstate gambling probe. The house has since been sold.

– November 30, 1990

A View to the Future

NOT MANY YEARS AGO, the buzzword among Vineyard planners was buildout — an ugly and ominous term for the possibility that the Island's 65,000 acres might soon be developed to the full extent allowed by zoning. Summer throngs of a quarter million people or more were seriously predicted. It was common to hear that the Vineyard is just 10 years behind the Cape, a statement whose overtones were guaranteed to chill any Islander just back from Hyannis.

But this week, the preservation of the Allen Farm in Chilmark stands as another sign that the Vineyard is rejecting this tragic future. Once again, the Martha's Vineyard Land Bank has provided leverage for this community as it turns away from the steady destruction of the environment upon which our economy depends. There is a danger of taking our land bank for granted, just as we can forget to appreciate our Martha's Vineyard Commission and every hard-working planning board, board of health and historic district commission on the Island. The saving of the Allen Farm — who could put a price on that grand sweep across open fields to the sea — is but the latest triumph for an agency that has now purchased 612 critical acres of Island property for enjoyment by future generations, and helps to control and protect 134 acres more.

If only we remain vigilant and take none of these hard-fought gains for granted, the word for the 1990s and for the new century beyond will be not buildout, but balance, as we seek to define a sustainable Island environment, a Vineyard that will mean renewal and refreshment for generations of Islanders.

– Editorial, June 1, 1990

Unprecedented Conservation Pact Adds Over 800 Acres to State Forest

By Julia Wells

SOME 830 ACRES of unspoiled upland property in the rural perimeters of Edgartown — part of the vast place known to many as Pohogonot, whose total land area at one time included some 5,000 acres of magnificent upland and coastal farmland — will be sold by the descendants of the late George D. Flynn to the state Department of Environmental Management (DEM) by the end of the month.

Once the purchase is complete the property will be added to the Manuel F. Correllus State Forest, bringing the total size of the forest to more than 5,000 acres. The acquisition is believed to be the largest single conservation purchase by DEM this year. Purchase price will be $4 million, a price which is believed to be under the appraised value of the land.

The property runs along the south side of the West Tisbury Road and is bounded by the state forest and also the secluded Oyster-Watcha compound. It also abuts the Wintucket land owned by the Edgartown Water Company and conservation land owned by Sheriff's Meadow Foundation. The land targeted for purchase by the state is all upland and sandplain and includes no coastal or shorefront areas.

Funds for the purchase reportedly will come directly from the DEM budget. The property is currently owned by Eric Peters, trustee for the Elizabeth D. Flynn Trust, and the trustees of the Pohogonot Trust.

The property will be sold to the state in what is termed a friendly taking — essentially an eminent domain proceeding which is undertaken with the full cooperation and agreement of parties on both sides. The purchase is the result of negotiations which have been underway for some three years.

The property was once part of the grassy sandplain where sheep grazed and the now-extinct heath hen roamed, and the potential exists for the property to be returned to this more traditional historical landscape. Although no formal announcement has been made yet about uses for the property, it is expected that it will be made available for public recreational use in a manner similar to the present state forest — including walking, bicycling and hunting.

The coastal sandplains of the Vineyard and Nantucket were named by The Nature Conservancy as one of the 40 Last Great Places on Earth in an unusual global conservation initiative two years ago. Once the purchase is complete, the property will become the largest piece of sandplain under single ownership in the entire region.

George Daniel Flynn, the patriarch from Fall River, began to assemble the vast family tract at Pohogonot in 1903, after he was injured in a train accident and was ordered by his doctor to rest in the country. He discovered a large home, the Crane House, on the open shooting grounds of the South Shore. Since then the Flynn property at Pohogonot has been used for farming and grazing, hunting and fishing.

And though the land has been sold off in portions over the years, the family has always had a strong bent for preserving the land. Oyster-Watcha, Bold Water and Swan Neck are all limited subdivisions with a conservation theme.

When George D. Flynn Jr. put the first of his vast holdings on the market in the late 1970s, Henry Beetle Hough, the late editor of the Vineyard Gazette, wrote: "The effect on the Island of the breaking up of large properties such as those of Mr. Flynn is bound to be profound. These old properties were bound to be called 'farms' or 'places' but never 'estates' and they were not walled off in the manner of mainland estates. To some extent, from what seems time immemorial, they remained more or less open to the public, sometimes more freely than in other instances. They contributed immeasurably to the vistas and general scenery as viewed from roads or hills, and the ambiance they gave to the countryside has almost always been considered a part of the character and quality of the Island.

"This passing of the old, whether one considers it with nostalgia or not, has become inevitable.... There are not only two horns of a dilemma, as between assessors and large property owners, but three horns, the last including the problem of a traditionally open Island with broad countrysides facing division and restriction dictated by economics and similar pressures."

— June 16, 1995

❧   ❧   ❧

Open Space Today, House Lots Tomorrow: Looking to the Future with 2020 Vision

By Julia Wells

THE STAGE IS MARTHA'S VINEYARD, the year 2020. The villages are gone. Hardware stores, grocery markets and post offices have moved to commercial strips on the outskirts of every town and the old town centers are a curious mix of pricey boutiques, restaurants and souvenir stores a little gone to seed.

In summer thousands of tourists still flock to the Island to enjoy the beaches, swim in the cold ocean water and visit the numerous wildlife sanctuaries. Many also come to gawk at the palatial waterfront estates owned by the wealthy people who summer on the Island. These lavish estates sprawl across places once occupied by rambling farmhouses or simple summer camps.

And as they sit in the ever-present line of traffic which snakes along the Beach Road between Oak Bluffs and Edgartown, parents tell their children stories of the days when they used to rake for quahaugs and go dip-netting for scallops in Sengekontacket

Pond. Now all the shellfish in the pond are dead, killed by a series of mysterious algal blooms.

An outlandish picture of Martha's Vineyard in 25 years? Perhaps not.

As the Island approaches the 21st century along with a rapidly rebounding real estate market, a burgeoning population of year-round as well as summer residents and a whole array of attendant social complexities, the dialectic between development and conservation once again comes into sharp focus. To some the questions may be shopworn, but when looking ahead they remain critical: Will there be another building boom? What are the lessons from the 1980s? And how can the Vineyard protect its rural character and rare natural habitats and still allow for development?

Some say it may already be too late.

"Will there be another building boom? The answer is it really doesn't matter because I think the die has been cast. The Vineyard in 20 years is going to feel just like any other suburb," said James Lengyel, executive director of the Martha's Vineyard Land Bank.

Mr. Lengyel and others spoke out candidly about the future of the Vineyard this week and the picture which emerged was unsettling. It includes the potential buildout on thousands of existing house lots created during the 1980s, pollution of many of the coastal ponds from too many septic systems, and fragmentation of many of the natural ecosystems by roads, street lights and swimming pools. It is a picture of the new-money Martha's Vineyard, a place where old summer camps and cottages are rebuilt into what some wryly call trophy houses — opulent homes which are more reminiscent of the Hamptons than the New England coast.

It is a picture which is not without beauty — the Vineyard of the future will undoubtedly include hundreds of acres of protected conservation land and a rich abundance of birds and other wildlife. But if many of the predictions are true, the Vineyard is sadly only a few steps shy of the devastating mistakes of Cape Cod.

"Frankly, I am not trying to be an alarmist, I am just being completely factual," Mr. Lengyel said. "If you work with town tax maps the way I do you will see that there are many, many house lots left to be developed. The public is driving by property today believing that it is open space, but in fact it is not.

"The Vineyard in 20 years will be a suburb but it will be one of America's most handsome suburbs," he continued. "This is not to say that we should be wringing our hands, because we have done a remarkable job. When you think of a suburb you think about what they call sprawl and of course the opposite of that is a village center. On the Island those centers are for the most part gone. Suburbs mean a rigid division between public and private land — in truly rural areas people do not feel the need to be so vigilant about protecting their boundaries. This used to be true on the Island but it is all changing now and in the future we are going to see more no trespassing signs and more fences," he said, adding:

"When all is said and done this is going to be one of the most beautiful suburbs in America. But there is going to be significant change to the character and fabric of this community."

The land bank, which collects a two per cent fee on most real estate transactions and uses the funds to buy public conservation land, was created in 1986 at the outset of the building boom. Since its inception the land bank has purchased 1,067 acres of land on the Island embracing property of virtually every type. But it is a small contribution on an Island of some 65,000 acres. "The word I use to describe the land bank's impact on the Island is 'trivial,' because we are going to work hard and keep purchasing land, but in 20 years the Island will only look trivially different because of the land bank," Mr. Lengyel said.

Others agree. "The Vineyard is moving in a direction that a number of people are not particularly comfortable with," said Brendan O'Neill, executive director of the Vineyard Conservation Society.

The numbers are compelling. The regional Island master plan done by the Martha's Vineyard Commission in 1991 shows that between 1980 and 1991 4,000 building permits were issued on the Island. Recent figures show that since then several hundred more have been issued. For perspective, between 1980 and 1991 in all of Berkshire County — which has a land area 10 times as large as the Vineyard and was under tremendous development pressure during the building boom — 3,000 building permits were issued.

Forty years ago 2.5 per cent of Martha's Vineyard was developed; today 33 per cent is developed and an additional 20 per cent has been subdivided. About 17 per cent is in conservation. At buildout the MVC master plan projects the year-round population of the Vineyard will be 23,000.

Mr. O'Neill said the conservation society did a calculation to determine how much of the remaining land needs to be protected and came up with about 10,000 acres. And this leads him to a conclusion echoed by others for years — that in the end private property owners will make the real difference.

"Start throwing the numbers around and you are going up into the hundreds of millions of dollars," he said, putting a rough dollar amount on the 10,000 acres needing protection. "And the land bank, with about $3 million a year — well, that brings us to the point of remembering Dick Pough [a noted Vineyard conservationist] who said in 1966 that if the Vineyard is to be protected it will be the private property owners.... There must be a major philanthropic contribution on this Island, or else we could go back to the Islands Trust bill and bring in the eminent domain powers of the federal government for a national seashore. We are at an opportunity juncture where the natural systems are intact and the lynch pin is really the private property owner."

In the debate between development and conservation the two sides are no longer very far apart. And there is a new theme in the dialogue: Along with the land, many say Island values are endangered.

"The most important thing people have to decide is if they want to save the values that make the Vineyard what it is and have brought people here all summer long each summer," said Charles W. Clifford, executive director of the Martha's Vineyard Commission.

Even real estate brokers these days are talking about conservation. "I think this Island is going to dictate its own limitations and we don't have enough land to continue this business of transforming the Island into a glamorous place with large houses with pools and all these amenities," said Justine Priestley, a Realtor and partner in Priestley and Smadbeck in Vineyard Haven. She continued: "The Island is itself an area out in the sea — it is kind of an escape and people have always been attracted to the Island for its simplicity, but now we have a situation which is sort of like when large herds of animals come to an area and the deer begin to strip the trees."

Mr. O'Neill also remarked on changing social mores. "There is concern and you hear it coming from a number of places, including from people who have been coming here for 50 years," he said. "The qualities that attracted them to the Vineyard included its isolation — these people sense that is changing and that the new people who are coming here have different expectations."

He added: "While it is true that simplicity is what attracts people to the Island, on an ecological level the essence of the Vineyard is its rich complexity. As suburbanization creeps in and these natural areas are increasingly fragmented by roads and lights and swimming pools, we will increasingly fracture that biodiversity."

Mrs. Priestley concluded: "At this stage we are in a very sanguine, very happy stage on the Island, but we really are having to confront the problems of overpopulation. We have a little bit of room left but not much — the difficult thing is to figure out a way to stop and I don't know what we can do.

"And in all the verbiage and speculation about the future, one single ingredient seems to be lost — just plain old common sense. I believe there are two ways out. We can use common sense and set our priorities in line, or we can wait until people don't want to come here anymore."

– May 12, 1995

❧   ❧   ❧

Is Bigger Better? It's Time to Think Again

By Phyllis Meras

BIG HAS BECOME BETTER FOR EVERYTHING — a bigger airport, a bigger Steamship Authority dock, bigger markets, bigger fairgrounds, bigger houses.

Like 9,999 others, I enjoyed the Livestock '95 concert on the Martha's Vineyard Agricultural Society fairgrounds last week. But now that West Tisbury has a bigger parking area — accommodating 5,000 cars, I am told — I cannot help wondering what bigger events, in seasons to come, will fill the fairgrounds and alter the quality of Island life.

For the quality of Island life is surely being altered by the economic urge that says that bigger is better. My credentials for thinking so aren't bad.

For the last two decades I have been living mainly by writing about travel. In those two decades, I have traveled the world, and I have learned a lot about tourism and tourists. Admittedly, they come in many categories, but I am principally acquainted with two of them. First, there are those who really don't care where they are as long as they are away from where they usually are.

These are the sort who frequent Hawaii's mega-resorts where Venetian gondolas take them to their deluxe grass huts along an imitation Venetian canal. Obviously, these tourists are not in Hawaii to learn about its culture and rain forests and lava flows. But nowadays, I wonder if it is not these we are attempting to attract with our bigger-is-better Island philosophy, and our sense that Dunkin' Donuts and Subway chains are mainland advantages those tourists surely won't want to do without.

But there is a better kind of tourist with whom I am acquainted, too. This is the tourist who travels intelligently to see and experience the unfamiliar. The unfamiliar, more often than not, is that which is quaint, picturesque or pristine. When bigger airports, bigger hotels, bigger shopping malls begin to sprawl across landscapes, at first, because they are new, they may be an attraction. But a decade later, their novelty has gone — and the landscape that was destroyed for their construction is gone, too. The trees have been felled. Their bird and animal inhabitants have gone with the trees.

Meanwhile, to justify the cost of the new facilities' construction, more air traffic has had to be solicited; more conventions sought. More T-shirt shops and hamburger heavens have been opened to supply the newcomers. These, like the landscape that had disappeared, are likely, after a short blaze of glory, to disappear, too. Higher rents force them out of business. Shortsightedly, many tourism officials fail to look ahead and consider the future.

Where once there were mullion-windowed storefronts in charming little communities, plate-glass storefronts replace them. High-class, high-rise hotels and condominiums that entrepreneurs like block the beachfront views to ordinary folk.

Happily, on the Island, all this hasn't happened — yet — but it is clearly just around the corner. The new Steamship Authority facility has much to be said for it, but the sheds to protect passengers from the rain also cut off a harbor view to townspeople.

New, bigger (and, therefore, better) passenger and freight facilities for the airport are just around the corner. These will make the Martha's Vineyard Airport a more appealing, more welcoming place for visitors, proponents of the grand facility are pointing out. Yet, rarely, when I have landed on a Caribbean island and been waiting for my luggage at a dinky shed, have I heard disgruntled travelers complaining that the facilities were not sleek and modern. More often they have been smiling and relaxed. Their vacation has begun at the funky airport where life is still laid-back and even amusingly inefficient.

I have long been a customer at Cronig's Up-Island Market, for it has been just the right size to get into and out of quickly. I could find what I wanted without referring to a giant table of contents on the wall. Because it wasn't crowded (lacking, as it did, absolutely everything a frenetic shopper might want), there was still time for country small talk at its checkout counters. It has been a personal sort of store. But now it is to be replaced by a bigger (of course better) impersonal one where, once I have ascertained which aisle carries which product, I will be able to shop without uttering a word.

To make way for it, a stand of Indian Hill trees is gone. And I liked those Indian Hill trees. It was foolish of me, I suppose, to feel fondness for scrub oak. Progress on Martha's Vineyard demands that tree after tree fall, berry patch after berry patch go.

My experience suggests that it's a pity to see the Vineyard go the unplanned way of growth and "progress," when other tourist destinations have found out that such unplanned progress, in the long run, isn't progress at all. I know there are planning boards and conservation commissions and watchdog organizations seeking to protect the Island, but unbridled growth seems *de rigueur*, regardless, when state or federal monies become available for improvements, or developers have innovative enough ideas.

In Maine, two decades ago, a study showed that tourism was downright detrimental to the state because of the impact it was having on the quality of life of Mainers. Roads were clogged. Beaches were crowded and the visitors who were coming were not contributing significantly to the economy with their purchases of souvenir coffee mugs and postcards.

Bermuda has limited the number of cruise ships it allows to visit the island, maintaining that smoke from their smokestacks blackens the roofs of their houses. The rainwater that runs off the roofs is their water supply and sooty water is unpalatable and unhealthy. Because their roads are narrow and picturesque — and they like them that way — they limit the number of cars on the island.

As recently as last summer, just across the water on Cape Cod, a distraught Cape Cod Commission, chamber of commerce and economic development council together hired an off-Cape planner to help them reassess if bigger is better; if more tourists really help the economy and if "expansion" actually is the be-all and end-all.

— September 8, 1995

INHABITANTS

*

THE CREED of the Vineyard Gazette is A Journal of Island Life, but perhaps it ought to read A Journal of Island Lives. In the broadness of mainland living, men and women may tend and harvest farms quite apart from one another. In isolation they may build and launch a boat, construct a home and raise a family, stage a play, show paintings, or hold a cultural fete. Not on Martha's Vineyard.

Here every important venture begun by one individual inevitably captures the interest of two or three others, who usually suggest the involvement of two or three more, onward and outward, so that every enterprise winds up stirring the consciousness of the Island in some small but significant way.

The Gazette has long recognized — ever since 1925, when it began to profile Islanders in a column called Interesting Men of Vineyard Haven — that the life of Martha's Vineyard is not led by agencies or boards of government, but by what its people think and do and say. Tell of a life on Martha's Vineyard, the paper believes, and you begin to take the measure of an entire time and a whole place. We are unique in this way. Municipal newspapers — indeed, most newspapers on the mainland — abandoned that idea long ago.

In the profiles, essays and conversations that follow, the great story is of diversity, vast and thrilling for so small and removed a place, and of a population mixing together in ways unimaginable not so long ago. In 1936, for instance, Henry Beetle Hough wrote of a widening division between summer visitors and year-rounders who, in a less refined era at the dawn of resorthood, had once met "on something like equal terms." He was writing and speaking of the same division at the end of the 1960s.

Now increasingly the population regards each Vineyarder and each faithful visitor as fully an inhabitant, potentially a vital investor in the life of the Island. The paper is mindful of the passing of eras, and sets itself the task of marking them in full, individual by individual. Yet in the last quarter century it has also paid closer attention to artisans and troubadours, to the outlook and energies of Island youth, and to those who have led in the worlds of politics and entertainment — these among many, many others.

This belief in each inhabitant as a contributor to the life of a place is the implicit theme of every profile it prints, a singular feature of Vineyard Gazette journalism.

– T.D.

Tapping Island Knowledge

By Garson Kanin

A STORY HAPPENED SOME YEARS AGO that I find very amusing. In Edgartown, which is part of Martha's Vineyard, where I live, we had a power outage, which meant that everything went out. We had no light; all the refrigerators went off. The air conditioning systems went off. And of course people panicked. And all the experts worked for two or three days trying to get the power on. And they couldn't. They even sent for people from Boston, and they couldn't get the power turned on.

And then someone remembered that one of the men who worked on the original installation, many years ago, was still around, had been retired, and was now living in an old retirement home in Gay Head somewhere. So they sent for him, and they brought him down, and this little old man about 87 years old came into the powerhouse, and he got down on his hands and knees, and he looked around, and there was a little switch box, and finally he took a mallet out of his pocket, and he went tap, tap, tap. And all the lights came on.

So being a Yankee, of course, the next day he sent the town of Edgartown a bill for his services. And the bill was extraordinary. It was for one thousand dollars and two cents. And it was itemized as follows:

Tapping: two cents.

Knowing where to tap: one thousand dollars.

– May 16, 1980

Captain Poole Speaks to a Life
In Good and Sufficient Boats

By Phyllis Meras

ORDINARILY, ALL WINTER LONG Capt. Donald L. Poole of Menemsha is out scalloping. It doesn't matter that he's 77, and that the temperature's down in the 30s. Donald Poole likes being out by himself in his Downeast 34, the Dorothy and Everett.

"Ever since I met my wife — I think 'twas 1926 — my boats have been named either Dorothy C. or Dorothy and Everett after my wife and son," he says.

But this winter, there was a spate of days when Menemsha harbor was frozen over and all her boats, including the Dorothy and Everett, were immovable in the ice. So on those days, Donald Poole was confined to quarters, so to speak, to the shack near his son Everett's fish market. There, in a red and black flannel shirt and gray and red socks and bright yellow wool gloves, with an eye to the coming season, he sawed lathes for lobster pots. Because, he maintains, he doesn't like to work in a hot building, he kept the door ajar and the winter wind whistled in, and every now and then picked up a wood shaving from one part of the floor and whisked it to another, the way it whisks leaves here and there in the autumn.

"I expect it's about 16 degrees here just now," he remarked of the temperature, as he paused in his sawing to warm up his nose by lighting his pipe. "It's got to be a minimum of 30 to go out scalloping. You know, I don't care what the scientists say, there's been a change in the weather and the height of the tides since I was young. I have contacts in Greenland with a half-Dane, half-Eskimo, and he cites the same thing up there and lays it to the fact that the glaciers are melting and there's less and less ice cap. I can tell there's a difference by the height of the tide going by Noman's Land and Gay Head. It was 72 years ago, you must remember, that I started fishing with my father in these waters, and the weather here is entirely different now than it was then. My theory is," and he took a long puff on his pipe, "that they've changed the jet stream in space by throwing all those spacecraft up there. Tom Tilton down in Vineyard Haven agrees with me, even if the scientists don't. But you know, sometimes even a damned fool comes up with something that means something."

That was more nattering than Donald Poole tends to offer most visitors. He clenched his pipe tight in his teeth and turned back to his saw.

Donald Poole was born in Chilmark, the son of Emily Howland Poole and Capt. Everett A. Poole. To the best of his recollection, he was six years old when he first went to sea with his fisherman father. "At least I was so small that all I could do was to steer," he remembers. "She was a 27-foot catboat my father had, and we'd go out lobstering. Like I said, nature is changing. I remember once on a two-day stretch with my father going from Gay Head to Noman's Land to Cuttyhunk, we caught a little over 4,000 pounds of lobster. We got 10 cents apiece for the counters — they were nine inches long — and 10½ cents for the full-sized ones. We used to sell a lot of them to big-welled smacks that would come up from New York. Can you imagine getting 4,000 pounds of lobster on a trip like that nowadays?"

But that early fishing was confined to vacation time. In winter, there was schooling to be attended to — part of it in Vineyard Haven and part of it in Rhode Island at the now-defunct East Greenwich Academy.

"Several of us from the Island went there — Sara West from Menemsha and Beatrice Gifford from West Tisbury and Russell Hancock, the son to the Hancock who ran the plumbing business in Vineyard Haven. It was a school that was strong on religion and damn weak on grub. Saturday night we got one frankfurt and black bread. The headmaster was a Methodist clergyman," Captain Poole said, and sighed unhappily at the memory.

So after two years, he returned to the Island, and finished high school in Vineyard Haven. "Bart Mayhew used to transport us down. He had a six-wheeler yellow Model T and he used kerosene instead of alcohol as anti-freeze in the radiator and sometimes the kerosene would catch fire. Not too seldom, as a matter of fact. It made for some nice excitement for school children. Yes, the old yellow-wheeler was quite a car. There was a series of pulleys and lobster pot rope that were the steering gear and sometimes the ropes and pulleys would part. But I s'pose half a dozen of us from Chilmark would go with him just the same. That was 1920 to '21. It took about three quarters of an hour, I expect.

"And then there was a girl named Aleta Flanders who lived very near Gay Head and when she was old enough to have a license, she took us. If I remember right, it cost us 35 cents a day for that ride. That's what they used to call the good old days," Captain Poole said, and stopped sawing again for a while.

"In those days, after I'd finished high school and went to work full-time for my father, he paid me $10 a month and 25 cents a week in spending money. But that was quite enough. A candy bar only cost a few cents and a good jackknife half a dollar. Why, I thought I was the richest kid you ever saw! And how I loved going out after fish!"

Not just Donald Poole's father, but his grandfather, Anderson T. Poole of Chilmark, had been a seafaring man. Indeed, Capt. Anderson Poole was Quitsa's sperm whaleman.

"From where I live," Donald Poole said proudly, "I can see the home where my father, my uncle, my great-grandfather and my grandfather all lived at one time or another. And an eighth of a mile across the road is the house where my great-great-grandfather and my great-great-great-grandfather lived. Some goddamned summer people live there now, I'm sorry to say.

"Where did my grandfather do his whaling? Why, he went

everywhere in the world except the Arctic. He lived to be 78. We lived at Quitsa in those days, and after he came home from sea I'd go down to see him and he'd sit there and tell me wonderful yarns. When I was a boy of eight or ten, there were still whalemen alive and they'd gather at my grandfather's house of an evening and I'd sit there quiet in a corner and they'd all go around the world many times in their recollections. It was quite exciting for a small boy. The stories they used to tell were unbelievable. All through the Pacific and the South Atlantic they went, and that takes care of a good part of the watery world. He always complained that he'd wasted his life whaling, though, and I'd say, 'Then why, grandfather, did you keep at it?'

"He never really answered, but I know the answer now. Can you think of any better way to make a living? The only things you have to contend with once you quit harbor and leave the breakwater behind are the weather and the Almighty — at least that's the way I feel about it. But when you come ashore, there are people to deal with, and that's bad. You know, there are some of us who don't feel exactly right ashore. Sometimes I almost wonder why God Almighty made the land, and the best reason I can think of is to separate the oceans. It's very convenient for that purpose. But we're a little different from most people, I s'pose, those of us who go to sea all our lives."

And with satisfaction, Donald Poole looked around his realm — at the nets that hung from the rafters of his fishing shack, and the rubber hip boots and the lobster pots and the anchors and the coiled lines, and he recounted a favorite tale about his father and the sea — how once, in pursuit of a 500-pound swordfish, he had driven it onto a shoal in his skiff, then jumped overboard onto the fish's back and wrestled it up onto the beach. There, he had finally felled it with an oak. "Did he have to? No, he didn't have to. It was just one of those things he wanted to do."

Reminiscing further about his father, Donald Poole remembered the day when the engine on his father's boat had stopped.

"Father was a man a good deal like I am — rather short-tempered. He simply gathered up his tools, dismantled the shaft, yanked the engine off and threw it overboard. 'Boy, let's put the canvas up,' he said then, 'and go to New Bedford and buy ourselves a new engine.' He never believed in going without a sail."

Although he never tackled a swordfish to get it ashore, like his father, Donald Poole has swordfished for years, though his first love has always been lobstering.

"Swordfishing was fun, but there wasn't so much money in it as in lobstering. In the days when I was doing it, most of the fish went to Woods Hole, to Sam Cahoon, who had a wholesale place — and a retail market, too, down there on the wharf near where the Steamship Authority is.

"What do I think of long-lining? It's strictly foreign to my bringing-up. Harpooning, it's rare to get a swordfish under 50 pounds and now, long-lining, they get them as small as 15 or 20 pounds. You just catch everything regardless of size. But on the other hand, you've got to remember that any change as you get older strikes you as being not so good as the way you used to do things. Changes simply are not acceptable.

"In the days when I was doing it, I was helmsman once aboard the Hazel Jackson out of Edgartown. We had eight men and four dories we'd drop overboard to go after fish. July was the best time to catch them. We'd start on the backside of Long Island, around Amagansett, and we'd go to Block Island for two or three weeks. We'd start about the 10th of June. Then the fish would move east'ard, southeast of Noman's and near where the Nantucket Lightship used to be.

"The trouble with swordfishing now as I see it is that the fish gets drowned. You see, they put weights on the line — you may let out as much as 20 miles of line — along with the hooks and the fish dies in the water that way and soaks in the water. When you harpoon a fish, you kill it straight out and haul it alongside and let the blood run out. That way it doesn't settle in the meat.

"But anyway, however it is you fish them, swordfish have become mighty scarce around here. We used to average 75 to 100 a season. Now the pleasure boats are quite pleased to get six or eight. No one knows what's happened to all of them, unless it's that the trash fishermen get all the fish the swordfish used to like to eat so there's nothing to come here for."

Talking was apparently warming Captain Poole up, for, the frigid temperature in his fishing shack notwithstanding, he drew a trademark red kerchief from a back pocket, wiped his brow, and the ear from which dangles a small gold ring, a gift some six years ago from his wife for their 50th wedding anniversary. Donald Poole remembers his grandfather's wearing gold earrings — the whaleman's sign of having gone around the Horn.

"My wife and I are double cousins, you know," Captain Poole offered. "She's part Hillman, part Cottle. My great-grandfather was a Hillman and my great-grandmother a Cottle, and she was a Cottle and her mother a Hillman. She was born and brought up in Brookfield. Her father was a lawyer and a judge up there and her mother went to teach school. Then her father died. Her mother came down to Edgartown for a visit and one day they came to call on my father. I was 19 then. We were married two years later when we were 21 and after she'd finished school. She went to Bridgewater, finished in June, and we were married in August. Was I smitten at first sight? Well, she says that *she* was.

"After we were married, she taught one year in Chilmark. Then Everett was born and she didn't go back to it till he got the size that he was going to school in Vineyard Haven. Then she started to teach again in Chilmark. But you know, no matter what she's been doing, there's always been a good, hot meal on the table for me when I got home. And sometimes it's been very late at night. I have 275 lobster pots, after all, and often I don't get home till around 10 o'clock at night because I have a lot of bait work to do after I get ashore. What time do I go out? Oh, usually around daylight."

Reminded of it, Captain Poole returned to his lobster pot making.

"You know, when I was a boy," he recalled as he sawed a lathe, "25 or 30 men built their pots here, and now I'm the last one who does. And I'll tell you, I love building my pots, so why should I stop?"

There was more buzzing of his saw. Donald Poole's chilled visitor took advantage of his attention turned to the saw to stamp her feet to keep warm.

Then, "I don't s'pose you've ever been to Noman's," Captain Poole inquired.

"Oh, what a lovely place it is. If it had ever had a natural harbor, it would have been settled 300 years ago. The soil is richer than the Vineyard's and they used to estimate that they could keep 2,000 sheep over there and not shelter them in winter. It's been years since I was there, but I carried the caretaker and his wife and chickens off the island when they left. It was Josh Crane who used to own it, but then he departed quite suddenly for France and the government took it over by eminent domain to use for bombing target practice.

"A lot of our fishermen used to go over there summers when I was a boy, but all the original houses are gone now, of course. There's a little graveyard there with a dozen stones all ruined. To all intents and purposes the island's all been destroyed.

"As many as half a dozen families lived there year-round once. They even had a haunted house and it's said there was a sea serpent off there. I know there was one instance of two men from New Bedford who claimed they'd seen it — though that was off Gay Head.

"Do I believe in sea serpents? I certainly do. I believe they're some sort of snake. After all, there are thousands of miles of ocean and unknown depths. Why shouldn't there be sea serpents?"

On the subject of the depths, Donald Poole admits that he has never — for all his years at sea — explored them. "No, I never did go swimming. Nine months out of the year, you wouldn't last if you went overboard, would you? You'd cramp right up and drown. The other three months, you gamble that you won't fall overboard."

It was getting to be lunchtime, and Donald Poole thought longingly of his iced-in scalloping boat.

"When the tide gets a little higher I ought to be able to get her out of the ice," he said. "It's high time I got out on the water again. You know, I enjoy my work more than I can tell you," he said, and sighed contentedly. "Even now, I wake up in the morning and roll and toss waiting for it to come daylight so I can get started out on the water again. I've been a very fortunate man. I would testify to that. I've had a wonderful woman for a wife and a son I'm very proud of, and good and sufficient boats. For what more than that could a man ask in life?"

– May 14, 1982

❧   ❧   ❧

Fond Memories of a Black Childhood

By Dorothy West

WE WERE BLACK BOSTONIANS on a train full of white ones. Because we were obviously going the same way, laden as we were with all the equipment of a long holiday, children, luggage, last minute things stuffed in paper bags, a protesting cat in a carton, in addition to the usual battery of disbelieving eyes, we were being subjected to intense speculation as to what people with our unimpressive ancestry were doing on a train that was carrying people with real credentials to a summer sojourn that was theirs by right of birth.

We were among the first blacks to vacation on Martha's Vineyard. It is not unlikely that the Island, in particular Oak Bluffs, had a larger number of vacationing blacks than any other section of the country.

87

There were probably 12 cottage owners. To us it was an agreeable number. There were enough of us to put down roots, to stake our claim to a summer place, so that the children who came after us would take for granted a style of living that we were learning in stages.

The early blacks were all Bostonians, which is to say they were neither arrogant nor obsequious, they neither overacted nor played ostrich. Though the word was unknown then in today's connotation, they were "cool." It was a common condition of black Bostonians. They were taught very young to take the white man in stride or drown in their own despair. Their survival was proved by their presence on the Island in pursuit of the same goal of happiness.

Every day, the young mothers took their children to a lovely stretch of beach and scattered along it in little pools. They made a point of not bunching together. They did not want the whites to think they knew their place.

There was not much exchange except smiles between the new and the old, no more was needed. Bostonians do not rush into relationships. Sometimes the children took their shovels and pails and built castles together. It was a pretty scene. The blacks in all their beautiful colors, pink and gold and brown and ebony. The whites in summer's bronze.

The days were full. There were berries to pick, a morning's adventure. There were band concerts for an evening's stroll. There were invitations to lemonade and cookies and whist. There was always an afternoon boat to meet, not so much to see who was getting off, but to see and talk to whatever friends had come for that same purpose.

For some years the black Bostonians, growing in modest numbers, had this idyll to themselves. The flaws were put in perspective because no place is perfection.

And then came the black New Yorkers. They had found a fair land where equality was a working phrase. They joyously tested it. They behaved like New Yorkers because they were not Bostonians. There is nobody like a Bostonian except a man who is one.

The New Yorkers did not talk in low voices. They talked in happy voices. They carried baskets of food to the beach to make the day last. They carried liquor of the best brands. They grouped together in an ever increasing circle because what was the sense of sitting apart.

Their women wore diamonds when the few Bostonians who owned any had left theirs at home. They wore paint and powder when in Boston only a sporting woman bedecked her face in such bold attire. Their dresses were cut low. They wore high heels on sandy roads.

I had a young aunt who would duck behind a hedge and put us children on watch while she rubbed her nose with a chamois when we told her it was shiny. We did not think her performance was unusual. It was the New Yorkers who seemed bizarre, who always seemed to be showing off wherever they gathered together.

The New Yorkers were moving with the times. They had come from a city where they had to shout to be heard. It was a city that offered much: judgeships, professorships, appointments to boards, stardom on stage and more. Whoever wanted them had to push. The New Yorkers wanted them. They were achievers. They worked hard and they played hard.

They would unwind in another generation. They would come to the Island to relax, not to race. They would come to acknowledge that the Bostonians had a certain excellence that was as solid an achievement as money.

But in the meantime they lost the beach for the Bostonians. That beach like no other, that tranquil spot at that tranquil end of the Island. All one summer the Bostonians saw it coming like a wave they could not roll back. It came the next summer. The beach became a private club, with a gate that only dogs could crawl under, and a sign that said, "For members only."

You lose some, and by the same token, you win some. The

world was not lost, just a piece of it. And in the intervening years more has been gained than was ever forfeited, more has been fought for and won, more doors have opened as fewer have closed.

Harry T. Burleigh, the composer, who left a priceless legacy in his long research of Negro spirituals — those shouts of grace and suffering and redemption that might have perished forever if he had not given his gifts to preserving them — he was the first to bring back glad tidings of the Island's fair land to his New York friends, who had always thought of Massachusetts as a nice place to come from, but not to go to unless bound and gagged.

Mr. Burleigh had come to stay at Shearer Cottage in the Highlands, a quiet boarding house operated by Boston friends, who had recommended the seclusion of the lovely wooded area, where New York's busy lights seemed as remote as the Island stars seemed near.

He was very good to the children of his friends. There were seven or eight of us who were his special favorites. He gave us money every time he saw us. We did not know any better than to spend it in one place. With abundant indulgence he would give us some more to spend in another. He rented cars and took us on tours of the Island. He told us about his trips abroad. To be with him was a learning experience.

There is a snapshot of him in a family album. Under the snapshot, in the handwriting of that aunt who could take us or leave us, there is the caption: H.T.B., the children's friend. He was rich and well-known in important circles at the time. There were a dozen glowing captions that would have applied. I think it is a tribute to him — and perhaps to my aunt — that she chose this simple inscription.

Mr. Burleigh's summers were spent working as well as sunning. Every weekday morning he went to a church in Vineyard Haven where he had use of the piano. Many of the spirituals sung around the world were given arrangements within God's hearing in an Island church.

In the course of time, Mr. Burleigh grew to regret the increasing number of New Yorkers who brought their joyous living to his corner of the Highlands. He had extolled this sacred spot, and they were taking over. Who can say they did not share his vision? They simply expressed it in a different way.

– June 25, 1971

❧ ❧ ❧

The Old Girl, Lenny and the Boy

By Michael F. Bamberger

THE OLD GIRL AND I met exactly a year ago, on a chilly night on the porch of her Main street home, across from the Dr. Daniel Fisher House in Edgartown.

She was 81 years old and the granddaughter of a whaling captain and the proprietress of the Charles H. Marchant House, named for her father who edited the Gazette from 1888 to 1920, immediately before Henry Beetle Hough. I was two days on staff of the Gazette and three away from college graduation, and could I take a room for a week upon return from Philadelphia?

Thus I entered the world of Elizabeth Marchant Sanchez and her brother Leonard Marchant. My week's stay lasted eight months and will remain with me forevermore.

The house was built by Mrs. Sanchez's maternal grandfather, Henry Ripley, in the middle of the last century. It is a white saltbox typical of the period, clapboard on the north side, facing Main street, and shingled south, to Pent Lane, and to the white houses east and west.

A large marble slab lies between the red brick sidewalk and the gray porch. From there Mrs. Sanchez, Mr. Marchant and Mrs. Elsie Wuerth, who lives across the way on Pent Lane, watch the Independence Day parade. Mrs. Wuerth is 92 and the two women have known one another for about five decades. Mrs. Sanchez says, "Mrs. Wuerth is the true grande dame of Edgartown, a woman of complete dignity," and the compliment of her friend is spoken with utter sincerity.

Madame Marchant — she gets a kick out of the French pronunciation I began to use out of ignorance — knows the meaning of friendship, the meaning of sincerity in a way far too uncommon. Above all the Old Girl and I are friends, kindred spirits linked by a deep affection for our newspaper, a hope to see the world and a plan to enjoy the backyard in the lingering sunshine of an August afternoon.

Our difference of 60 years is indiscernible, so joined were we by our love for cranberry juice. Not long after we hit upon that interesting fact a new practice was begun. Every morning as I descended the steps for work I found a cool glass of the familiar red juice. Every day, without fail, without effort, without comment (unless I failed to finish) the juice waited on the marble-top night stand. The Old Girl stands for sincerity without even trying.

Every night for eight months, returning home after selectmen's meetings, planning board meetings, a late night at the Gazette, or a movie, I found a note from Madame on the same table where the cranberry juice awaited that morning. They have all been saved, over 200 of them, and hidden carefully in my desk. Here's one:

Dear Mr. Pulitzer,   9 p.m.
    Your dad phoned. We had a little chat, which I enjoyed. He said they are retiring early tonight so it's best not to return the call tonight. David is at home studying for his bar exams.

                                        Tally ho! and -30-
                                        Ye Olde Madame
(Two "tonights" in one line — give me an "F")

I especially enjoyed this one, Madame showing her usual keen insight:

Flash! Flash! Hot News Item!
A Caller from New York:
Could It Be,
Could It Be?
It's SALLY!
(who undoubtedly anxiously awaits your call)

The upstairs of the old house has three bedrooms: the Blue, where I first took up Edgartown residence; the Pink, also known as the Honeymooner's Special; and the Northeast, which has a small bedroom attached. There is a single large bathroom with a large old tub, the kind with the curved legs.

"Do you think the floor needs a touch-up?" Mrs. Sanchez asked the other day as we toured the floor of the Northeast. "The great romanticists push the beds together, which is fine if that's what they want to do, but in so doing the paint chips off. So every spring before the season I find myself in a pickle, should I re-paint the entire floor, or should I just do a touch-up?

"The whole matter is complicated because years ago I painted the floor with a mix of royal blue and black, so whether I do a touch-up or the whole thing, I have to match the same mixture, which is no easy trick."

"I think a touch-up would be fine," I said.

"Oh, good, boy. I can always count on you for sound advice," said the Old Girl, who commonly refers to me as "boy."

There is a third floor where Mrs. Sanchez used to take guests but no longer does. It now houses enough material for about three yard sales, four with the stuff I have contributed.

On the wall along the stairs between the first and second floors is a print entitled One Hundred and Ten Edgartown Whaling Captains. Four of those captains are Marchants — Charles, the most direct to Mrs. Sanchez, her grandfather.

Downstairs is the bedroom of Mr. Marchant, who is known to generations of Edgartonians as Lenny, earning love and respect and many friends as a grocery man for Connors Market and later for sweeping town sidewalks.

Mr. Marchant's disabilities, which are physical and mental, have made his life difficult. And yet Mr. Marchant is to me the true old-fashioned Edgartown gentleman, always ready with a smile, a handshake and a "How are you today?"

Madame says these often lost qualities came right from the Old Editor, who would not walk the streets of Edgartown without a necktie, and who would not pass a new face in town without a hearty welcome.

Also downstairs is a sitting room, from which Mr. Marchant, now largely confined to the house, can watch the flow of eastbound traffic on Main street and the flow of pedestrians in all directions. Across the street and slightly to the east is the Old Whaling Church.

Mrs. Sanchez refers to the famous town edifice as the Edgartown United Methodist Church, which she attends every Sunday, holding equal her responsibility to choir and her responsibility to God.

Since 1951 Mrs. Sanchez's greatest responsibility has been to Leonard, who requires an attendant. She left the Island in 1923 to work for Boston newspapers; she was a fast Linotype operator in the days when fast Linotype operators were highly valued.

She fell in love with Boston and with Francis John Sanchez, a newspaperman whom she married. They returned to Edgartown in 1947 to care for Leonard and Charles Ripley, the oldest brother, and to begin the guest house.

Her rates are very reasonable and her guests are loyal, many coming back year after year.

"Oh, hello," she says to a Connecticut couple making plans to return again. "We're looking forward to seeing you," speaking, as she always does, to include her brother.

"We" is the word because stuffiness and self-indulgence are

not a part of her life. She's as unstuffed as the colorfully striped sheets that billow on her clothesline.

It is "we" because she does not believe life is an isolated affair with self-achievement. The sharing makes it worthwhile, regardless of what "it" is — the Sunday choir, the call from Connecticut, the boarder for whom she found a special place.

On the topic of me, Madame is unpardonably generous, and I pray I never disturb that. For Mrs. Sanchez is a small and wonderful woman, with snow white hair, with fine creases that age has brought on gracefully, and with blue-framed glasses of the style popularized by school teachers of generations ago. Her cotton blouses are always buttoned to the top, and her dresses are always as colorful as her smile and her language.

That is how I found her when I returned home each day for lunch last summer, walking from the Gazette office down Pent Lane, through the backyard and to the back kitchen door. We bantered about finer points of the English language, of which she knows a great deal. She taught me the word "euphony."

Madame Marchant taught me, too, the difference between a bungalow and a fishing shack — the Island does not have the former — and I taught her how to use the broiler. That feat earned me the title Conqueror of the Kitchen. She taught me, not very well, how to waltz and I taught her to use a hand-held can opener.

Madame showed insatiable curiosity for Judaism and New York city and college and the welfare of my parents, for whom there is great fondness, which is mutual. And I showed the same for old Edgartown, on going away and coming back, the sense of family responsibility uncommon today and the facing of old age with life.

"We cannot lay aside the pen without saying ... we have loved the paper and the work it has imposed upon us," the Old Editor, Mrs. Sanchez's father, wrote once long ago.

The Old Girl applies that lesson to life, and taught it to me without even trying.

— May 13, 1983

Cafe Finds Happiness with Young Clientele

By Jason Gay

THEY ARE KNOWN AS THE GET-A-LIFERS: the legions of teenagers and twentysomethings who congregate at Vineyard Sweets, a coffee shop on Tisbury's Main street. Sporting nose rings, dreadlocks, goatees and other Generation X accessories, they huddle around the shop's outdoor red tables each afternoon at about 2 p.m., swilling java, smoking cigarettes and discussing everything from Kafka to Kahlo to Kato Kaelin. It's a scene resembling coffee haunts in Cambridge and Berkeley, but on Martha's Vineyard, the resident beatniks are often boat builders instead of filmmakers, and the curbside poetry is more likely to be about beach walks than existential angst.

The proprietors of Vineyard Sweets are Leon and Anne Bennett, a couple from Tisbury who had no experience in the coffee business before opening their store in 1993. Despite their lack of training, the Bennetts have witnessed their business grow to one of the most successful in town: On peak summer days, Vineyard Sweets will sell as many as 1,200 cups of coffee from behind its polished wood counter top.

But it's Vineyard Sweets' eclectic cafe denizens, and not its coffee, that attract the most public attention. Potential customers are either enticed or turned off by the parade of hipsters who settle their young bodies at the outdoor tables from early morning until darkness, drinking concoctions like hazelnut and French roast. The group is so ensconced in the image of Vineyard Sweets that the Bennetts have made the Get-a-Life Cafe the shop's official second name, and now advertise it on its purple outdoor awning and soon-to-be-released T-shirts.

"The Get-a-Life Cafe is sort of a joke among the people who hang out here," says Anne Bennett. "But the kids that hang out here have been really good."

The Bennetts admit they were unnerved at first by the bereted and body-pierced crowd, fearing they would intimidate customers and scare off business. But a few minor incidents aside, the Get-a-Lifers and Vineyard Sweets have become a perfect — and profitable — business marriage.

"There are some in the older generation who are completely turned off by the group," Anne says. "But more of them are intrigued by the young people."

At first glance, the Bennetts and the Get-a-Lifers couldn't be stranger partners. Leon, a tall and soft-spoken man with elaborate tattoos on each of his forearms, is an electrician by trade and a diehard conservative. Both he and Anne vote Republican. But Leon isn't bothered by the Get-a-Life crowd, and he doesn't mind mixing it up with a clientele whose youthful politics tend to fall somewhere left of Ché Guevara.

"People just come in to get good coffee and enjoy themselves," Leon says. "Sometimes people and I disagree, but there's no fighting."

The Get-a-Life crowd is new to the landscape of traditional Main street, where the average shopper can look like someone removed from the pages of the J. Crew catalogue. Indeed, the coffee kids have raised a few eyebrows: Last year, the few nearby businesses were irked when kids hung out after hours on the street, occasionally harassing passersby and blocking storefronts. But the Bennetts say that troublesome crowd is gone.

"We had problems last year, like everyone else did," Anne says. "But they never abused the place."

And the Get-a-Lifers are good business, the Bennetts say. Among the younger customers, the get-up-and-go hazelnut is the coffee of choice. More adventurous tastes reach for regional blends like Guatemalan Antigua and Jamaican, and there's an assortment of cappuccinos, lattes and espressos to boot. And even the hard-cores have their own house drink: The Get-a-Life Blend.

If you're working behind the counter at Vineyard Sweets, what's the most difficult thing to make? The question is put to employee Tabitha Grasing, a young woman bedecked in a black shirt with a red necklace around her waist.

"A half-caf, half-decaf double mocha cappuccino," she says. "That's the worst."

Anne and Leon chuckle at the fickleness of coffee customers, many of whom analyze blends like fine wine tasters. Before they got into the business, the Bennetts were strictly a Folger's instant crystals household. Today, Anne doesn't touch the stuff, but Leon still knocks back "about 15 to 16 cups a day." But even his intake doesn't hold a jittery candle to the local plumber who comes in and orders a quadruple espresso every afternoon.

"There are people who just want coffee to feed themselves," Leon says. "And there are people who like good coffee and like to know how it is prepared."

Ironically, the "Sweets" in the coffee shop's name comes from the Bennetts' passion for chocolate making.

When the store was originally opened, it was intended as an outlet for their various candies, which they make daily in their Tisbury household. But when Anne and Leon learned that coffee was going to be their number one export, the chocolate operation was reduced to expand the java selection.

And no deadbeats, please: If you bring your young artistic temperament to Vineyard Sweets, bring some change to spare. The Bennetts have a quid-pro-quo agreement with the Get-a-Lifers, one that states you must purchase something to sit down, and you mustn't wear out your welcome. Loitering at the tables is okay in the middle of winter, but don't try to do it in summer, or you'll be asked to leave.

"They know that in the summer, they have to move on," Leon says.

But most of the year, the outdoor cafe at Vineyard Sweets serves as a classic coffee hangout, where a cup of joe, maybe a smoke and a novel can pass you through an afternoon. The Get-a-Lifers commandeer the late afternoon hours, but the outdoor tables are also occupied during the day by retirees and nine-tofivers on a break. It's part of a national trend, the Bennetts say, where coffee houses have replaced bars as the places where America sits down to socialize.

"It's like what the old pubs used to be," Leon says. "A place for conversation, shooting the breeze."

And the Get-a-Lifers must be loyal if Vineyard Sweets is to survive. The young crowd is critical to the coffee house's defense against its most formidable opponent ever: Dunkin' Donuts. Next month, The Vineyard Haven Coffee Shop will debut across the street with the franchised donuts, muffins, croissants and beverages. But while some residents are appalled at the invasion of the "Double D," the Bennetts believe the competition will be friendly.

"We're pretty hopeful that we have a little bit of a following," Anne says.

If Vineyard Sweets continues to thrive, will Leon and Anne become king and queen of Vineyard coffee? It's impossible to say: Opinions on who serves the best java are varied and impassioned, and a consensus winner is seldom declared. But the Bennetts think they have come a long way from their days of drinking instant from a can, and there's a loving — albeit unkempt — group of customers to thank for their success. Says Leon: "I feel this place has become an important part of Vineyard Haven for a lot of people."

– March 31, 1995

❧ ❧ ❧

Extinct Abilities

The dinosaur, for what it's worth,
No longer dominates the earth;
The penguin can no longer fly,
And Vineyard men can't tie a tie.
D.A.W.

99

Horacio Malonson Was Unique Spirit

By Richard Russell

"I lived my soul of life at Martha's Vineyard island...."
– Horacio Malonson, 1954-1984

HORACIO MALONSON, a Wampanoag Indian of the Gay Head tribe and the son of Chief Donald Malonson, died last Saturday on his 30th birthday, after being hospitalized for a prolonged illness. The Indian names he took were Sea Hawk and Sabbath of Moon and Stars.

All his life Horacio had been well-known among the people of Martha's Vineyard. Although deaf since birth, he worked at many different jobs, had hundreds of friends, and held an abiding love for the natural wonders of sea, sky and earth. He spoke in sign language, and through feeling, and lived in the richest of silent worlds.

He could often be seen helping his father, then the fire chief of Gay Head, in rescue operations, or doing landscaping for residents on various parts of the Island. For a time he drove a truck for Trip Barnes, making long-distance journeys through the Pennsylvania mountains, to New York city, as far south as Florida.

"Everything was a new experience to Horacio," Mr. Barnes remembers. "He had amazing strength and a wonderful sense of humor. When he learned how to do something, he always did it with such care. He was very fond of children, loved showing them how to do things, and they felt such trust for him. I don't know anyone who didn't like him. A part of me goes with Horacio, because he gave me the spirit to go on during a hard time in my own life."

When he worked on the Vineyard Haven docks, Horacio was greatly respected by the fishing fleet. The men would always ask him to be on board when their catch was being unloaded and weighed. Supervising the buckets being sent down chutes for sorting, he would know the exact numbers of the day's haul simply by watching it tumble past him, and fishermen would marvel at his uncanny accuracy.

Horacio loved to fish, and to gather clams and mussels and scallops for his friends. When he caught his first striped bass from his little dinghy, his tumultuous shouts and laughter echoed across the clay cliffs of Gay Head. And when he had the great fish close, he leapt overboard, fishing rod in hand, and came up with it cradled in his arms.

In many ways, Horacio was a guardian of the natural world. Living with friends on a farm in Kansas, he raised seven baby rabbits that he rescued from a huge snake, feeding them goat's milk through an eyedropper for several hours a day before finally returning them full-grown to the wild.

On Vineyard beaches he would chase people who drove over clams, horseshoe crabs, and the other creatures he loved. In his old four-wheel-drive truck, he was always stopping to see people, shopkeepers and boatmen, and he always seemed to know when someone was ill or needed help.

There was always an aura of mystery about Horacio. He felt personally responsible for the condition of the ancient Common Lands of the Gay Head Indians, keeping vigil over the Cliffs, the herring creek, the cranberry bogs and the beach plum bushes. He believed himself linked not only to his Indian ancestors, but to the Vikings who first came to the Island many centuries ago.

Remarkably, he was considered a fine dancer and often made music on various instruments. Despite his inability to hear, the notes Horacio played were never off-key. They produced a strange, haunting sound that friends often referred to as "the music of the spheres." His favorite song was Amazing Grace.

Although his formal education was very limited, Horacio devoted himself to learning of many kinds. With a dictionary at his side, over many months he absorbed Woody Guthrie's Bound for Glory and Steinbeck's Grapes of Wrath. He painted pictures of Vineyard vistas, and of spaceships hovering over waters. He wrote many poems, bearing titles like Feel of Dream and Great of World, Soul of Beach, and Soul of People. He always said that he had a secret, but would someday tell his story.

A year ago, Horacio wrote: "I didn't find any friends in the city. I did want friends. I looked at the stars in the sky on the Island. I wished to hear a spaceship on its orbit. Then I met a people on the Island and Fort Hill and I thought 'Friends' and it was my soul and my life, too."

His death was as mysterious as his life. Beyond any known medical possibility of consciousness, Horacio communicated with his family in sign language. His final message was: "Soul is real. I am Soul. I am who I always was."

Horacio lives through his wife Liz, his father Donald, his mother Pat, his sister Bettina and brother Ryan, his aunts and cousins, his tribal family, and his wide family of friends.

He lives on, too, through his poems, like this one:

> *As I look at the moon from the beach*
> *and stars shine,*
> *I will walk along the long beach.*
> *I like to look at the moon*
> *brightly shining over the sea.*
> *The surf rolls in toward me.*
> *I go to the cliffs by the lighthouse.*
> *The cliffs of clay and rock*
> *which I climb on Martha's Vineyard.*
> *I can see my zodiac in the stars*
> *of my soul.*
> *My life like the moon shining on the beach.*
>
> *– May 11, 1984*

Aviatrix Carolyn L. Cullen Flies Trade Winds of Oak Bluffs

By George W. Adams

DRIVING SOUTH ON COUNTY ROAD a little past the Registry of Motor Vehicles, the curtain of scrub oak is suddenly broken on the east by a gently rolling, closely mowed field opening a vista to the woods and fairways of the Island Country Club.

Across a row of white painted posts strung with a piece of rope, you see a trim white building, the flight shack of the Oak Bluffs Airport. There is no sign — but if you have a doubt, a red windsock atop the hangar is a dead giveaway, and if you happen by on a busy summer weekend, you will see as many as 60 small airplanes lined up with military precision.

Somewhere amongst the planes you will see Carolyn L. Cullen, owner of the field and head of the Trade Winds Flying School. You can't mistake her — whether she is digging a post hole or subtly suggesting a different landing approach to a visiting pilot who takes himself too seriously, her appearance is as trim as her field's.

"This is my kind of weather," she said, taking a break from her lawn mower on Sunday a week or so ago. "The air is crisp, but when it is clear like this, with no pollution, the sun feels so warm. Did you hear the front go through last night?"

An airplane appeared in the sky to the west; she excused herself and hurried off to greet the pilot and show him where to park. Shortly she returned with two new visitors to the Island in tow, cheerfully suggesting places they might stay, things to do, and she offered to call a cab or rent them bicycles.

"This place is sort of a port of entry to the Island," she said when they had departed. "Part of the job is like running a little chamber of commerce. At some airports, you have to hunt for a place to park, then wander around to dig up someone to help you. I try to greet everyone the minute they get to the ground."

Whether accustomed to the hospitality or not, the sight of her trim figure stepping out vigorously to indicate a parking spot must be welcome. A silver barrette, likely to be complemented by Indian silver about her neck and wrist, holds back her dark hair, now graying, in a ponytail. Her tanned face and ruddy cheeks, her erect posture, her open manner fit the picture of a woman aviator to perfection; the twinkle in her blue eyes and a constant smile stem from a youthful enthusiasm about life that belies 35 years of experience as a flight instructor.

In the beginning, hers was the footloose life of the barnstorming days. During the war, she rose to the rank of captain in the WASPs, after being chief pilot in primary instruction at a Navy training base. In 1947, she came to the Island with a flying friend, Rachael Williams, to run the Oak Bluffs Airport. "And that was it," she says.

"What do islands — all islands — do to you? I don't know, but they are fun. And I love the ocean. There are wonderful people here. I guess there is just something here that satisfies your inner soul." As she talks about her walks on the beaches and through the woods, and as she reminisces about the early days of her flying career, she gives listeners a glimpse of a frontier spirit which loves the wild not because it stands to be conquered but because in its vastness man can watch life without seeing constant reflections of himself.

"When I came here, you could walk for miles and miles on the beach. But it's getting harder and harder to get access to the beaches, and the beaches are getting more and more crowded. But the Island is attractive, and what can you do with a place like that — run only two boats a day?" she says with a laugh.

That hint of regret appears every now and then, usually accompanied by a thoughtful bite or two at a piece of chewing gum always tucked in her cheek, but it quickly fades in the brightness of her enthusiasm.

"I love to sightsee," she says. "Right now, with the fresh spring growth, the Island looks so soft and lacy — it's like a medieval tapestry. That doesn't last long — just a few weeks. In the winter, when the leaves are off the trees, you can see mile after mile of walls, beautiful stone walls, and streams you have never noticed. I'll spot something from the air, then walk in to see it.

"I keep pretty good track of the building going on, too. I love houses — when I see something new going up, I'll drive over and have a look at it. There is a lot of skillful building going on — less of it than last year, I suppose, but I doubt you'll find any of the reputable builders out of work. Maybe what is leaving the Island are a few kids who can hardly hold a hammer, yet call themselves carpenters.

"I have a great admiration for people who are truly skilled in any problem. To be truly skilled there has to be a basic love, and a patience and devotion to the task. It's true in flying — it takes time to make a good pilot. You have to teach your instinct to the student. The first few hours are very important — that's when the attitude is formed. There has to be a love of it, a respect for it. That's why I use the Cub in training — it's so basic."

She points to the hangar where sits her humble Piper Cub, a little two-seat fabric-covered airplane built in 1946. The plane shows every sign of being babied — Miss Cullen says it's because there are so few of them left, but visitors watching the tender care she gives it will suspect there's more to it than that.

"The Cub has got a stick," she says. "A stick is great — I think they should use nothing else in training. A student is so used to driving a car that when he gets behind a wheel in a plane it's hard to shake off the conditioning. You always have a great feel for the plane with a stick — besides, it seems more natural to put pressure in the direction you want to go than to turn a wheel. There is no substitute for learning on a short grass field, either. There is just no way you can simulate short-field takeoffs and landings on a 10,000-foot jet strip.

"I never get over flying. It's a thrill every time. You can tell just by the way they take off and land which pilots have a real feel. I don't want to train airplane drivers — hell, you can teach a chimpanzee to drive a car, but what does it prove?"

— June 6, 1975

❧ ❧ ❧

Eddie Heywood: Touch of Gold And a Soul Full of Music

By Richard Reston

THE GOLD IS IN HIS FINGERS and the beat is in his soul. When he plays, he plays from the heart and not from the head. He has a left hand in the bass range like no other pianist in America. On a dirty street corner in New York not so long ago, a stranger approached to ask his name. And when the stranger confirmed what he already knew, he said: "Man, I want to tell you, you are a living legend."

The musician thought about that a little later and decided the remark was just about the nicest compliment one person can pay another. But he didn't dwell on the adoration very long because that's not his style.

The other night at the Harborside Inn he played a concert, not for himself, but for the benefit of others, in this case the Nathan Mayhew Seminars. His generosity on the Island is well-known — the benefits are always for something or someone other than himself, the hospital, free books for children, education.

After the concert some young people came to him for autographs and to tell him they never heard the piano played with such feeling.

The man is Eddie Heywood Jr., and feeling is what he plays

with. His fans may call him a living legend but he's just plain Eddie to anyone who knows him.

In 1969 Eddie and his lovely wife Evelyn moved to the Vineyard permanently. They have two sons, Edward 3rd, 28, and Robert, 21, who is studying at the University of Massachusetts. Both are accomplished musicians in their own right.

The Heywoods live in a beautiful ranch-style home on Hines Point. Eddie says the sweeping view across Lagoon Pond is a source of inspiration in his work, as is the whole of Martha's Vineyard. "As a kid I used to have to go to the zoo to see a swan. Now I have them swimming in my front yard," he says.

At 61, what can you say about Eddie Heywood, about the twinkle in his eyes, about his flashing smile and, more important, about his musical and human spirit that never dimmed even in times of hardship and suffering?

He is not your ordinary jazz piano player. At the keyboard he is a master of technique. He is an arranger, composer and consummate performer. He has written more than 100 songs, all of them published, some of them classics.

Eddie began young making music in his home in Atlanta, Ga. He started at three banging on the piano and he did it so often his father, also Edward Heywood and a well-known musician, writer and conductor, gave Eddie's mother these instructions: "Let him bang away. He's having a love affair with the piano."

At five Eddie was playing the piano for real. No more banging.

"I don't have large hands. My father, who was really the only teacher I ever had, felt I wasn't going to be able to span as great a range as other piano players. So he made me work hours and hours, hundreds of hours, on my left hand. It was his foresight as the years went by that led me to develop my own style. By 18 I didn't sound like the rest of them."

By the time he was 10 Eddie was going to the theatre every Saturday night with his father. After several months of this, his father, much to Eddie's surprise, simply informed him that he would play the show that evening. His father disappeared and out walked Eddie to play his first public show with adult musicians. He was a rousing success, and all at the age of 10.

And then his father went on tour with what Eddie says was a great act called Butter Beans and Susie. His father would return from New York and other road trips with arms full of records. Eddie listened for endless hours to the likes of Louis Armstrong, Jelly Roll Morton and Ethel Waters.

Vaudeville was at its height when Eddie was growing up. Many of the greats in those days were friends of the Heywood family. Many of them came to Eddie's father to get him to arrange or write their shows. So Eddie grew up listening to and even talking with certain artists he would later play with in New York.

He would go to New York in 1938 where he began to play and record with artists he had dreamed about. They were all there and so was Eddie. Armstrong and Morton, Fletcher Henderson, Coleman Hawkins, Shelley Mann, the late Johnny Hodges and Billie Holiday.

"Here were all these greats and now they were saying, 'We want you to record with us,' " Eddie recalls.

"One night I went to an after-hours joint and Billie Holiday was there," Eddie says. "Everyone wanted her to sing but there was no piano player around good enough to accompany her. Someone said: 'This boy over here, he can really play.'

"Because of all the training my father had given me, I knew how to play behind a singer. I played two songs and Billie stopped me.

" 'From now on,' she said, 'you're going to play on all my records.'

"Billie's style was a lazy style and her arrangements were too busy for her," Eddie says. So Eddie Heywood started with Billie Holiday by rescoring such classics as In My Solitude and Georgia on My Mind.

And there were all the places he played in those years, the Savoy and down in the Village at Nick's, the Vanguard and Barney Josephson's Downtown Cafe Society. "One night I walked into Nick's and asked Bobby Hackett if I could sit in on a jam session with his band. I played and he hired me right then and there."

Eddie moved uptown to Swing Alley along 52nd street between Fifth and Sixth avenues. "That was it in those days," he says.

He played at a place called the Three Deuces. By now all his friends and fellow performers were storming the musical world along Swing Alley: Duke Ellington, Count Basie, the late and great Art Tatum and, yes, Billie Holiday.

And then it happened, in 1943. Eddie Heywood began to play Cole Porter. And nobody played Cole Porter quite the way Eddie did.

It started with Begin the Beguine. People jammed the places Eddie played to hear his Begin the Beguine. A record was made. It was a smash success and so was Eddie. One radio station played the song eight straight times without interruption.

Eddie Heywood went to Hollywood to play and to accompany the musical giants on the West Coast. He played and wrote arrangements for the likes of Ella Fitzgerald, Bing Crosby, the Andrews Sisters and, as always, Holiday.

And as they had in New York his fans mobbed him wherever he played. Burns and Allen were constant visitors, as were Fred Astaire and Barbara Stanwyck. It was something Astaire did in 1945 that was later to change the whole course of Eddie Heywood's life.

Astaire asked Cole Porter whether he had ever heard Eddie play. The answer was no and one night Astaire brought Porter, by then in a wheelchair, to hear Heywood on Porter.

When it was all over Porter and Heywood met for the first time. "You're a born composer," Porter said. "You must compose and play your own songs as well as those of others."

But for a little while longer Eddie would play only the songs that other composers had written. He played and played and played. He played at night, recorded during the day, wrote arrangements in between. He ate little. His only diet was music. By the end of 1945, Eddie had played himself into exhaustion, into a nervous breakdown and into what doctors described as an occupational disease that left him with frozen hands. Both his health and his hands gave out completely. The doctors put his hands in casts and they were to stay on for months. Rest and a new diet were prescribed.

The most serious part of the condition was to last two years. And even by the late 1940s Eddie still could not play more than about 15 minutes without severe pain in his hands. His hands had shrunk while in the casts and he could no longer reach his old range on the piano. His wife, Evelyn, recalls the period of suffering and agony.

"He was fatigued like a soldier in the front line. His hands were overworked. He would sit with his hands in warm water and I would swirl the water around with my fingers.

"Eddie would sit at the piano trying to play for hours with tears streaming down his face. We all prayed and it pulled us through and gave us courage."

By now a first child had come. It was 1954. "My hands still were just not strong enough," Eddie says. "Without her I don't really think I could have pulled through. And we were pretty broke."

It was at this point Evelyn told her husband something had to be done and reminded him of Cole Porter's words. Eddie began to write.

His first song was Land of Dreams, a smash hit. More songs. And in 1956 Canadian Sunset, now a classic. It received an award several years ago for being the most played song on radio and television, more than a million times. It was used last year as the television musical theme for the Olympics coverage.

And there were more songs and hits such as Soft Summer Breezes.

"I feel an artist some time in his life has to suffer," Eddie says.

"The good Lord and my wife were in my corner when I was down."

Now Eddie was back composing and arranging. His hands and health returned so he could play and record again. With a new dimension to his musical world, Eddie was able to avoid the nightly circuit that once had broken both his hands and his health.

In 1970 Eddie began on the Vineyard a project as ambitious as any he had ever undertaken. He began to listen to the sounds of the Vineyard. He would begin to write a Vineyard suite.

It was to be a tone poem about the Island's seasons. Poetry of Martha's Vineyard, he would call it. The capturing of nature in music proved more difficult than he had first imagined. He wrote and rewrote and put it aside and came back to it. Eddie was not happy. "At first I was overusing my craft and not using my heart and my imagination enough."

He talks of sitting on his Lagoon bank and listening to the grass. He listened every day and every night, each time concentrating on a new sound.

"I found out a little about spring," he says. "It's like a whirlpool. You never know what is going to happen. All the sounds, the birds, the colors. I had to understand that."

When the beauty and strength of summer comes the whirlpool disappears, he says. "But it took me six to eight months to learn how to go from spring into summer. I knew I had to integrate the strength of the summer theme into the whole."

Eddie and his wife traveled the entire Island to listen to the Vineyard speak. They went to Gay Head in howling winds. They recorded the winds and then listened to the tapes by the hour. They went to the Indian burial grounds at Christiantown in deep snow and sat for hours trying to capture the sound and historical meaning of that place.

"I tried to feel the Island at every time," he says. "February sunsets in Menemsha. This spot, this Island started it all. It's something Martha has that other islands don't."

Eddie found he was getting into European themes at times.

But this work was to be American, pure American, and that meant jazz, soft jazz. He weaves it into his fall theme with the touch and glide of a ballerina in flight.

Winter notes are shrill, icy. The howl of musical wind has texture. The spring is discordant.

Eddie wrote and rewrote it all, even the parts for background strings. His bold summer theme which carries through the entire suite is one of haunting beauty.

It is finished now. His next album entitled The Versatile Eddie Heywood is built around Poetry of Martha's Vineyard.

Listen to it and you will hear the magic of musical poetry in Eddie Heywood's soul.

– July 26, 1977

Chappy Has Its Problems Too, but How Near Heaven Dare You Go?

By Vance Packard

IT IS EASIER TO EXPLAIN why my family came to the Vineyard (Chappaquiddick) than why we have stayed 24 years, in view of recent irritants.

By irritants I am referring to the tract developers now starting to block out their grids even on Chappaquiddick. I am referring to the fact that Chappy residents — and contractors brave enough to serve them — often must wait in 40-car lineups consisting mainly of sightseers at the Chappy ferry to get their cars on or off Chappaquiddick. And I am referring to the way Chappaquiddick taxes skyrocketed a couple of years ago. More than 40 families on Chappy must pay from $1,000 to $10,000 in real estate taxes to Edgartown, whereas in the roughly comparable landscape of Chilmark it is hard to find a family on the tax list who has to pay more than several hundred dollars. I suppose Edgartown has more need for money, but it still seems odd. Martha is being mauled if not yet raped. But still my wife Virginia and I find ourselves spending more and more months each year on her Vineyard. Two years ago we got off just before pipe-freezing time.

I guess it is because Martha's Island still offers greater opportunities, in my view, for experiencing tranquility and community than any place on the 3,000-odd miles of seaboard stretching from Brunswick, Me., to Brownsville, Tex.

There are still thrilling, unspoiled vistas of sand, sea and sky peopled only by egrets, herons, hawks, terns and gulls. The blues still run in great numbers and the horseshoe crabs seem to be making a comeback (while the blue-claw crabs seem to be losing ground). The wild turkeys are gone, but pheasants and deer are still around, but more wary. And if you stick to the dirt roads the many bicyclists aren't too much of a hazard.

Virginia and I spent our first visit to the Vineyard as cyclists while on a sort of delayed honeymoon-vacation in 1940. We stayed at the Pequot Inn in Oak Bluffs and came away heavily bruised from cycling but happy.

Ten years and three children later we needed a place to spend August because we had rented our New Canaan, Conn., house for the summer. We happened to see, in the real estate section of The New York Times, a small ad for a rambling house on Chappaquiddick. In our cycling we had never gotten onto Chappy. It had been considered wilderness in 1940. But we rented the old Garrett house (now the Stephens house) unseen, and adored it, even though it then had oil lamps, lumpy, wire-sprung beds and an erratic gasoline-powered refrigerator.

That August was probably our family's greatest experience in Togetherness. After a morning dip, breakfast and cleaning up the house we spent the day on walking expeditions, mostly looking for blue-claw crabs. At night we read The Deerslayer aloud. It came with the house. Or we read from a whaling captain's handwritten journal of around 1848 that one of the children found in a closet.

During this first August the only island people we knew beyond nodding were the ferry operators. We were back again for two successive Augusts; and then in 1953 we heard that over the hill a long-abandoned, turn-of-the-century 12-room house with five outbuildings and more than 30 acres facing Katama Bay and the ocean was for sale.

Virginia and I went to look at it. All the porch stairs were crumbled but we managed to climb up and peer in the windows. Maybe it was the magnificent sunset reflection on Katama Bay that helped sway us. At any rate within three hours we had found the owner and put down a deposit. The sale price was $8,500. The next summer we furnished it for $213, mainly by going to auctions and picking up useful items from the beach and the Chappaquiddick dump. And the following year my young sons and I began building a dock, mainly by using timber on the beach that had floated in from the sea.

As the summers passed we came to know just about everyone on Chappaquiddick, most of Edgartown's merchants, a number of town officials and a good many up-Island Vineyarders.

We have known dozens of Chappy families for at least 15 years. The "summer" ones keep coming back each year, from California, Kansas, Missouri and other distant points. Some have moved their regular urban homes a number of times due to job transfers or other reasons.

For them and for us "home" emotionally is the Vineyard, not some urban suburb or high-rise apartment. Many of us have come to feel more passionately about Island affairs than the affairs at our official voting residences off-Island.

But most of us are relative newcomers as Vineyard enthusiasts. Our own nearest neighbor, Mrs. Georgie Thomas, has lived on Chappy since about 1884. Indifferent to the material world, she refuses to go to the "city" (Edgartown) in the winter months even though her cottage by the sea is heated primarily by a small wood-burning stove. She has inspired all our family and taught us a great deal about love of the sea, the joy of beach-strolling and about the flora and fauna found in and near the sea in our corner of the Vineyard.

My own children now are all grown and widely scattered, but a summer never passes that they don't come back to Chappaquiddick. In fact our oldest son took a year off while in college in order to spend a winter on the Vineyard.

As for Virginia and myself, if we ever decide to settle down in just one place we know where it will be, provided that the developers can be induced to show a decent respect for the fragile nature of the Island. It probably will be on Chappaquiddick. Certainly it will be somewhere on Martha's Vineyard.

– June 21, 1974

✤ ✤ ✤

Milton Jeffers Carries Forward Island Blacksmith Tradition

By Mark Alan Lovewell

MILTON JEFFERS is the last Vineyard village blacksmith. At age 61, Mr. Jeffers still sends the bright sparks flying like fireworks into the air at his old barn-sized shop in Edgartown. He cuts a piece of metal to be fastened to a floating dock. With his bare hand not far from the flame, he begins bending the metal.

Mr. Jeffers runs his business in much the same manner as he did when he graduated from welding school in 1940. Not a great deal has changed. Many of the same old-fashioned tools are as valuable today as years ago, and they hang on post and beam, within easy reach.

Near the back of the shop, a blacksmith's forge sits idle. Mr. Jeffers doesn't use it any more, he says, because it takes too much time. Welding tools have taken over most of the forge's duties. There are a few new additions in recent years, a drill press and a band saw.

The pounding of hammer against anvil is still heard occasionally, but Mr. Jeffers relies more on the heat of his welding equipment to do the "persuading" of bending or finishing a piece.

Mr. Jeffers says he remembers with affection his predecessor, Edgartown's late Orin Norton. Mr. Norton used to shoe horses and repair wagon wheels down by the waterfront, where the Wharf restaurant stands today.

Mr. Jeffers doesn't shoe horses.

"I worked on and off with Orin. And we used to have a few clashes," Mr. Jeffers recalls, "but all in all the disagreements were usually over the old way of doing things versus the new way of doing things. We got along."

Today, Mr. Jeffers still uses Mr. Norton's anvil and a lot of what Mr. Norton taught him.

Not long after Mr. Jeffers applies the bright blue flame from his welding torch, a bright white glow illumines his whole working area. The light is blinding. The metal's temperature quickly moves up to a workable red glow, between 1,600 and 2,500 degrees Fahrenheit, depending on the metal.

Welding is the newest addition to a trade centuries old. "There is arc welding which uses electricity, oxyacetylene which uses oxygen gas and acetylene gas, and finally there is heli-arcing which uses electricity combined with an inert gas," Mr. Jeffers says. "Each has its own special purpose.

"Today welding is a much larger science and requires further training," he says.

Just as the blacksmiths before him, when Mr. Jeffers wants to know what the temperature of hot metal is, he'll spit on the metal. The speed with which it vaporizes, Mr. Jeffers says, tells him the temperature.

No shingle hangs from a signpost or a wall in front of Mr. Jeffers' Pine street shop. No sign announces the way Mr. Jeffers makes his living. A large pile of steel in a variety of different shapes lies on the ground. The steel and more than 40 years at the same location brings his customers from all over.

"If no one showed up from here on in," Mr. Jeffers says, "I'd be busy for the next two weeks."

That's why his customers show up so early. They come from all over the Island. A Menemsha fisherman needs a length of rigging repaired. A farmer brings a broken plow.

"There is always something different to do," Mr. Jeffers says. And he adds that he's worked on just about everything from an artificial limb to a naval submarine.

Mr. Jeffers says his steadiest customers are the Vineyard fishermen. "The Menemsha fleet — they're always needing something to be done to their fishing gear. Something needs fixing."

Fishermen also congregate in the off-season inside Mr. Jeffers' workshop, a building made from the remains of a shed blown down by the 1944 hurricane. "It used to be located at the coal dock. My father Lawrence and my brother Lowell helped me build it."

And in winter these fishermen and other customers are usually not far from Mr. Jeffers' wood stove, which he keeps hot.

On one cold winter day last February with snow in the air, a group of fishermen was waiting for Mr. Jeffers to heat and loosen a rusted turnbuckle. While they waited, they talked of the man they come to so often for help.

Edgartown fisherman Peter Vann, captain of Miss Jean, said: "Without Milt the whole fleet would be tied up. This man can fix anything. Without him we'd be in tough shape."

"Sometimes when I come out here in the morning, there are five guys waiting for him," Mr. Vann said.

Some regular customers are free to walk in and help themselves from Mr. Jeffers' collection of nuts and bolts. Those acquainted with the practice, after filling their order, step over to a table and write their orders in a smudged and dog-eared notebook.

"They trust me, so I trust them," Mr. Jeffers says. He smiles and adds, "Maybe not all of them."

Mr. Jeffers, who grew up on Chappaquiddick and whose parents were part Christiantown and Gay Head Indian, says he has never been much of a businessman.

"When I was growing up on Chappy, there wasn't much money around. You did what you could. We grew vegetables. We had chickens. You did the best you could without money."

Mr. Jeffers' memory is precise and full of detail. For Chappaquiddick, he is a walking history book. And the number of tales he can tell might fill several volumes.

How did he become a welder and blacksmith? By accident, he says.

"A woman set up a scholarship fund at the high school for anyone who wanted to seek a higher education, and I applied and got it. I wanted to be an artist." But a good elder friend, Dr. Joseph Frame of Chappaquiddick, suggested he go to welding school.

"Orin was 60 years old at the time and Joe Frame said to me, 'You know somebody has to be able to take Orin's place someday.'

"So I spoke to my parents. Tuition for the welding school was $180. The scholarship was for $750."

The scholarship, according to Mr. Jeffers, paid for everything: tuition, room and board.

And except for an occasional itch to draw, which he still does admirably, Mr. Jeffers says he's been happy and satisfied as a welder.

During World War II, he furthered his experience by working at a Quincy boat yard where he participated in building warships for the military which later went to battle in the Pacific and Atlantic.

"I worked on aircraft carriers, destroyers, cruisers and invasion barges," Mr. Jeffers says. His handiwork saw duty, as he figures it, in sea invasions at Normandy and in the Pacific theatre.

"I worked a whole summer on the aircraft carrier Bunker Hill. So I've worked on just about everything," he says.

No one has dropped by for an hour needing something mended. It is dinnertime, and Mr. Jeffers has finished his day as a welder and he won't think about beginning again until 4:30 tomorrow morning when he takes an early walk with his dog.

"I'll probably do some bookkeeping in the morning too," he says. "There aren't any interruptions."

He pauses before going indoors, through the kitchen door.

"You know the only things I haven't worked on?" Mr. Jeffers asks. "And I would like to someday: a helicopter and a spacecraft."

– July 24, 1984

❧   ❧   ❧

Maynard Silva Picks His Moment
To Feel and Play the Blues

By Jason Gay

WITH A SIX-STRING GUITAR, a heart full of emotion and a dizzying talent in his fingertips, Maynard Silva is the prince of Vineyard blues. After logging years on the road in smoky bars and jam sessions, he returned to the Island like a prodigal son, full of memories and moments with the greats of the business: Buddy Guy, Junior Wells, Bukka White. Maynard Silva, a local kid who bought his first harmonica at Bunch of Grapes Bookstore, left the Vineyard and played with them all.

But while the youthful days may have passed him by, Mr. Silva's talent remains. He's still a student of music, and his hands move up and down the neck of his wood-body National like an

18-year-old's. Actually, better than an 18-year-old's. Because when you play the blues, the living is everything. The more you have lived, the better you are.

And Maynard Silva, at 43, has *lived*. He's not even fifty, but you could fill an encyclopedia with his life story.

"I had this gig, it must have been '71 or '72," he recalls this week, celebrating the release of a new CD entitled, appropriately, Maynard Silva. "I played in this place called Alice's Moonlight Lounge in St. Louis. I played for guys who were off their shift, they were factory guys who had been up all night. They would be in there, drinking their lunch, and it was a black bar. I'd play Jimmy Reed songs and Elmore James, 'cause that's what they loved. They'd sit there and sing along with it."

This was 1971. Maynard Silva was a Vineyard kid in St. Louis, learning blues the hard way — the right way, the only way. He can't understand the new blues scene, the yuppie rebirth subsidized by corporate America, full of big money and clubs serving wine coolers and imported beer. It's not the kind of blues Maynard Silva learned. It's not real.

"It's hard to see this big explosion of BMW blues, you know?" he says. "I mean, Eric Clapton, a multimillionaire, singing about five long years working in a steel mill?

"I go into the city and play blues gigs and it's just crazy. It's really weird, because the people that come and listen to you, they want to see if you have the right kind of hair, the right guitar, the right amp, and if you can do all those things that all the popular people can do. And not to knock the people that are real popular, but man, it was a lot better when it was innocent."

When Mr. Silva was on the road, blues wasn't played in yuppie bars. If you played the blues, you were lucky to get a stage and a chair, never mind a sound system or lights. Sawdust on the floor? Fine. No mirrors in the bathroom? Better. This was the blues.

"When I was playing pretty extensively around New England, most of the places I played in were biker bars, working-class bars," he says. "They related to the music instantly. When you went onstage, you were looking at 'Nam vets, divorced mothers, and disgruntled, confused college kids. There was a racial mix, an economic mix, and they just had this gut thing. You just went in, and you'd start playing — we were usually out of our minds by the time we got onto the stage — and there would be this gut response. People were really into it on an emotional level."

Maynard Silva can't imagine any other level. To him, emotion in music is everything, ever since the night he heard the blues for the first time, on a windy October night in Vineyard Haven.

"My English teacher my junior year in high school, Leroy Hazelton, he took me over to his apartment and put on a Howling Wolf record," he remembers. "He showed me all these pictures of people named Buddy and Lightning, and it was otherworldly.

"Howling Wolf is this guitarist, and he's got this distorted sound, and it's kind of droning, bommm, bommm, bommm, over and over, like death bells ringing. And there's this big voice going, 'Woooi,' and he's wailing, and it's a windy October night, trees are shaking outside, and it was like, 'Wow, this is amazing.'

"And Leroy says, 'You think that's something?' and he puts on this Little Walter tape, and this guy is screaming like he's getting cut up. And he started playing the harmonica, and it's so far down in its echo that you think it's coming out of a tunnel. I was afraid. I didn't even drink, and I was hallucinating from this music."

The rest is Vineyard blues history. The next day, teenage Maynard went downtown and bought his harmonica. He sat out in the woods in Vineyard Haven — "Back when there still were woods," he says — and practiced.

A few years later, he moved to St. Louis to attend college, and it's safe to say he majored in the blues. He began playing guitar, and soon he and a friend were on the road, on to Memphis, looking for legends.

"We went down to Memphis, and we looked up Bukka White and Furry Lewis. We went to their houses and drank whiskey," he says. "If they liked you, they would show you stuff. If they didn't, they wouldn't show you a thing."

They liked Maynard, the white kid from Martha's Vineyard. Bukka White liked him enough to invite him onstage.

"When Bukka White said, 'I want you to play a gig with me.' I've got to say the only thing that ever happened that was bigger was when my kid was born," he says.

The memories of Memphis and Bukka White are still fresh in Mr. Silva's mind, but times have changed. He still plays a gig once in a while, but he also runs a successful sign-painting business. He spends time with his seven-year-old son, Milo. He still has the blues, but he picks his moments now.

"The economics of playing music here is kind of spooky," he says. "There's basically room for a big party band every year. This year it was Entrain, one year it was Johnny [Hoy and the Bluefish] and Michael [Johnson] had a year at it.

"I've never been responsible enough to try and do that. I'm not really interested in that type of audience response. People always come up and ask, 'Are you going to have a band this summer?' and I usually find some way to duck out. I'm not really interested in playing for a bunch of people that come in with Day-Glo shorts and baseball caps on backwards, have chug-a-lug contests and try to figure out how to get laid. I just don't care about that. I've done my time."

Maynard Silva has done his time, and plenty of it. He's seen sadness and tragedy; he's wrestled with his dark side and loss in his family.

But every time he is down, there is the blues. His music. His remedy.

"Yes, it's a sad thing that we don't live forever," he says. "We don't get to be with the people we love all the time. Bad things happen to people. How do you accept that? That's a question I'm not equipped to answer. I'm not a philosopher, I'm a guitar player.

"But I know the way I finally stopped running away from sadness. I had so much built up inside me that I couldn't get away from it, but the music somehow worked with it. Sadness was the spaghetti and music was the sauce. I wasn't about to eat a bowl full of raw noodles."

– September 30, 1994

❧ ❧ ❧

Henry Beetle Hough, Country Editor, Led the Gazette for 65 Years

By Phyllis Meras

HENRY BEETLE HOUGH, for 65 years the editor of the Vineyard Gazette and one of the most esteemed members of his profession, died yesterday at his home on Pierce Lane in Edgartown. He was 88. Newspaperman after newspaperman came to the Gazette office to see its country editor, who achieved special fame for both himself and his paper with the book by that name, Country Editor, published in 1940, the first of his 24 volumes of fiction and nonfiction.

They found a slender, balding man with rich brown eyes, a shy, almost tentative manner, but a ready wit, and a mind as well-informed about all manner of things and a pen as sharp as any city editor's.

The difference was, as Henry Beetle Hough told the late Edward R. Murrow on a radio broadcast, that the country editor believed that "a big world is not necessarily a grown-up world, and the values of life are not measured by any standard of size."

When he and his bride, Elizabeth Bowie Hough, received the

Gazette as a wedding present in 1920 from his father, the New Bedford Standard's executive editor, George A. Hough, its circulation was 600. By the time of his 50th anniversary as its editor, the circulation was more than 6,000 and today it is 13,000. The Gazette has never been a paper that concerned itself with national or world issues, but with local events. "Weekly newspapers," Mr. Hough wrote in Country Editor, "… are a sustained chronicle of the life which they report and represent. There are certain threads which carry through, year after year, recurring as the seasons recur in nature. Most often the best front page stuff is acutely typical rather than violently exceptional, a respect in which the weekly newspaper differs radically from the daily." Henry Beetle Hough was not unacquainted with city life. He was born in New Bedford, Nov. 8, 1896, the younger son of George A. Hough and Abby Louise Beetle, the daughter of a Martha's Vineyard whaling captain. (Their older son, George Jr., became editor of the Falmouth Enterprise.)

As a boy he lived in the city, but his love of the Vineyard was nurtured during summer vacations on the Island. All the same, he did not decide as soon as he was an adult that this 18-mile-long Island of scrub oak and pine, and golden beaches and white colonial houses, was to be his home. He went from New Bedford to New York city, to Columbia University and then to its School of Journalism, where, in 1918, he was awarded a Pulitzer Prize for a history of the American press. A fellow student there was the blue-eyed young Pennsylvania woman who was to become his wife and fellow editor.

He did not return to the Vineyard until he had served in the Naval Reserve, working principally in Naval Intelligence in Washington, and not until he had tried his hand at public relations for the Institute of American Meat Packers in Chicago. Then there was one more year in the city — a sort of leave from the Gazette some years after he and Betty Hough had come to the Island — when they returned to New York where Henry Hough worked in public relations for Western Electric.

But it did not take them long to return to the familiar and beloved Vineyard sights "to see the round yellow moon at the foot of Main street at seven on a winter morning, and the white breath of the harbor, and the brown slopes of Chappaquiddick against a slowly lightening sky," Mr. Hough wrote in his 1950 sequel to Country Editor, Once More the Thunderer.

He was devoted to Martha's Vineyard, and he was devoted to newspapering, and was fortunate enough to be able melodiously to combine the two. Although he once said that he feared that instead of making himself qualified in the profession of journalism, he had taken root in a place, he expressed no great dismay at it, remarking that "to each there must be some particular spot on the surface of the globe, and I rejoice that this is mine."

Fellow newspapermen, however, certainly never felt that he lacked professional ability. For years, he was on the Pulitzer Awards jury. He was the recipient of one of the Columbia School of Journalism's first annual alumni awards for having "labored steadfastly in his own New England community to make journalism a learned profession and keep it a free one." He was awarded the Columbia University Medal of Excellence, the Elijah Parish Lovejoy Award for courage in journalism, the Massachusetts Audubon Society's Conservation Award citation and the New England Press Association Award. He received honorary degrees from Columbia University, Simmons College, Yale University and Southeastern Massachusetts University.

"His influence on country newspapers throughout the entire nation has been inspiring and distinguished and his pithy editorial articles and nature writings in the spirit of Thoreau have been highly praised by leading newspapers from coast to coast," one of his Columbia University citations read, while the New England Press Association in honoring him noted: "For many people, Henry Beetle Hough is symbolic of the Island of Martha's Vineyard itself ... blessed with longevity which has withstood the ravages of time while providing a sense of continuity in a changing society, drawing on knowledge of the past as a benchmark by which to judge the present and as a certain and steady guide when charting the path for the future."

And it was not only journalists and conservationists who honored him and sought his company. He numbered among his friends the actress Katharine Cornell, novelists William Styron and John Hersey, playwright Lillian Hellman, and the artist Thomas Hart Benton. His advice on living with one's fellows in an insular community, on collie dogs (of which he was inordinately fond, always having one as a mascot in the Gazette office), on real estate problems and literary matters was constantly sought. Young people writing theses about the Vineyard, older people writing books, turned to him for the historical and genealogical information and the natural history that bubbled in his brain. They were always welcomed graciously, and their manuscripts assured a thorough reading.

His knowledge of plants and birds was phenomenal, for, even well into his 70s, he was still walking 10 miles and more a day with his collie, through the meadows and along the beaches, noticing that the red-winged blackbirds were back and the mayflowers peeking from beneath the leaves, the purple of myrtle brightening the spring grass. Roses and blackberry vines tumbled over the Gazette office. For years, until Mrs. Hough's death in 1965, they kept one of Edgartown's finest rose gardens in the front yard of their white house. He was a past president of the Thoreau Society.

He always wrote reverently of nature, and determinedly sought to preserve the beauty of the Vineyard's woods and waters for future generations. With that in mind, he and Mrs. Hough donated 60 acres of their own land to start Sheriff's Meadow Foundation; "a living museum" of some of the Island's loveliest acreage was what the Houghs called it, and, after their initial gift, many another conservation-minded landowner gave his property, until, last year, there were more than 800 acres of the Island saved from development, and open to nature lovers to ramble through.

Mr. Hough's incisive and poetic editorials preserved trees whose limbs were about to be lopped off to make way for tour buses; brought a handsome white lighthouse to Edgartown to become a landmark when an open ironwork structure was in prospect; fought to make the Island a national trust when there seemed no other way to save it from builders' bulldozers, stayed the arrival of McDonald's, preserved wetlands from the intrusion of houses and tennis courts.

Not all of his battles, of course, were successful ones, but he fought them with a fury of which many were in awe, and at no time was he happier than when he was crusading. If a good cause was likely to be furthered by printing two extra pages of the Gazette, even if there was not the advertising to justify them, they would be printed.

"If we printed millions or hundreds of thousands of copies, the use of a little extra white paper in each copy might ruin us, but with a run of 4,000 or 5,000 copies, even at the burdensome high cost of newsprint today, an extra page or two does not come to too much. It does not ruin us. It puts us in the happy position of being able to write and to print in lifelike proportion what we write and others write for us, to edit the paper for our readers, and, to an extent, for our own satisfaction as newspaper people," he explained.

In an old-time tradition, he was a jack of all newspaper trades. He could, and often did, set his own copy on the Linotype. He even invented and patented a special typewriter keyboard. He could run the presses. He inserted and wrapped newspapers for mailing when he was needed; he carried them to the post office for mailing. He gathered ads.

In his use of language, he was a perfectionist and a purist, and demanded the same high standards of his staff and of any writer he was called upon to criticize in a national publication, as he frequently was.

Although he was 40 when his first book was published, that publication sparked him in a long literary career. He was regarded as especially able in the art of the essay and editorial. Singing in the Morning, a collection of his nature editorials, and Tuesday Will Be Different reflect this especially. But he also wrote novels and history and biography and a juvenile. Most of his fiction was set in New England small towns or in the New Bedford he remembered from childhood. Among the magazine publishers of his stories were the Saturday Evening Post and Esquire.

Above all, however, he was the newspaperman's newspaperman. Any number of times, after Betty Hough's death, he tried to retire to devote himself entirely to his literary output, but he never could. There were still too many people who would stop him on Edgartown's Main street and ask him to espouse their cause and right their wrong in his editorial columns.

But at the end of his 87th year, he said he simply had to stop. He was not getting out and about as he always had, and was not keeping abreast of Island events as was his wont, he insisted. He was impatient with the arthritis that prevented his legs from taking him on his accustomed journeys. So he said that he had to stop, but he didn't really mean it.

In 1979 he had married Edith Sands Graham Blake, a former Gazette reporter and photographer 30 years his junior, and an Edgartown visitor since childhood. With her, there were still some outings — mainly dinner parties with friends — but they were hardly the same as briskly making his way through the bull briars by the Sheriff's Meadow Pond or along Main street with a collie nipping playfully at his heels. (There had been a long line of collie dogs — Rikki, Captain Matrix, Dundee Bold, Lochinvar, Graham, Killiekrankie.) He felt out of circulation when he no longer could be totally independent, and, the good newspaperman that he was, he knew a newspaperman belonged on the streets.

He did manage, however, to enthusiastically welcome admirers to an open house at the renovated and much expanded Gazette office. As always, there were autograph seekers asking him to sign his works for them. And, as always, with infinite graciousness, he was pleased to oblige.

Though he was doing virtually all of his writing at home by then, and had finally grudgingly agreed to have his editorials picked up much of the time (in his 87th year he was still writing six of them a week when necessary), he always maintained an office at the Gazette.

Some 30 years earlier, he had written: "How to resign the duties of a country editor — that is what we would like to know ... how to step through the door as an editor for the last time, into a street of mellow twilight — twilight, of course ... with the white houses of the town early in shadow and the stores already lighted as one walks through the creeping, aromatic New England dusk."

In the nature of things, with new ownership at the Gazette, and his advancing years, he had left off many of his old duties, but he never did step through the door as an editor for the last time. He never did grow too old to write — and to plead and to fight for his Vineyard.

— June 7, 1985

❈ ❈ ❈

Heroes, Heroines and Real Principles

By Everett S. Allen

IN THIS SMALL ISLAND TOWN where I grew up, a friend and I were talking about our nation's need for heroes and heroines and for reaffirmation of the principle, particularly American in concept, that neither fame nor fortune can separate friends.

As a consequence, I walked down Union street toward the wharf and stood for a few moments at the site where Laura Johnson, born in this village, used to be a clerk in the American Railway Express office. She had neither husband nor children, but people were her concern and she would open her office cheerfully at virtually any hour of day or night to satisfy a need. She handled shipments of everything from baggage and meats to live baby chicks and a couple of burros, and she had worked for the company so long that she could remember when its messenger rode the Island steamers daily to make deposits in mainland banks and even match calico samples in mainland stores for Islanders.

No one, even the quite young, called her Miss Johnson; she would have decried that as a meandering approach. A woman of slight build and great candor, Laura exuded forcefulness, even in silence. She wore skirts with pockets, into which she hooked her thumbs; she strode through life with feeling but without fear, chin first. Her humor was laconic and memorable; she told this anecdote of herself: When young, she was an adroit "brass pounder," fast and accurate with the telegraph key that sent company business messages in Morse code. One day, back in the horse era, she walked past a couple of men standing next to a hitching bar, made of pipe. One of them tapped on the pipe with an iron ring, in Morse: "Peculiar looking woman." Laura walked to the next hitching bar, tapped back: "You're right," and proceeded on her way, without even looking back.

Laura, whose peanut brittle I have eaten, would not thank me for suggesting that she was of heroic proportions, but she was, essentially because of overwhelming spirit that knew no insurmountable barriers.

Her friend was Katharine Cornell, a fellow Islander and a first lady of the American theatre, something of a heroine in her own right in both obvious and lesser known ways. On behalf of the Red Cross, Miss Cornell once pitched a whole inning in a game between the Edgartown Hell Benders and an all-star team that included Denys Wortman and Thomas Hart Benton. And playing second base, she drew a roar of approval from the bleachers by leaping into the air to snag a fly, even though "it felt as if every bone in my right hand was broken."

"It was because of Laura Johnson, who was then head of the Island U.S.O.," author-journalist Henry Beetle Hough once wrote, "that Katharine Cornell put on her benefit show at Vineyard Haven in the summer of 1942. This was the first big tribute to Laura...."

In 1948, actor Gregory Peck was asked if he could name his favorite picture. "I could," he replied, "but it's not the sort of picture you mean. It was made in the summer of '42 before I ever went to Hollywood, on the stage of the high school in Vineyard Haven. It moves me every time I look at it because beside me stands Katharine Cornell, singing a song in a show that she put on for the U.S.O.

"She sang it beautifully. Her husband, Guthrie McClintic, was terrified, said she shouldn't try to do something she'd never done before, but there was a persuasive and wonderful little woman, Miss Laura Johnson, who said, 'The people on this Island love Katharine and they'd like to see her doing something informal.' So there she was, and there was I; a photographer snapped the picture and it's my favorite."

In the fall of '47, Miss Cornell opened in Antony and Cleopatra on Broadway. From the beginning, Laura planned to see the play, but she was terminally ill. She was hospitalized during that winter, and it didn't seem as if it would be possible for her to go to New York until her friend Miss Cornell chartered a plane for the purpose and made all other arrangements, in March of 1948. An hour and a half after taking off from the Island ("Without a bump or a jar," said Laura), she was in bed in the hotel in New York.

"It was matinee day," Laura recalled, "but Katharine came over very soon after we arrived and we had a good visit. Our friendship is the sort that does not require a great deal of conversation. We sat and enjoyed each other's company.

"We had a box seat in the theatre, made especially comfortable for me, and the play was the most marvelous thing I ever saw. Katharine glowed, positively glowed. She had lived her part until the light of her inspiration came to the surface and became visible."

On the following day, Laura's plane was grounded by weather. Among those who came to see her were Brenda Forbes, Noel Coward and Brian Aherne — and Miss Cornell came again "for another nice visit."

"The next morning," Laura said afterward, "we started for home in a pouring rain. In less than five minutes, we were above the storm and shortly after, the sun was shining. I said, 'My cup runneth over.' "

Those were her first and last plane flights.

The other day, I walked along South Main street to look at the house where Laura lived, where I once swung in her backyard hammock. Someone else lives there now but the window panes glisten in the early sun as they used to and the backyard will be filled with flowers this summer, as it always was. I thought, "What does it mean to me to know what these two women were, and were to each other."

I submit there was a nobility in their relationship that persists even in the recollection of it. Their affection and mutual respect, in the most civilized tradition, surmounted lesser differences that might have proved stumbling blocks to lesser principals.

"Heroes are created by popular demand," Gerald White Johnson wrote during World War II, "sometimes out of the scantiest materials, such as the apple that William Tell never shot, the ride that Paul Revere never finished...." But that, of course, is something else. This is not an essay on heroes and heroines born of dramatic action. Rather, it is concerned with those uncommon members of our society whose grasp of what we are and ought to be, on an ordinary Tuesday, is so extraordinary as to be elevating. True heroes and heroines reassure because of the way in which they live, especially as this pertains to their association with, and their concern for, their contemporaries.

I am the better (and so is the nation) for the relationship between Laura and Miss Cornell because its sparkling worth inhibits — perhaps even logically prohibits — subscribing to lesser and sometimes popular theses. Among these are the suggestions that mankind has within itself the seeds of its own destruction, that the human is basically evil and weak and dominated by lesser, rather than greater motives. With the end of her life in sight, Laura said, realistically, as always, "My cup runneth over." She knew precisely what she meant and the sentiment itself, under the circumstances, is sufficient to dispel any number of lesser theses.

I ask for the betterment of America and the world, not more William Tells but more Laura Johnsons. And more Katharine Cornells, for that matter.

– May 21, 1982

✻   ✻   ✻

Inside Baseball with A. Bartlett Giamatti

By Richard Stradling

A DRAFT COPY of Angelo Bartlett Giamatti's new book sits on the coffee table at his Edgartown home. Rings show where the president of professional baseball's National League and his family have used the book as a coaster for drinks.

Due out this fall, the book is a collection of essays and addresses from Mr. Giamatti's years as president of Yale University from 1977 until 1986, when he stepped down to return to teaching. When he became president of the institution he told reporters, "All I ever wanted was to be president of the American League." Less than 10 years later he got the next best thing, when he was offered and accepted the presidency of the National League.

"I didn't have any idea this was going to come along," Mr. Giamatti said. "I was very happily contemplating being on the faculty at Yale. I had an office, I had a parking space, I had everything important. I had a reading list. I mean I was ready to go."

It has been nearly two years since Mr. Giamatti became head of one of the oldest sports organizations in the country. And while the switch from academia to athletics seems on the surface a drastic one, Mr. Giamatti maintains it is not.

"It's not as big a move as it looks. I, after all, was not teaching at Yale when I left, and I'm not playing baseball in the National League," he said. "I'm a facilitator. That's what you are as a president of a university, and that's what I am here. So that while the context is very different, a lot of it is not. In both cases you have people who are pursuing intensely and competitively and in a very focused way goals that are not necessarily compatible with other people's."

On Tuesday afternoon, Mr. Giamatti sat beneath the skylight in the living room of his Edgartown home, talking of baseball, the place of sport in society and his new book.

"It's a good coaster. I hope it will prove to be as good a book," he said.

The National League was founded in 1876, and the game of professional baseball has not changed fundamentally since the 1890s. It's this sense of tradition that is the appeal of the game, Mr. Giamatti said.

"As professional sports go, the National League is about as old a structure for the maintenance of a competitive grid as there is. That means there is an awful lot of accumulated history, and baseball is tremendously conscious of its history. The statistics every day are merely the most recent snapshots in an album that goes way back.

"I understand how slowly baseball changes. I understand why it's slow to change, and why it's essentially conservative of itself. I think that's one of the reasons it appeals so profoundly to the country. People like something whose tradition is to be traditional. It is still in that sense of the word a 19th-century game. That's part of the appeal."

Mr. Giamatti said baseball is part of the entertainment business, and that the league he presides over is made up of 12 highly visible small businesses. And, he said, baseball is essentially tied to larger issues that confront the country.

"I don't think that it can be in any fundamental sense exempt from the country," Mr. Giamatti said. "Baseball reflects issues of social justice for example, affirmative action, the role of minorities, issues of substance abuse, whether alcohol or drugs, labor and financial issues, municipal issues. These are all American issues. If these games, and baseball in particular, were somehow viewed by the culture as so completely separate from these issues, no one would be interested.

"You don't go out there to get away from the world, you go out there to see a better one. But it's not a separate one, and people who say politics and other matters ought to be kept out of sports have misread the history of sport. These forms of leisure distill a culture's interests. How a culture takes its leisure is more indicative of its health and basic interests than how it goes about its work. To pursue leisure is a matter of choice. That tells you an enormous amount about a culture."

One key social issue surrounding baseball is the acceptance and mobility of blacks at various levels within the major leagues. Mr. Giamatti points to the relatively early effort baseball made to allow black players into the league.

"Baseball integrated itself before the United States Army and certainly before Brown versus Education in 1954," he said. "That isn't to say it was at the time of the Civil War. But America had not fully faced up to its racism until after the Second World War forced mobility and upheaval, and forced it to look at itself. If you go off and defend American values against fascism worldwide, you'd better examine what they are. It's not an accident that baseball integrated itself early. It thought of itself as quintessentially American.

"Baseball has more to do. I don't know how much more, but it certainly has more to do. Baseball has made tremendous efforts and strides in what I would call opening up equal opportunity in terms of front office jobs. It's certainly under way. It seems to me in that respect not unlike a lot of other American institutions which have racist pasts and have to expunge whatever vestiges that remain, and let's be candid, baseball's no different."

Mr. Giamatti said there is also concern for the place of minorities as welcome spectators of the sport.

"The number of black Americans in the stands is lower than the percentage of the black population at large," he said. "It was not viewed as accessible because it was not accessible to blacks at the major league level until 40 years ago. It therefore has not made the black American feel welcome in the stands, not in some obvious way, but in some deeper sense. And that will take time. And when baseball as an industry — not just as a game, but as an industry — reflects the complexion, the pluralism, the diversity of America, you will see a gradual change in the stands. I think it's a longer term, subtler, deeper issue, which has now surfaced and people are talking about, and I think that is a good thing."

In these years of huge salaries, drug problems among professional athletes, and highly publicized disputes between athletes and their managers and owners, the vision of the sports hero in society is changing. But Mr. Giamatti believes the human qualities and faults in athletes put their achievements in perspective.

"The fact is that sports heroes are among the only authentic walking-around heroes. That's just a fact," he said. "When someone does something that is better than anyone else in the world can do, and yet that person is alive and in all other outward respects looks like you and me, but has this capacity to do things that you know are virtually superhuman because your humanity can't do it, and who picks you up out of yourself because they can do it, that person is treated with a kind of awe.

"Nobody ever said that because we treat them with this awe that they also weren't human. That's, of course, one of the reasons for the awe, that they are human. Most people aren't astonished when human beings have human frailties. What astonishes us is the capacity to do something that frankly most people can't do.

"Now what happens on the sports pages — America's love of sports, its worship of sports — should not amaze us in a culture that has always admired the individual who can reach farther than anybody else."

– August 26, 1988

❧ ❧ ❧

Enchanted Island

By William A. Caldwell

YOU ASKED, YOUNG LADY, WHETHER PEOPLE who live on Martha's Vineyard aren't glad to see you summer persons go. You expected the old gent who had stopped his car to pick you up and your big backpack and small dog to say yes. He has been wondering why you wanted him to say yes.

The answer is no.

"The crowds," you said. "The traffic. The noise. The litter. How you must hate us!"

The answer is no.

I am not authorized to speak for Islanders — indeed, after all these years I'm a stranger here m'self, a traveler from a distant place and time — but I think it is safe to say they aren't very good at hating anything except maybe dog ticks and Ceratostomella ulme, or Dutch elm disease.

But why do so many of you ask, and why do you pursue the question?

After you're gone, you've told me again and again this summer, you and your brothers and sisters in uniform dungarees and beer-ad sweatshirts — after you're gone, then silence and blessed solitude and peace will flood back into this Eden, and....

And what?

One morning not long ago a woman stood leaning against the rail of the ferry Islander's crowded upper deck. Goodbye, she called to someone on the wharf below, goodbye and thanks for everything, goodbye, and the engines pulsed and the boat creaked away from its slip and she composed herself in a deck chair and opened a book. But when it cleared the breakwater and turned into the long run to West Chop — the leg of the journey that parallels the beach road — she put down the book and rummaged in a rattan bag and hauled out an immense red towel.

This she unfurled, and, taking it to the rail, she waved it almost frantically, almost desperately — perhaps (one did not ask) to someone she knew would be watching from a cottage on the shore or a car on the causeway, perhaps to the whole of the Island — and at last she turned away and came back to her chair and covered her face with a corner of the blanket and wept.

There went summer.

I take you now to the porch of a house along the shore or the seat of a car idling along the causeway abreast of the now hurrying Islander, or to the doorway of a home at the end of a lane in the woods, and here is a family of year-round Islanders waving farewell. Goodbye, they'd be saying if they could trust themselves to speak; thank you for being our children or parents or dear friends; goodbye, and come back soon. Oh, for God's sake come back now and never go away, but the boat or the car or the Day-Glo backpack has dwindled out of sound and sight. They are gone.

There went summer.

What we all of us rue is that a moment of high beauty and

shared delight is ended, but there is more to it than that. There is also the premonition, or rather the absolute certainty, that one of these times will be the last time. In his beautiful new book *To the Harbor Light* the editor of the Gazette, Henry Beetle Hough, refers to a column the philosopher Erwin Edman wrote 20 years or so ago in The American Scholar about first things and last things, first times and last, and the exquisite but difficult art of living each experience as if it will never come again. It was the last such essay Professor Edman ever wrote. He proceeded forthwith to die, leaving to his friends such comfort as they could find in his assurance that in large things and small, indeed it is world without end. A personal reminiscence may be excusable. In the summer of 1922 took place an immense reunion of the interrelated families that farmed the stony moraine between Keuka and Seneca Lakes. The feasting and merry-making went on for some days, and folks told each other, of course, that we must do this more often. My father came home pensive. No, he said, it would never happen again. The we who had been there would not be together again. It was a last time. He had to go away on a trip later that summer — I remember watching him striding off to the little railroad station on his long legs and I remember wanting to run after him and ask him not to go — and a few days later he was dead.

There's some of that, which is morbid, in our wishing summer might not ebb away like this. But there's something unselfish too. On our part it is a wish we might go with you and share your joys and dangers. It is on your part, I suspect, a yearning to remain on this Island when the world and its clamor and busyness recede.

It can't be done. And shouldn't.

We've made our choices, and although these are subject to change, for now the decision is final. Someday you may come to stay. Perhaps, later, we shall board the Islander, wave farewell to Martha's Vineyard, and go to seek our fortune. But in the meantime, though we follow your steps to the ends of the earth, we can never get to where you're going. Though you leap overboard and swim ashore and persuade us to take you home with us, it would not be Eden you returned to. It would be the chill gray reality that for a few months, always perhaps for the last time, you summer people have transformed for us into an enchanted Island.

Hate you, child?

The answer is no.

— Column, September 3, 1976

NATURE

❧

ONE WARMISH AFTERNOON roughly 12,000 years ago a southeastern lobe of the great Laurentide glacier advanced its last few inches along a front running from the Lagoon up to Quitsa or thereabouts, and in the days following, it began to retreat. The waters came roaring in, surrounding the gray landfill of boulders and gravel and sand dumped upon the crust, and some of the organisms left behind took root or dug burrows in the grit, setting off down their evolutionary pathways completely unacquainted with everyday mainland behavior.

Pummeled by thundering ocean breezes, smothered in fogs, routinely burned by salt and fire, these biota began to do weird things, scientifically and metaphysically. Wildflowers and shrubs kept their heads down, spreading outward rather than rising upward, grabbing the sandy soil more tenaciously, blooming more darkly, craving riots in the atmosphere and landscape more ardently than their cousins on the continent.

Act differently long enough, scientists will tell you, and you become a different creature, an Island creature, right down to your classification in the reference books. The planet thrives on the sort of genetic diversification that Islands create. And the Gazette rejoices in it.

The newspaper knows that mankind rules the roost on Martha's Vineyard, but it sees strange insurrections everywhere — in the near conquest of Tisbury by feral turkeys, for example, or in the Edgartown pig who ate poison ivy and cars. The newspaper clears front pages and editorial columns to mark a return to Gay Head of a bird from the tropics, or record the manner by which a wild goose or a family cat passes from the scene. It admires the strength and craft by which a spaniel survives the most brutal test of Island life, and the cunning of catbirds, and the vanity and patience of gulls.

The Gazette is a newspaper that celebrates the tenacity of weeds, the refinement of skunks and the songs of frogs.

And from an amazingly early date, 1933, it grasped the idea that the Vineyard encompassed an entire habitat away and apart from the rest of the world. That year the last survivor of an eastern strain of prairie chicken — a bird of almost explosive courtship rituals known as the heath hen — died somewhere on the outwash plain, where circumstance and savagery had cornered the race. The Vineyard had witnessed an extinction — "the utmost finality which can be written, glimpsing the darkness which will not know another ray of light," said the Gazette that spring in an editorial, now famous, called A Bird That Man Could Kill.

Too often now, Martha's Vineyard serves as just this sort of refuge, a final retreat for plants and animals dependent on an open seaward place where salt and fire scour, where fog and wind blast. The Gazette argues plainly that the osprey and the piping plover — and by scientific extension, the world at large — deserve a chance the heath hen never got. Indeed, the paper believes in deference to any creature wise enough to choose a home where the water meets the land.

– T.D.

* * *

Night Transition

THE NIGHTS ARE STILL FILLED WITH MUSIC under the high and thoughtful stars, but the music is not quite so confident. As the air cools and fresher winds blow, the sound of the insects becomes a slower, softer orchestration, the effect comparable to that of another lonesome phenomenon, lights going out one by one. But the diminishing of the early autumnal chant is, all in all, a pleasant transition. Summer's destiny, in part, is to be piped out by this strange music, practically all strings without support of wind instruments unless the wind itself takes part, and with no conductor except the great spirit of the night.

The retreat of insect sounds takes place at no prescribed or regular rate; both volume and authority rise and fall with the temperature and the nightly aspect until some final chill imposes an ending.

By the chirping of the cricket it is entirely practical to tell the temperature of any September night. Count the number of chirps a cricket makes in 14 seconds and add this number to 42. You will have the temperature within a degree. No computer can do better.

It is partly the insect noises that make these nights so vast and impressive when they are clear, partly the quality of the starlight or the moonlight — especially the moon glade on the water — and partly the strong hint of prophecy. What is to happen tomorrow night or on any night this week or next, no one can say. But the season should bring some of the old familiar interludes when the stars that have written in the heavens of the past seem to be writing of the future. Pools of warm air are cradled here and there, but a new cooling takes charge. Summer is ending, everything says, and the future is whispering along the passages of time.

In the morning there is a residue of night — dew glistening on the grass, white haze rising like a sorcerer's smoke from field and marsh. These and other signs show that night was busy and significant; it knew what it said. The turning cannot be put off longer.

– Editorial, October 1, 1971

      ❧   ❧   ❧

Cap'n Norman Benson Tells Salty Tale of the Past

By Norman G. Benson
(As told to William L. Peltz)

"SMARTEST DOG I EVER HAD WAS BUFFY, no doubt about it. He was a real knowin' dog. He could do everything except talk. An' a great dog to take gunnin'. He could smell ducks the way hounds can smell rabbits. Sometimes he'd follow along the shore, sniffing for the scent and then when he'd found it, you'd see his tail waggin' in the grass. But if he had a crippled duck, he'd bring him back careful in his mouth, or sometimes he'd just turn around and look at me to let me know and ask me what to do. I would just wave him on and he'd do what I wanted. I never licked him. I'd talk sharp to him but never lick him.

"Buffy was buff-colored and a sea-goin', duck-huntin' spaniel.

"Back in those days, we used to use live decoys for gunnin'. We used to put a strap on their legs an' then put 'em out along the shore and leave 'em there right through the season. Of course, we'd feed 'em every day an' take 'em home when we was done gunnin'.

"On this particular night it was dark. In those days, you could shoot as late at night as you wanted to. You didn't have to quit at sunset like you do now.

"Well, it was dark, like I say, an' this duck started quackin' offshore. After a while, this feller who was with me says, 'I think I see him.' I said, 'Give him a gun. Go ahead an' try it.' So, he fired. The minute he did, that duck flapped his wings an' started for the shore.

"I said to Buffy, 'Go git him!' Buffy was a dandy dog an' never jumped a gun, but as soon as I said 'Go,' he was off. He'd always come back with the duck. This time though, he went over and after a while he came back without the duck.

"I said to him, 'You git back there an' git that duck!' So, he went over again but this time he didn't come back. I knew somethin' was wrong, so after four or five minutes, this feller and I walked over, and there was Buffy with his paw right on one of our live duck decoys who'd got loose. He hadn't wanted to hurt it, so instead of takin' that duck in his mouth like he would've if it was a crippled wild one, he was holdin' it down on the ground with his paw. Pretty smart, I thought that was!

"Bein' a spaniel, Buffy loved the water.

"He always went out on the Riverside with us, when we hauled trap. Even when he got to be old, he'd want to come along, just as loyal as a hired man.

"He'd usually lie on the afterdeck, which was his favorite spot, and after the day's haul when we got back to Lambert's Cove, where we anchored in those days, he'd come ashore with us an' ride back in the truck.

"Well, this particular day when we came ashore about midday, we figured he was with us till we got home an' everyone said, 'Where's Buffy?' We was awful upset when we realized he was missing. All the children cried and everyone said I'd have to go back to Vineyard Haven an' look for him. So I went, but he wasn't at the dock or anywhere else I could see. We searched everywhere we could think of.

"Then I recalled that when we came out of Woods Hole, it had begun to get mighty choppy in a tide rip, an' with him sittin' on the afterdeck, he must have been pitched clear overboard 'way out there off Woods Hole. I felt awful bad.

"Back home, I got out the almanac an' figured there was four hours of tide goin' to the east'ard, an' that would be enough to sweep Buffy clear around Cape Pogue, over to Chappaquiddick or maybe even beyond.

"That was an awful unhappy night at home, I'm telling you.

"Next morning my son Franklin, who was a little feller then, said he'd had a dream. 'I could see him,' he said, 'an' he was alive, crawled up on a high place an' was all tuckered out.'

"When we went over across the Sound to haul our traps that day, we kept a sharp lookout for Buffy. We looked all along the shore by Woods Hole up past Nobska and then back down along the shore of Naushon, 'way past Tarpaulin to Black Woods, but we never see'd no sign of him. When we landed our fish at Woods Hole, I asked Sam Cahoon if he'd seen him, but he hadn't. He drove us up to where there was a female dog, just in case Buffy'd come ashore an' headed there. You can imagine how unhappy we was all day. When we got home that night, the kids were terrible upset, Franklin especially.

"About nine o'clock that evening, Brett Stokes called me up an' said, 'I've got Buffy. I'll bring him right over.' He musta landed way over on the south side of the Vineyard an' walked clear across the Island.

"Seemed hard to believe, but I was sure it was Buffy, 'cause Brett and I used to go gunnin' together an' everything, an' every time we'd go, we'd take Buffy along, so he knew him well.

"When they arrived, Buffy was plain wore out. His eyes was bulged, his hair was covered with salt, an' he just was so sore he could hardly walk. Dog tired, you could say.

"Came over an' put his head in everyone's lap, an' then he just flopped right down an' jus' lay there an' didn't stir the rest o' the night.

"Thing about it was, Buffy'd learned never to buck a tide. You see, I'd hunted lots o' times with Buffy along the North Shore an' he'd come to know how strong the tides are there. When I shot a duck, he'd never go straight out and fight the current to get it. Instead he'd swim out and take advantage of the current, until he could turn and pick the duck up easy as anything. Like I say, he'd learned not to swim against the current. Sometimes he'd come ashore a long ways, maybe a quarter mile down the beach, but he'd never fight that current. I'm convinced that that's what saved his life when he got pitched overboard. He just swam an' swam along with it until it turned and landed him over beyond Cape Pogue on the South Shore of the Vineyard. Eight or ten miles, it musta been from where he went overboard.

"I had other good dogs," Norman said, sort of in conclusion as it were, "but he was the best of them all and far and along the most intelligent. He was a dandy dog, and a real knowin' one, too, like I said before."

— June 23, 1972

❧   ❧   ❧

A Weed by Any Other Name

Instead of yanking weeds for hours,
Learn their names as native flowers;
Though they violate decorum,
Smile and just take credit for 'em.
D.A.W.

Helen the Pig Is Dead After Two Beers And Half a Ton of Love

By Mary MacDonald

AFTER ALL EFFORTS TO SAVE HELEN the pig failed this week, the 600-pound resident of Chase Road in Edgartown was given one of her favorite treats, two cans of beer.

And then she was put to sleep, leaving behind a loving family and many friends.

Helen was an Edgartown landmark: a point of destination for curious schoolchildren and a good direction point to guide visitors. She was, perhaps, one of Edgartown's most famous residents.

But after more than 10 years of living a happy existence in the care of the family of Jesse Morgan, she succumbed to an intestinal blockage and was put to sleep on Wednesday.

For a domestic pig, one that for a period of time weighed in at well over 700 pounds, 10 years is a remarkable age, said Stephen Morgan, the son of Jesse and the late Anna Morgan.

Along with beer, which Stephen said she drank "like there was no tomorrow," one of Helen's favorite snack foods was poison ivy.

In her front yard enclosure, Helen had within reach all the poison ivy a pig could want.

"I'm allergic to it, so she used to get rid of it for me," Stephen said. "She used to suck that stuff up like spaghetti."

He noted that she was named Helen for her uncanny resemblance to the Aunt Helen of a family friend, who will remain unidentified for that reason.

She came to be the Morgan family pig almost by default. Raised from birth in the company of two boars, Helen was originally destined for the slaughterhouse. After it was discovered she was expecting, the Morgans decided to keep her and she soon became a part of the family and a fixture in the community.

As domesticated as a family pig can get, Helen was described by the elder Mr. Morgan as well-behaved, when in 1982 the long-time Edgartown animal control officer was interviewed by the Gazette.

But, as Stephen explained this week, the pig also had a knack for getting into mischief.

Once, in the early autumn, before storm windows went up around the neighborhood, Helen broke out of her pen and embarked on a tour. Pushing her broad snout against their screen doors, the visiting pig shocked some neighbors.

And then there was the time she took a liking to metal, locking her teeth into a neighbor's car hood and creating $146 in damages. That perhaps was the first time a pig was held liable for damaging a car.

"The insurance company covered it," Stephen said. "It was on the homeowner's policy. It was a liability. It did need a special note though."

— November 11, 1988

      ❧   ❧   ❧

If You Know Your Catbirds

THE COUNTRYMAN WHO WRITES the nature editorials in The New York Sunday Times is Hal Borland, and he lives in Connecticut. Is it possible that catbirds are not the same familiars of home premises in Connecticut as they are on Martha's Vineyard?

At any rate, Mr. Borland, in a recent tribute to the catbird, otherwise beyond criticism, says, "He won't come and eat from your hand." Not eat from your hand? How different and deficient must be the customs of Connecticut.

On the Vineyard, catbirds absent over thousands of miles and long winter months that seem as protracted in their monotonous way, arrive punctually in early May at the same windowsills they left behind last fall, ready to eat raisins from the same hands. This has been so for years and decades, proving that the intimacy of catbirds in their chosen Island neighborhoods must be passed on from generation to generation.

Sit out under a spreading elm on a Sunday morning, and not one but two or three catbirds will drop to your shoulder, your book, your knee, or your head. They make the situation quite clear. They expect raisins or, better, currants which can be devoured more easily. Their confidence is complete. They know. They have privileges that are as good as rights.

Leave an unscreened window open, and catbirds will enter to discover the raisin supply for themselves, and often they will find it. Or, try walking around the yard or the nearby field, and observe how closely the resident catbirds follow, perching as closely as possible, reminding you that you are remiss in an important duty. Then hold out your hand with a few raisins and see how quickly your gray friend will fly to it.

– Editorial, May 2, 1972

     ❧   ❧   ❧

A Task of Frost and Iron

By Everett S. Allen

IT IS SOME TIME BACK NOW and there is no need for fresh mourning — death is, after all, inseparable from life — but standing at the place of now-mellowing earth and blackberry thorn the other morning, I was moved to remember that Sunday in winter when I dug a grave there with an ax. It was hard earth that no one had a right to turn. The frost glinted through, the ax struck sparks, each stroke never lifting more than a splintered fragment of stubborn dirt. This is how it was:

Chip, strike and spark. There was no room to stand erect because the grapevines, a durable net to protect nature against the human interloper, created such a low ceiling. On one's knees, white breath blowing with the effort, chop and pry as if the earth were stone; the little pile of soil in claylike crescents grew with painful slowness. Somewhere a church bell rang, not the warm bronze of summer but cold steel striking a brittle sky. Nobody came by; it was too bitter for traveling. For the moment, the solitude and nature of the work made getting below the frost line life's only important goal.

There was no one to ask how long or how deep a grave should be. Deep enough, long enough, that was all. Smooth the sides, square the corners. If you do not do this out of honest feeling, why do you do it at all? And if it is out of honest feeling, then do it as well as may be.

Finally, it was done. I lowered him in, wrapped in a white wool blanket so that I would not have to look at any aspect of what had been for so long, even up to an hour ago. Why is it that one does these things gently when it no longer really can be important? Still, there persists the compulsion older than time to whisper, to redistribute the earth neatly, as if there were only one acceptable way in which such things may be performed. I even took pains to shovel a half-dozen unearthed bulbs back into the hole, hoping some still might live because, I told myself, "When spring comes, there must be, as there were in all the years when he knew this place, the white narcissus, the nodding tulip, which he seemed to appreciate in a wordless way that said much."

For he was not one to pass by anything indifferently — not one cricket, cobweb silvered with dew, or a splash of sunlight in shade. The one I buried was a tiger cat, male, 17½ years old, found abandoned and leaf-chasing in a Vineyard Haven alley-way when the world and he were importantly younger. From the first, he brought to our home the impression that he had been assigned by Somebody to fill a gap — of which, frankly, I had been unaware — and that it would be no trouble to do so. His self-assurance was obvious; he knew, early on, that most of life's annoyances were not worth the effort of chasing them over the fence and that eventually they would go away of their own volition. In summer, he contrived to appear pale purple and I do not know how he managed that.

He ate with gusto, as if he deserved it because he had brains enough to appreciate good food, which he did. I often have won-dered how other cats eat asparagus spears. He confronted the stalks end-on, like pale-green cigars, and inhaled them. I can-not remember whether it was a pint of clams or a quart of clams that he consumed at a single sitting but whichever it was, when he had finished glassy-eyed with fulfillment, he reminded me of W.S. Gilbert, who once observed, "I see no objection to stout-ness, in moderation."

Over the years, he assumed — especially in the presence of children — that his age and experience entitled him to respect, which it did. This included going through doorways first. In due course, it became as simple to understand what he wanted, what his attitude was in any given circumstance, as it was to com-prehend that the cobweb, narcissus, and clam deserve more at-tention than many humans are inclined to give them. There were, of course, some humans with whom he could not communicate at all but I did not find that strange because even other humans have that problem.

Digging the grave was an ambivalent experience — there are a few in life; I had not wanted it to be necessary; once neces-sary, I had not wanted to start it; having started it, I did not look forward to having it end, because there was only one way in which it could end. I submit that even the most matter-of-fact among us is sobered when forced to be reminded that finalities may not be postponed, continued or amended and that whereas much of nature has solved the miraculous equation of wintering under and reappearing in spring, some of us have not. I mounded the earth and thought briefly of marking the place but decided I would let whatever came up there in April mark it and that would be better. It was a reasonable decision; already, there are green shoots showing.

Once, I knew an old woodcutter who lived in the up-country where cold weather translates into days and nights that try the endurance. He said, "I never been to Florida or them other places where there's no hard ground any time of year because they don't have it cold the way we do. And I know these days folks, even country people like me, don't have to dig graves for their kin because there's somebody else to do it. But I had done it twice before I was 30 and I tell you maybe sometime during their lives everybody should have to dig a grave when the dirt comes up full of frost and hard as iron.

"Death ain't thoughtful. Sometimes it comes when nothing's blooming. And if you really have to work at it to put somebody away, before the job is done you get a proper idea of what it is you're doing. You believe it."

I believe it.

– Column, March 24, 1989

❧ ❧ ❧

On the Wings of Spring

SNOW ON THE GROUND and spring in the air. Nothing unusual about that, not in New England in these first uncertain days between winter's end and the start to a new season, the prelude to summer. The search now is for signs of seasonal confirmation, for the color of crocuses, the song of pinkletinks

153

and soon the cream and pink of shadbush or wild pear, the yellow flash of daffodils and forsythia. These are signs closer to us, familiar to Island soil and woodland.

But look up to find in the distance the true majesty of spring. On the breeze high above the Vineyard an observer will discover the new season painted in silver streaks and graceful patterns of gliding flight. And this is the surest sign of all.

Spring is to be found in the golden eye of the osprey. They arrived up-Island on Tuesday, as if to confirm that all is well in a world otherwise troubled by the less important business of daily life. The return of the ospreys. It is now a ritual as important as any on the Island's seasonal calendar. These great sea hawks, the feathered fishermen of our waters, are here for the spring and summer and early autumn before taking leave for the south and warmer climes.

They are here for the season's first alewives and to fish the Island's herring runs. They are here because the Vineyard is home to the largest concentration of ospreys in this part of the country. And they are here as witnesses to a great conservation story written in the efforts of leading Island naturalists over the past 20 years, especially the work of director Gus Ben David at the Audubon's Felix Neck Wildlife Sanctuary.

Two decades ago there were but two pair of ospreys on the Vineyard. Today the ospreys number closer to 130 and the Island has become the seeding ground for these sea hawks on the Cape and in Nantucket, across the state and throughout the rest of New England. Last autumn Mr. Ben David and friends planted the Vineyard's 100th nesting pole and it is to these sturdy homes that we now welcome back our ospreys on the wings of spring.

– Editorial, March 27, 1992

Pinkletinks!

MICHAEL WILD, WHO LIVES NEAR the Edgartown Great Pond, called the Gazette Monday to report hearing spring's earliest pinkletink. The weather conditions were ideal. It was warm. The sun was out. Mr. Wild said he heard the little tree frog at 10:38 a.m. "It happened when the temperature hit 50, this little guy came out," he said.

– March 12, 1993

Frog Retraction

MICHAEL WILD VISITED THE GAZETTE yesterday to offer his sincere public apologies, and to retract his claim to have heard the first pinkletink of 1993 in song at Katama. He has traced the apparent peeping, he said, to a vent in his furnace.

In other, similarly distressing news of the season, William Marks called this week from West Tisbury to announce that he had just picked the first wood tick of the season from his dog, Puppy.

– March 19, 1993

❧ ❧ ❧

Vineyarders Dream and Scheme
To Spread Butterfly Weed

By Amyas Ames

SEVERAL YEARS AGO, as I pursued my hobby of wildflower photography, I came to love the butterfly weed. It was not only the clear orange color, or the multiple clusters of blossom, but as I lay watching in a summer meadow, I saw the intense, almost passionate eagerness with which insects feasted on the lovely flowers. The blossom is not only beautiful, it is a nectar champion in the world of flowers.

Butterfly weed is scarce in North Tisbury and I went on a trip cross-Island with Kib Bramhall — another addict of this "weed" — to see the rich display in fields near Edgartown. We marveled at the many thousands of plants and speculated that the seed, born on thistledown, had been concentrated there by prevailing winds and that if we could establish a source in North Tisbury, our westerly winds would populate the Island with blossom.

This led me to gather seed pods in the fall, maroon-colored and erect on coiled stems, and, sitting in the cool sunshine of October, to pull off the thistledown skirts so the seed could be stored, safe from mice in an unheated shed until spring. Scattered on moist earth, with an eight-inch cover of compost and an occasional watering in dry weather, the seed proved easy to propagate. I had to learn that it took two years of growth before the young plants blossomed — but I had my source.

It was when I extended the project to planting the year-old "weeds" in our little meadow of about an acre that I realized I had a problem. I had always cut my field in June or July to keep it from going wild with briar, sumac, ivy and various woody plants that seemed to love it as their home. Now that my meadow was my garden, I could no longer cut it.

I took my problem to the New York Botanical Garden Institute of Ecosystem Studies at the Cary Arboretum in Millbrook, N.Y., asking one of their ecologists — Mark McDonnell — how to nurture blossom in a meadow without fostering unwanted growth. He told me that the mechanized cutter-bar, when improperly used, was the enemy of all blossoming field plants and that mankind in this century was endangering many species of flowers — including butterfly weed — creating in effect "great mechanized deserts of grass" across our land.

He recommended that a field should be cut in the first surge of spring growth, before the butterfly weed, a late riser, has grown to the height of the mowing blade. It was just reaching this height in North Tisbury by May 25, so the best time to cut a Vineyard field is early in the last week of May. An earlier cutting, about May 1, will increase the control of unwanted growth. He further advised that a September or October cutting is not helpful in meadow culture as by then more food is stored in the roots, and it will result in more unwanted shoots in the spring.

I have been following this advice in developing my little meadow garden for several years, and am pleased to report that my one-acre field is filling with flowers. The butterfly weed is starting to spread from its own seed, giving an overlay of orange bloom and butterflies, and I am now planning for the day when black-eyed Susan and goldenrod will in turn bloom in wild profusion.

— July 7, 1989

❧   ❧   ❧

Katama Plain Burns in Flames For Rare Island Species

By Dorsey Griffith

To THE ISLANDER Sunday's dry, cool and sunny weather meant a first seasonal bike ride, outdoor yardwork or a picnic on the beach.

But to a group of conservationists, the conditions were perfect for the torching of 16 acres of grassland at the Katama Plain nature preserve.

By setting fire to the grasses on one portion of the property adjacent to the Edgartown Air Park runway, state and local environmentalists hope to promote the continued existence of rare animal and plant species. The burn is part of a management plan for proper stewardship of the Katama land. The plan was developed by Nancy Braker, an entomologist who worked on the Vineyard as a field assistant for The Nature Conservancy last summer.

Miss Braker and a team of burn experts from across the state and local conservationists, volunteer firefighters and airport officials have been waiting to conduct the burn since early April. But it wasn't until Sunday that Mother Nature provided the prescribed burn conditions: wind between 8 and 15 miles per hour; relative humidity between 25 and 50 per cent and air temperature between 50 and 60 degrees.

According to William Patterson of the Department of Forestry and Wildlife Management at the University of Massachusetts, Amherst, Sunday might have been the last day of the season to set fire to the Katama Plain. "In two or three weeks the grasses will start greening. Now is a time when it is a minimal risk to nesting, fledgling birds," he said.

By 7 a.m. the Katama airport was closed and the runways marked with huge white Xs to discourage hovering planes from landing. Christina Brown, a member of the Edgartown Conservation Commission, warned neighbors of the upcoming event. Two Edgartown fire trucks arrived with about 1,000 gallons of water and by 11 a.m. the burn specialists were ready to put the first match to a specially marked area of the 193-acre Katama prairie.

The burn, designed and led by Peter Dunwiddie, a plant ecologist at the Massachusetts Audubon Society, was conducted in two, eight-acre sections. The boundary where the fire started was marked and soaked with hoses from a moving fire truck. Using drip torches with a mixture of kerosene and gasoline, burn specialists set backfires, fires that move against the wind at about three feet per minute.

The flames rarely reached heights greater than five feet. With hand water pumps on their backs, team members maintained a wet line along the edges to contain the fire within the area designated for the burn. The 15-member team controlled the burn so accurately that a lone wooden sign in the middle of the flame zone was left completely intact.

"When people think of burns, people think of raging wildfires. What we're doing is very different. We are able to control the burn. The difference between wildfires and prescribed fires is the same as the difference between crashing a car at 20 miles per hour and crashing a car at 60 miles per hour," said Dr. Patterson.

Dr. Patterson, who has conducted prescribed burns for 17 years, explained to observers that burning has been used as a land management technique for the last 10,000 to 12,000 years, beginning with early Indian settlements. "The last 40 years are the only times when these areas have not been burned frequently. The Smokey the Bear campaign has given the impression that all fires are bad. But the effect and damage of this type of fire is different than a wildfire," he said.

Caren Caljouw, director of science and stewardship for The Nature Conservancy's office in Boston, said there is historical data to support the belief that grasslands were maintained as open moors and were burned frequently for centuries.

The Katama land was used for farm pasture and the burns continued throughout the 1800s and on into the 20th century. Although the area had not been burned for 20 years before Sunday, Stephen Gentle, former owner of the 128-acre air park, periodically used controlled burns to keep the Edgartown airport free of brush.

Miss Caljouw said the burning has helped maintain the grassland in its original state and has created a diverse community of animals and plants. During a presentation to Edgartown selectmen last fall, Miss Braker said ground-nesting birds like the northern harrier, short-eared owl and grasshopper sparrow, which have been spotted in the area, are sensitive to their habitat and do not tolerate encroaching trees or shrubs. Periodic burning of an area, she explained, keeps out trees and shrubs and reduces leaf litter, providing a better habitat for flora and fauna.

Miss Braker also monitored the existence of insects, including the regal fritillary butterfly, a rare and endangered species which feeds only on violets. Sunday's burn, Miss Caljouw explained, will result in a more vigorous growth of violets and perhaps more of the rare butterflies will appear when new growth occurs.

According to the management plan, burns will occur in the spring and fall and each area will be burned every four to five years. To maintain a buffer area for animals displaced by burning, no more than 20 per cent of the entire property will be burned in any one year, Miss Caljouw said. In addition, 29 acres of the Katama Plain will be mowed periodically and the results of that management technique will be compared to the effects of the burns.

— May 1, 1987

❧   ❧   ❧

Two Chicks at Cape Pogue

YOU COULD SEE THIS DAY COMING on the Vineyard as surely as the rise and fall of the tides that wash the Chappaquiddick shoreline from East Beach north to the tip of Cape Pogue. You knew this day was coming, perhaps as long ago as 1933 when the world's last heath hen sounded a final, dying cry on the Island. The silence from that extinct species remains with us today, a haunting symbol of the ever growing collision between the human world and the natural world upon which all of life itself depends.

And so this week, with great anguish and under pressure from federal and state officials, The Trustees of Reservations acted suddenly and forcefully to protect the piping plover — like the heath hen, another endangered species. The trustees closed more than 500 acres of the Cape Pogue sanctuary to all vehicular traffic by night and only limited traffic by day. This closure, the largest of its kind on the Vineyard, was taken to protect two plover chicks, all that are left of eight, some destroyed by natural causes, at least one mashed beneath the tires of an off-road vehicle. There are only 900 pairs of adult plovers left on the Atlantic seaboard, 11 of them nesting on the Vineyard, a prime breeding ground, with the Cape, along the eastern coastline.

Already there is grumbling, even threatening talk, from within sport fishing circles on the Vineyard. But such talk, this destructive dialogue of confrontation, from whatever quarter — fishermen, environmentalists or others who drive these barrier beaches — is at best selfish and uninformed.

Accordingly, we believe the action undertaken by the trustees to protect the plover population here and thus elsewhere in the nation represents a necessary and intelligent decision. The move to close Cape Pogue deserves the full and outspoken support of the whole Vineyard community. The trustees acted, first and foremost, on behalf of environmental sanity and, secondly, on clear and indisputable grounds of federal and state laws tied to the Endangered Species Act.

The fate of two plover chicks in a protected wildlife preserve on Cape Pogue is not the issue here. Nor is it simply a Vineyard issue. And most of all, the decision to close Cape Pogue for the next couple of weeks is not directed at any single party or group properly concerned about access to the shrinking public coastline of America. The trustees are not acting out of malice or in any way that deliberately targets the interests of fishermen, bathers or anyone else who drives overland vehicles to the water's edge.

Two chicks at Cape Pogue. They seem so inconsequential, even if vulnerable, at the height of the summer season on Martha's Vineyard, a tourist resort. But the survival of these two tiny plovers stands today as a small and very important part of a much larger crisis — the environmental crisis that confronts the Vineyard, the nation and every other country on this planet now under siege.

What is happening at Cape Pogue these days, the plover patrols and the closure of conservation lands, is no less a symbol of the global environmental threat than the destruction of the rain forest in the Amazon, the pollution of our coastal waters, the building in America's vanishing wetlands, the choking smoke and acid rain that rob our clean air and fall from our skies.

These baby plovers can't just move "somewhere else" because there's not much left of "somewhere else" anymore. The issue is not that there are only two chicks and so why worry; it is that only two remain and that should be of great concern to everyone. Efforts to ensure the survival of plovers at Cape Pogue are no different from strict environmental measures to ease the threat against striped bass and swordfish, against the evaporating fish stocks on the Grand Banks or the snail darter in the Little Tennessee River or the spotted owl in the timberlands of the Pacific Northwest.

We call on officials from The Trustees of Reservations and the fishermen and all other parties affected by beach access questions to meet together to resolve any differences or misunderstandings. There is an urgency to this call for a dialogue of cooperation if we are to prevent the destructiveness of confrontation.

Preservation of the earth's environment remains a common goal for all and not a matter for warfare to determine the rights of one special interest group or another. We shall either address these environmental crises together — from the two baby plovers at Cape Pogue to the smog hanging over Los Angeles — or we shall fail together. And if we fail in the end, nobody will have to worry about the earth's environment, about fish in the sea, wildlife on land, about the air we breathe and the water we drink.

Because there will be none.

– Editorial, July 17, 1992

Tisbury Turkeys Go Cross-Country Bound for Louisiana

By Jason Gay

TISBURY IS GETTING A LITTLE HELP from the Bayou State in solving its feral turkey epidemic.

Mark Klemperer, a zoologist with a degree from Louisiana State University, has adopted six male toms and one female turkey from the town. Mr. Klemperer learned about Tisbury's turkey overpopulation problem this summer while visiting his grandparents in Chilmark.

Tisbury executive secretary Peter L. Fohlin said the zoologist is "fascinated with our domestic feral turkey population because they are so much heartier than the average domestic turkey and they are not afraid of people."

Mr. Klemperer will relocate the turkeys to his home in Louisiana, where he also owns other birds, including peacocks, pheasants and "one other lonely wild turkey," Mr. Fohlin said.

Tisbury's feral turkey overpopulation attracted international newspaper headlines this spring after roving bands of the large birds caused trouble in residential neighborhoods. The flocks can number as large as 50 turkeys, and are known to eat homeowners' gardens and peck at house shingles and automobiles. They are primarily found in the wooded areas around Tashmoo and Lagoon Pond.

The birds have also chased pets and Tisbury residents. One elderly woman in the Tashmoo area was knocked down after a turkey gave chase in her driveway.

Mr. Fohlin was charged by the Tisbury selectmen to find foster homes for some of the turkeys. "As far as I am concerned, the turkey problem is solved," the executive secretary said at the selectmen's regular meeting Tuesday.

But selectman Henry Burt, who has witnessed turkeys gathering at his home on Lagoon Pond, said he did not think the adoption of seven birds solves the Tisbury turkey dilemma, speculated to include some 200 birds.

Mr. Fohlin said Mr. Klemperer was last seen in a compact car with his seven adopted turkeys at the Vineyard Haven Steamship Authority terminal.

– September 22, 1995

❧ ❧ ❧

A Visitor from the Tropics Sojourns Again at Cliffs

By Gus Daniels

NO BEATING ABOUT THE BUSH. No whimsical little ticklers. Just a straight, flat-out, stop-the-press news lead: The red-billed tropicbird is back. Phaethon athereus, the bird of our hearts last fall, has returned to the Vineyard after an absence of almost exactly nine months.

What fabulous news. Can you believe it? Can anyone believe it? This fantastic rarity coming back for a second time? But there it was before my wondering eyes at 9:32 this morning, August 6, just as sleek and gorgeous as ever, beating swiftly past the Gay Head Cliffs and showing off its vermilion red bill, black-marked, snowy-white wings and those magnificent streaming white tail feathers.

All birders nourish wild dreams; we're a little like Red Sox fans in that department. And when the tropicbird finally departed our fair isle early last November, we all dreamed that maybe, just maybe, it might return. It was forlorn, of course. Tropicbirds are what their exotic name suggests, creatures of warm climes and 85-degree waters. The red-billed colonizes a few islands in the deep Caribbean, also off Africa and in the Pacific; occasionally, a bird is seen out to sea from San Diego and there are a very few records for the southern Atlantic coast.

So when Dooley Rosenwald found our red-billed last September, it was the bird of a lifetime, an ornithological event so momentous that people came from all over the country to see it — everyone knowing that there would never be another chance. Those who missed it were plunged into the depths of despair. They may not have wept, but there was that awful hollowness, that sickening ache that comes with such a hideous miss.

Still, hope is the birder's great analgesic. Everyone remembers Ludlow Griscom's classic line. "Birds have wings," the father of field birding once advised, "and sometimes they use them." Good point. And there were other little bits to fuel our fatuous hopes.

Sometimes, when birds get turned around, when their marvelous navigation system gets a little bent, it happens that they become programmed to make the same mistake again — and again.

Some years ago, Gus Ben David and I found a western grebe off Nashaquitsa on a Christmas count; this terrific bird was about 2,000 miles out of range, one of only a dozen or so occurrences on the East Coast until then. Guess what? It kept turning up in New England waters — though not the Vineyard that we know of — for the next seven years. Then there was a pair of Brewer's blackbirds, also westerners, that I happened to find at Herring Creek Farm one winter; they came back a couple of times and were seen on the Cape and South Shore for some years after that. What about our burrowing owl found again on Katama Plains after an eight-year absence? And who will forget the pair of gyrfalcons, greatest and most northern of the falcons, that found happiness among the pigeons in a Pennsylvania rock quarry and returned for three or four winters in a row?

So an impossible dreamer might make a case for our tropicbird. It has obviously found the Vineyard waters and bountiful squid to its liking, making the circuit between Noman's, Gay Head and the Elizabeths for eight weeks in September and October and part of November. That was astonishing enough; no tropicbird had been observed off U.S. shores for more than a few hours. But then there are lots of amazing things about the Vineyard.

At any rate, an incurable optimist might speculate that our tropicbird, staying strong and healthy on squid, or whatever, might merely have left because food became temporarily scarce. Might it not have spent the winter and spring somewhere down south, far out to sea, perhaps in the Gulf Stream? We thought last year that the bird, fully adult, might have come from the colony on the Cape Verde Islands, off Africa, and that population pressure might have encouraged it to seek a new home, with cliffs to burrow in and plenty of food.

If it had once found a suitable summer habitat — though no mate, alas — might it not try again? Why not, indeed — except that tropicbirds are largely nonmigratory, and unlike terns, do not fly thousands of miles between summer and winter grounds.

Ah, but then about three weeks ago, little rumors began buzzing and hearts started beating faster. On July 20, Chip Vanderhoop called Sue Whiting to report that he thought he had seen the bird at Gay Head. I don't think he had binoculars with him that day.

Almost two weeks went by — and nothing. The dream started to fade. But then on August 2, Hollis Smith was sitting on the beach, around the corner from the Cliffs on the Lobsterville side, when something flew by flirting its long, lovely tail. Tropicbird? Holy cow, tropicbird!

But again, no binocs.

At this point, Sue decided to lead off this week's Bird News column with a note that word was in the wind of Phaethon's miraculous return. But no "birder" — that's somebody who falls down a lot because he's always looking up — had seen it with binocs. Yet how could anybody make a mistake on a tropicbird, you may ask?

Easy, says I, or so I thought Wednesday morning, August 5.

I got to the Cliffs bright and early, feeling midway between euphoric expectation and cynical disbelief. As it turned out, disbelief carried the day. For two hours I stood there on the Cliffs, scanning into the teeth of a rising northwest wind, a cement doughnut from a shall-be-nameless shop sinking slowly through an ocean of viscous coffee in my stomach.

Then, Omigod. A flash of brilliant white over the Cliffs. Up snap the binocs. Nothing. Zero. Zed. Zip. Xerox. It's a pure white pigeon, flying around all alone out there. And for a second, it looked just like....

So home we went, disappointed, but smug in the knowledge that only birders can identify birds. What those guys obviously saw was the pigeon. Right? Well, um.... When I told our pal Vern Laux about it, Vern said, "Gee, Gus, I dunno. Hollis Smith said it flew right down the beach."

So back I went next morning. The chastening came at precisely 9:32. This time, a leaden English muffin was sinking through the coffee, and I was about to depart, when BINGO! There it was in all its astounding glory. As always, the bird seemed to come out of nowhere. An apparition — even an impossible dream.

I rushed for the phone. Five minutes later, the bird was gone from the Cliffs. But I soon found it again around the corner, flying around the terns, dwarfing them and looking majestic. Also right at home.

— August 7, 1987

❧ ❧ ❧

Feathered Frenzy

In winter's freezing cold and drear,
    The birds behave like people here:
They either live from hand to mouth
    Or take a long vacation south.
                    D.A.W.

On the Conceit of a Gull

By Arthur Railton

MOST OF US have moments when we feel more important than we really are. It doesn't happen often, but occasionally a certain smugness takes over. And why not? We're living in an age of conspicuous self-importance. It's the current talisman.

Self-hype is very much in the air. Humility, it seems, is a sign of weakness. Being humble, along with a nickel, will get you, as we used to say, a cup of coffee. In a world of Donald Trumps, of athletes holding out for an extra million, of football players dancing in the end zone, it's easy to believe in ego. Try to think of a national hero who's humble.

So who can blame us ordinary folks, you and me, if on occasion, our tiny ego takes over and we feel important.

After a couple of years as head of a committee, we're handed the inevitable token of appreciation as our successor states how impossible it will be to fill our shoes. The members duly assembled, happy to have found a successor, applaud. It's only human that for a few moments our ego blossoms and we allow ourselves to believe what we hear. We are, it seems, important after all.

Occasionally, someone will tell me how great my last Gazette piece was and visions of Thurber and Andy White and other greats dance through my head. It's good for the soul, unwarranted though it is. Just don't let it last.

I have a cure for it. Whenever such a surge of self-satisfaction pumps me up, I remind myself about my summer friend, the sea gull. Like many folks who spend summers by the ocean, we have a pet sea gull. Well, he's not really our pet. We didn't adopt him, he adopted us. We are, in fact, his pet. And each summer we feed him and each summer he repays me with a lesson in humility. Not that sea gulls are humble, quite the opposite. That's where the message is.

Every afternoon when I stoke up the grill on the deck, getting ready to prove I can cook if I have to, our friendly sea gull takes his position on the chimney, watching every move I make. He knows what's going on. He's watched me for years. I am, in his mind at least, making his dinner. He waits patiently, standing guard, chasing off all other sea gulls, as I baste the swordfish, or the chicken, or carefully turn the hamburgers, until they are done just right.

Then, as he stares down at me, I put the carefully prepared food on a platter, take it inside, and some time later, I return to serve his dinner — a plate full of delicacies. To me, it's a plate full of leftovers, scraps none of us will eat: carcasses of chickens, bones of fish, trimmings of steak. But to him, it's a perfectly prepared, precisely trimmed selection of tidbits. Dinner in the grand style. I carefully place them on his usual feeding place, he struts up like the Lord of the Manor, tucking on a figurative napkin, and arrogantly gulps down the meal — the meal that I have prepared just for him.

That's what he thinks. And why shouldn't he? He has watched me lovingly cook the meat, then carry it into the kitchen where I and everybody else thoughtfully cut it up into small pieces before taking it back outside for him. Surely, he (and here I must admit I'm guessing) thinks we went to all that trouble just for him. It's so obvious. Why shouldn't he think that? Why shouldn't he think he's more important than he really is? He doesn't realize he's really a convenient garbage dispose-all, not a dinner guest. His arrogance, his strut, his noisy and animated fight when another gull shows up, make it clear that he believes the whole thing is in his honor.

So whenever I'm tempted to think I'm more important than I am, I tell myself to remember the sea gull. That brings on a quick surge of humility.

Maybe we should send a few sea gulls to Washington. There are folks down there who could use such a lesson.

– Column, September 13, 1991

Hunting for Blueberries in the Wild

By Phyllis Meras

NOW THAT SEPTEMBER IS HERE, the wild blueberries and the huckleberries are almost gone, and I have picked barely a pint. Partly, it is because the four cultivated blueberry bushes in my West Tisbury yard have been so bountiful. I really have no need for wild berries to fill pies and to make breakfast muffins plump. But going blueberrying and huckleberrying in the wild has never, I suspect, been to put berries on the table for me.

I have gone berry picking in woodsy places in the early morning to listen to the birds, to be alone with the fragrance of cedars and pines before they are swallowed by car fumes, to see the mushrooms and toadstools that have erupted overnight and the cobwebs glitter with dew. And, I am sure, to remember past berrying times — on the Downs at East Chop with my grandmother from New York when I was a child, above the Lagoon when I was a teenager picking with friends so we could sell the berries for pocket money.

I was reminded this week of those entrepreneurial teenage berrying times when I went into the Wesley House lobby in Oak Bluffs just after the President had visited. It was the first time, I think, that I had been back since my four baskets of hand-plucked fat huckleberries had been disdainfully turned down by the chef when I was about Chelsea's age.

A friend and I had picked all morning long to gather the four quarts the chef had told us he would buy. I remember we had even encountered a snake as we picked, and had fled, terrified, from the hill thickest with ripe berries.

When, at last, we arrived at the Wesley House and proffered our morning's work, looking forward to the two movie tickets our proceeds would buy, the chef snarled that we had brought him seedy huckleberries and he would only buy blueberries.

Now there is a division among berry connoisseurs about which is more flavorful — the blue or the huckleberry. Even if huckleberries are seedier, they have a more remarkable, wilder taste. My brother was remembering the other day the succulent huckleberry pies that the grandmother who lived with us made for summer Sunday dinners, served at midday, of course, after she had gone to Christian Science Society services on New York avenue.

Reflecting on all this led me out yesterday on a last berrying expedition of the season. No berry picker, of course, gives specific information about his or her favorite patches. But I could not help noticing from the top of the bank where I was gathering late high bush blueberries firm and perfectly round (the Wesley House chef would have approved) that the cyclists and joggers and even the walkers who passed by down below were looking neither left nor right at the riches — berries and goldenrod and sassafras mittens — on the banks along the road. (They were not noticing either the bottles and cans that have been a less happy aspect of Island roadsides this past summer.)

I could not help thinking how much they were missing hurrying by on their morning constitutionals. One can always go on vigorous jogs on the tow path in Washington and in New York's Central Park. But there one cannot enjoy the so-fast-disappearing Island beauty that still lies, here and there, in quiet woods and sprouting fields.

Of the berrying places of my childhood, few remain. The Downs is riddled with roads and houses. What has become, I wonder, of the gold metal candy box in which I buried a dead bird I had found at a sandy Downs crossroads because crossroads were, somehow, an evocative place for a burial.

Above Lake Tashmoo, the finest berrying place of all has given way to a development. There are still, happily, berry bushes that grow undisturbed on the Vineyard Haven side of the Lagoon. I cannot speak for the Oak Bluffs side.

On the Middle Road in West Tisbury, I did not find the berries abundant, but at least they are still there, not dug up or trampled down to make way for new houses. And if I found few, to some extent it may have been my fault.

I do not mind the fact that I have trouble nowadays trying to thread a needle — that my eyes simply cannot find the needle slit. But I do resent it when my eyes miss the blueberries under the leaves. That shouldn't be.

For so many reasons — disappearing Vineyard landscape, eyes and ears that lose their keenness with the onset of age — those younger bodybuilders who race by along the Middle Road on an early morning should slow down a little to listen to the cawing of the crows and the pecking of woodpeckers, the soughing of the pines, to smell the wetness of morning, to be bedazzled by gleaming cobwebs, to consider whether fairies perch on toadstools — and enjoy a wild blueberry now and then. It is these things that Martha's Vineyard is all about.

– September 2, 1994

✻　✻　✻

Starring an Island Lab Named P.J.

By Julia Wells

H E WAS A BLACK DOG whose picture appeared in the pet adoption section of the Vineyard Gazette a little more than a year ago, an Island Labrador without a home. Nobody else wanted him. But Bryan and Elaine McCarthy of Oak Bluffs saw his picture and it did something to them. They went to the MSPCA in Edgartown and took him home. They named him P.J.

Call it providence.

Because this week something happened that made the McCarthys know they had made the right choice. Bryan McCarthy is working at a job site in Makonikey, and one day this week he was working alone. He tripped and splashed paint thinner in his eyes. Mr. McCarthy was in pain and could not see, and there was no one around to help him.

Except P.J.

Mr. McCarthy remembers: "I was shouting for someone to come and help me. I wear contact lenses, and I was really hurting. I could hear the chain saws of people working at the next lot over in the development. But no one could hear me. I kept shouting. Then P.J. came over and tugged on my pant leg. I swear, it was like something right out of Lassie. I couldn't believe it. But he had come over to get my attention. He knew I was in trouble. I held onto his collar and he led me over to the next job site, where I yelled to the people working there.

"They helped me and we got my eyes flushed out with water right away. But I could never have gotten over there without him. He did it."

P.J. is the local hero now. All the McCarthy's friends have heard about what happened, and have congratulated P.J. He is feeling a bit proud of himself, the McCarthys say, but then he should.

"He is a great dog," Mr. McCarthy says. "I always knew he was going to be great. But now I really know it. He is feeling good."

Did the McCarthys give P.J. a reward for his heroic efforts? "Oh, yes. We gave him a pound of hamburger."

Lassie couldn't have done any better.

– May 9, 1986

❧ ❧ ❧

Perspiration

Cats can't. Therefore they pant.

D.A.W.

Of Skunks and Skateboards

By Everett S. Allen

I WAS SITTING IN MY BACKYARD thinking generally benign thoughts about man and his world — which I do on occasion — when out of the gathering darkness, there ambled a self-possessed skunk. On second thought, that is redundant. I never heard of a hysterical skunk.

This one was bold as brass. Six feet from me, he hunched up on the rim of a low stone birdbath and had a leisurely drink of water. I was fascinated but decided I would not move even if I ceased to be fascinated because I did not wish the skunk — which had a relatively small head — to misunderstand my intentions.

Seated beside me was a male Siamese cat of some years. He is called "The Father" because he is old enough to have seen and done everything at least once. "The Father" did not move except to raise his right eyebrow, a reaction to the skunk that I found singularly intelligent because I had thought of doing it myself. Although there may be humans who were raised far enough from the boondocks that they mistake skunks for cats, cats do know the difference. "You are very smart, Father," I whispered, "and just keep it that way."

Finally, the skunk stopped lapping water and faded back into the darkness. The next morning, because I felt it was the responsible thing to do, I went looking for the skunk's residence. It was beneath my toolshed. In such moments, one turns instinctively to friends and neighbors for solace and wise counsel as one does, for example, when the furnace blows up or pipes freeze and the dining room ceiling falls.

The question of ownership of the skunk was established with remarkable speed. I do wish that solutions to major social problems might be half so quickly arrived at. With an attempt at levity, I said to one of my neighbors, "You'll be interested to know that we have a skunk problem." With what I thought was most uncharacteristic grimness, he replied, "What are you going to do with or about your skunk, and when?"

"My skunk?" I said. "I didn't invite it here. I don't even know its name."

"Everybody knows its name is Jimmy," said my neighbor with a leer. "Meantime, I will use the other side of the street when I go by your house. By your skunk, that is." And he walked away, leaving me to reflect that even if my neighbors had not found me lovable in pre-skunk days, they had at least regarded me as bearable. Now, all that had changed.

The skunk had constructed front and back doorways for his home. I thought it reasonable that if I filled them with something he did not like, he would leave. In deciding on this course, I chose to reject the advice of a fellow across the street who said glibly, "It's simple. Get a cage-type trap and put it outside the hole. You've got two holes, get two traps. When you've caught him, put a blanket over the cage, put the cage into your car, drive out into the country, and release him." I said, "What is he going to be doing during all of this lengthy procedure?" This fellow looked at me with disapproval, and said, "This great country of ours was not settled by cowards."

So I got a bucket and poured into it the contents of a box full of mothballs and a bottle of unutterably awful after shave lotion given to me by a friend (?) who lives in Des Moines. I stirred this concoction thoroughly and poured half of it into each of the skunk's doorways. "There," I said to myself with satisfaction, "that will suggest strongly that I would like him to find another place in which to live."

I could hardly wait for the next morning to examine the holes. As far as I could see, nothing had been disturbed. I was confident that the skunk had abandoned the place in dismay. I spread the glad tidings among my neighbors. They smiled upon me once more, shook my hand, said they really never had doubted for a moment that I would turn out all right in the long run, and resumed borrowing my lawn mower and hedge trimmer. In return, I celebrated my social reinstatement by signing a neighborhood petition in behalf of seedless-only raspberry jam.

That evening, while I was sitting in my backyard with "The Father," the skunk ambled out of the gathering darkness and had a leisurely drink of water at the birdbath.

In desperation, I consulted my 15-year-old granddaughter, who somehow knows everything I do not. "You used the wrong approach," she said; "you were rude. Rudeness produces a reaction of defiance. Skunks are courteous. Even in the face of threat, and before producing the characteristic odor for which they are noted, they exhibit a definite warning behavior, performing a highly-stylized display dance, including foot stamping. They are polite; they prefer to warn, and to annoy only as a last resort."

"Who says so?" I responded with skepticism.

"Dr. Wolfgang J.H. Wickler, professor of zoology at the University of Munich, and an authority on behavior physiology," she replied, as quickly as that.

I was impressed. "I'm sorry," I said; "I did not mean to hurt the skunk's feelings. But what on earth do I do now?"

She said, "I'll take care of it."

That was three weeks ago. I have not seen the skunk since. So I asked her what she did.

"First," she said, "I found a nice place where I would like to live if I were a skunk. Right on the edge of town. There are trees, and water. Then I wrote directions on how to get there from here. I tacked the directions on an old skateboard that I don't use anymore. I put the skateboard with the note near those holes under your toolshed."

"That is absurd," I said.

"The skunk's gone," she said. "So is the skateboard. What more do you want?"

— Column, August 25, 1989

Gift of the Manitou

T HE WAMPANOAGS OF GAY HEAD recalled an ancient legacy on Tuesday when they settled among the dunes at Lobsterville and plucked the wild cranberry from its sandy, dry bog. With wooden, tooth-edged scoop and paper bag, they gathered the last fruit of the season and reclaimed the native American heritage that reaches centuries back, to a time when the Vineyard was theirs alone.

Cranberry Day, ceremonial and unusual as it is, probably did not start with the title it acquired in this modern century. In another age the crimson harvest meant more than ceremony. The harvest meant survival itself, the gift of the Manitou — the Great Spirit who watches over and cares for a native people in harsh winter.

One has only to stand along the white shores of Lobsterville and imagine an Indian sachem ordering tribal members to erect their teepees for the duration of the two-week harvest, or the medicine man performing his solemn ritual, imploring the Great Spirit for safekeeping of the land. There were oxen teams, there were outdoor games and there was a bountiful harvest, by the barrel, not by the hand basket.

The hurricanes of previous decades burned out the bulk of the wild crop with their windy, salty blasts. Not even President Roosevelt's crews from the Works Progress Administration could revive the wild cranberry bogs, and the Gay Head natives poked fun at the man-made, fumbled effort.

Old Gazette files describe a three-day harvest in the 1930s and 1940s. But in subsequent years the crop dwindled and in 1954 the last oxen team vanished from the holiday scene. It was Nanetta Madison who grieved for the loss of "the last touch with the past."

Now is the call from some in the tribe to turn Cranberry Day into an official homecoming of Gay Head Indians, many of whom make their homes in far corners of the continent. It is a fitting challenge during a formative stage of the Wampanoag government, which was granted tribal status from the federal government in 1987 and is at work on a new constitution.

– Editorial, October 13, 1989

❧   ❧   ❧

The Death of Kings

By William A. Caldwell

THE THERMOMETER OUTSIDE the emergency quarters in which I am working this morning assures me the temperature is eight degrees above zero, and having just tacked upwind to the woodpile and sailed home across the yard without moving my feet, I can assure myself that, considering what the radio forecasters call the wind-de-chill factor, it is 165 below. It is the last gray day of a grim gray month. I am warned by a farmer who established his credentials by predicting the freezes of mid-December and Jan. 17 that the first week of February will be crueler yet. It does not surprise me that as I stand at the window staring out at the waste of crumpled ice between the hither shore and Chappaquiddick I find myself thinking of death and funerals.

What does surprise me is that there's nothing gloomy or depressing in this. I recall the dignity of the old monarch's going.

He was a goose, to be sure, a Canada goose, one mere bird among all the tens of thousands that have frozen to death this terrible winter, and I am aware that a man might better be thinking, for whatever good that could do, about the endangered species called humanity, than about the epidemic of rigor mortis among the local poultry.

"The barge with oar and sail moved from the brink," chants

Tennyson in the last of the Idylls of the King, and I can't get
the rest of it out of my mind:

> *Long stood Sir Bedivere*
> *Revolving many memories, till the hull*
> *Look'd one black dot against the*
> * verge of dawn,*
> *And on there mere the wailing*
> * died away.*
> *But when that moan had passed*
> * forevermore,*
> *The stillness of the dead world's*
> * winter dawn*
> *Amazed him, and he groan'd*
> * "The King is gone."*
> *And therewithal came on him*
> * the weird rhyme:*
> *"From the great deep to the*
> * great deep he goes."*

We noticed the old goose first because, of all the company he
had led to the edge of the only streak of open water on the bay
through which geese could browse on eelgrass, he was the only
one that remained erect and alert when the shadow of the bluff
crept out across the ice. The other 50 or 60 huddled on black
feet facing into the shrill north wind, and tucked their black bills
under a wing and slept, but the old goose stood tense and watch-
ful. Something was coming. Something besides the night.

I think it was Drew Marvel who told us this attitude of wari-
ness is a symptom. A goose seems to sense it's running out of
time. Old folks in my family insisted there's a Caldwell ban-
shee that wails, in a way audible only to one whose number is
up, before a death in the house. You're supposed to excuse yourself, take to bed, and go peaceable. We shall see. In due time.

He detached himself from the company — just drifted away
across the ice, no snit, no heroics — and before dark we heard

the rest of them pull out, yammering like Boston taxi drivers, for some upland meadow. Next morning the old goose lay dead not far from shore. He seemed to have sought some shelter in the lee of our mooring stake. Sometime in the night the cold had stopped hurting, and he had dozed but had not withdrawn into the warmth under his wing. The head had been poised high on the craning neck. So he lay next morning, outstretched.

The crows circled and landed. Gulls came. The monarch was carrion now, and they are scavengers, skilled and faithful to their trade. I tried once to reach the goose so as to fetch it in and give it decent burial, but the ice was mushy and I dared only a few feet from shore, not enough to hook the body with a clam rake.

That afternoon the wind blew from the south, and felt south, and the ice in the bay began to break, first into fields separated by rivulets of black water, then into rafts, drifting and bobbing, then at last into dwindling shards and fragments, as if some god had dropped and shattered a vase. On one of the rafts lay the goose. We stood on the brow of the beach and watched him go.

"Sorrowfully they cast loose the funeral boat," Tolkien tells us of the death of a warrior of Middle Earth; "there Boromir lay, restful, peaceful, gliding upon the bosom of the flowing water. The stream took him ... and slowly his boat departed, waning to a dark spot against the golden light; and then suddenly it vanished. The River had taken Boromir son of Denethor ... out into the Great Sea at night under the stars."

For a while the old goose's funeral boat drifted until it lodged against the skirt of ice below the Chappaquiddick dunes. The body was a black dot, then a dark spot, but the light was fading, and there was nothing to do or say or stay for. Next morning there was nothing to see. From the great deep to the great deep a king was gone. It occurred to us that Nature, who has no traffic with such human concerns as mercy and justice and nobility, still sometimes makes funeral arrangements with more taste than we do.

– Column, February 4, 1977

F A M E

❦

UNTIL THE PRESIDENT began to vacation here, the name of Chappaquiddick was better known across the country than the name of Martha's Vineyard. That's one of the odd tricks of fame. Odder still might be what happens to a place when its separateness from the world attracts luminaries who bring the whole world with them when they come.

Make no mistake about it — the events, the people and the headlines of the past quarter century have been momentous.

Here a $3 million horror flick goes three times over both schedule and budget and becomes the most successful motion picture up to its time, and for the rest of the decade too. Here the most famous woman in the world builds her summer home, a president takes two weeks off and a princess seeks refuge. Here also, of course, marks the site of the most consequential car accident in history.

Nantucket, meantime, waltzes out of the 20th century known across the country for a sitcom about its airport (Tuesdays, 8 p.m. Eastern). Such are the vagaries of fame.

The road to Vineyard stardom was probably a dirt one, curving through the hills of Chilmark in the early 1920s, when a small clutch of artists, writers and academics happened upon the village because it was just about as far as their money could take them by train and steamer, and it was cheap.

There they could live in their old clothes, rent a shack for $25 a summer, swim naked in the surf and begin to mix with folks who knew how to fish and farm, who sat around a stove in the country store telling old stories in musical idioms with glorious endings that freeze-dried the concepts of socialism and concomitant secular theorizing. All the city boys had to do was check their pretensions and their tongues at the door and listen. Hard to ask of a young Thomas Hart Benton, Walter Lippmann or Felix Frankfurter, maybe, but they did it, happily.

The Gazette paid only occasional attention to them, and to those of greater candlepower who came later, like Jimmy Cagney and Katharine Cornell. They made themselves anonymous on Martha's Vineyard by making friends, with whom they learned to lobster and to sail, open scallops and plow fields, break bread, play baseball and dance at village revels. They sought not so much to disappear from the larger, fawning world, but to enter a more real one. They were esteemed by Vineyarders because they esteemed Vineyard life.

It was the lengthening shadows of this philosophy that attracted Jacqueline Kennedy Onassis to Martha's Vineyard 18 years ago, and shielded her here. The Island, as ever, encouraged her to play a regular, neighborly role. It was this sort of thing President Clinton was looking for when he first arrived with his family in the summer of 1993, and what drew the Princess of Wales a year later.

But look at the distance we've come from Benton and Frankfurter, a journey from old clothes and life on a dirt road to life inside a bubble. It was inevitable that the old arrangement in the stars should begin to fly apart — that the friends of the celestial pioneers should introduce other friends who would value the remove of the Vineyard more than the customs of it, who would seek out comfort and size more than simplicity and scale, and the company of each other more than the company of the town.

Once the spotlight swings your way, everything begins to glitter and shine. And everyone comes to stare. An exegesis on Vineyard life boils down to a three-minute analysis by a man with a microphone, a haircut and a tan.

The Gazette tries to examine the fame of the place with greater care than that, recognizing that those who make headlines everywhere else cannot be ignored while they are here. The challenge, as always, is to tell the Vineyard story, to find out what the person or the event has drawn from Island life, and what has been contributed. There are enough of these stories to fill a chapter in a book. Benton, Lippmann and Frankfurter would have been surprised.

– T.D.

❧ ❧ ❧

Tourists and the Bridge

THAT THE DIKE BRIDGE on Chappaquiddick should have become a tourist attraction is one of those deplorable things which can be dealt with only through an appeal to the taste and better instincts of the sightseeing public. Such an appeal is difficult, the more so in a summer of idle time, and there is always a question whether the sightseeing public, which by definition is a part of the public on the loose to peer at almost anything, is sensitive to matters of taste. Isn't taste what you leave behind, along with other forms of personal selectivity, when you buy your ticket?

When the curious have seen the bridge on Chappaquiddick, have they been brought closer to the tragedy of a year ago in which a young girl was killed? Does the holiday spirit allow of so sober a reflection?

In some states there are highway markers, monuments of a kind, giving notice that at this corner or at the intersection a mile or so farther on, a man, a woman, or a child, often more than one, suffered death in an automobile accident. These are grim markers, perhaps useful in moderating the speed of passing cars, and in promoting safety. No sightseeing buses pause to allow their passsengers a closer look. No vacationers get out of their cars to stare.

If the bridge on Chappaquiddick is a memorial, it is of this sobering kind. Though tourists may whittle away at their souvenirs to take home, and pose on the bridge for snapshots to display to friends at home, the only meaning the bridge can really have for them is tragic, all the more because of their callousness.

— Editorial, July 14, 1970

❧   ❧   ❧

On Vacation

The head of the nation
Arrived on vacation,
But most of the mess
Was because of the press.
D.A.W.

Memories of Jaws: Residuals
And Rubber Sharks

By Peter Blumberg

IT WAS 13 YEARS AGO that the Vineyard's place in Hollywood history was assured, and the career of filmmaker Steven Spielberg established, with the making of a movie called Jaws.

The best-selling novel turned blockbuster movie is just a memory in the minds of those who were around when it came out. Thirteen years and three Jaws sequels after the original Universal Studios film was released and broke all previous box office records (amounting to $130 million in ticket sales through 1987), most agree it is finally safe to go back in the water.

Nevertheless, the oversized mechanical man-eater's presence is still felt here, as a subject of endless fascination for tourists.

It is difficult to put a monetary value on the total economic impact Jaws has had here. But depending on whom you ask, Jaws was either a prize catch for the Island economy or a nightmarish exercise in commercial exploitation.

Robert J. Carroll, a longtime resident and one of several Islanders who played a small role in the movie, says the movie rescued the Island during hard times.

"In 1974 we were deep in recession. We all needed the business. It worked for everybody," he recalled this week.

Fred B. Morgan Jr., a selectman in Edgartown both now and then, says Jaws is something the Island did not need, because it created more nuisances than benefits for all but a few people who were connected with it.

"That summer they were here filming the movie was probably the worst experience I have ever had since becoming a selectman," he said, noting a range of problems it created, from noise disturbances to a police chief payoff scandal.

In any case, estimates at the time of production were that the movie's producers pumped upwards of $30,000 per day into the Island economy while filming, for a total of $1.5 million out of an $8 million budget. The local people involved, said to be half the Island's year-round population, pocketed about $100,000 in wages.

And for the dozen or more locals lucky enough to have been cast in the movie with speaking parts, Jaws income is still pouring in. Those people, by contract with the nationwide Screen Actors Guild, are guaranteed residual payments on a regular basis according to how many times the movie is shown at the movie house or on television.

Another segment of the population continuing to benefit from the movie is those who sell souvenirs.

A perusal of the Island's novelties shops and drugstores suggests that selling the terror of the sea, while perhaps not as easy as it once was, is still quite a business. From gray rubber sharks to bright-colored Revenge of Jaws beach towels, from so-called authentic sharks' teeth wrapped in cellophane to a Jaws-like creature made out of pecan shells and imported from North Carolina — all of it is available.

Jaws postcards are another favorite with visitors. Edward Thomas, who distributes Island postcards out of Vineyard Haven, says that a card depicting a great white killer and carrying the message "Enjoying Martha's Vineyard" has for some time been one of his top sellers. As with other Jaws items, postcard sales have dropped off considerably, from about 7,500 per year when the movie debuted to about 5,000 now, according to Mr. Thomas.

Merchants say the most convincing testimony of Jaws' selling power is the constant market for spinoff T-shirts. The shirts, which are priced at $10 and up, feature such variants on a theme as an obscenity-yelling windsurfer clearly in peril of being attacked and a character named Land Shark who resembles Budweiser Beer's mascot, Spuds MacKenzie, in his party spirit. One shop in Oak Bluffs has as many as five different shark T-shirts.

The merchants note that the primary customer base for Jaws

novelties is young boys who were not even born when the movie was released.

For those boys and others who want to rush out and see the movie, they may be out of luck: The Edgartown Library reports that there is always a waiting list to borrow its video copies of the film.

— July 15, 1988

❧ ❧ ❧

Flag for the Vineyard State

AT A CEREMONY in the State House's Hall of Flags, Rep. Terrence P. McCarthy was presented with a flag for the new state of Martha's Vineyard and Nantucket.

The flag shows a white sea gull in upward flight, against a red-orange sun, all on a field of deep blue.

The flag was presented Tuesday by Eric Davin and Fran Forman, both of Cambridge, and both active members of the Martha's Vineyard Statehood Support Committee, recently formed to "support the independence aspirations of the Islanders and to draw attention to the gerrymandering disaster which has linked Martha's Vineyard and Nantucket with the outer arm of Cape Cod in the new state representative district proposed by state Rep. George Keverian." The group is composed entirely of non-Islanders, though many of them are frequent summer residents.

Accepting the banner, Mr. McCarthy thanked the group for their support and concern.

He also said final choice of a state flag would be up to the people. This flag is the first entry.

The proposal to secede has continued to draw attention from the nation, and the flag presentation added to it.

Yesterday, Sen. Edward M. Kennedy released this statement:

"I fully understand the deep sense of frustration of Island residents as a result of the loss of their seat in the House of Representatives of the General Court.

"Since the beginning of this nation the unique resources of the Islands of Martha's Vineyard and Nantucket have provided all of us who represent these residents with an opportunity and a challenge to find ways to protect this uncommon, natural, scenic, and cultural heritage.

"I hope that a way can be found to ensure that Martha's Vineyard and Nantucket are fully represented in the House of Representatives. I am confident that the Island residents who have proposed secession in order to focus attention on their concern prefer to remain fully represented participants in the commonwealth. All of us understand that the special qualities of these Islands make Massachusetts the special place it is."

A White House spokesman this weekend said he doubted the White House "would have a comment on the matter, as it is a state's rights problem." Asked whether the government would attack the Islands if the Islands declared war on the United States, he said the nation might "if it became a matter of national security."

The response to the secession move has been favorable in Nantucket, although there are early signs of conflicts between the two Islands over appointments to high offices. Like Vineyarders, Nantucketers have begun nominating officials.

According to the Nantucket Inquirer and Mirror, the Nantucket selectmen's office has already received a telephone call from New Hampshire, recommending the sales tax advantages of deserting Massachusetts and joining its northern neighbor. The phone call was anonymous.

The state flag presented to Mr. McCarthy was designed by Fran Forman, one of the members of the support committee. She is a professional designer of flags and banners, employed by Signage Associates of Boston. She says the elements of the flag "represent not only the proud and independent spirit of the Islanders, but also the Islands' rich resources — wildlife, air, and water — which are becoming increasingly endangered by human pollution."

"There is neither a direct air route nor a direct ferry route from the Islands to the rest of the proposed state representative district," Mr. Davin said at the flag presentation.

"If Island residents wish to talk to their state representative on the outer Cape, they would be forced to make either a long-distance telephone call or take a long and ridiculous ferry and automobile ride to reach the representative.

"If the district lines are not redrawn to take into consideration the special circumstances and problems of the Islanders, they have no reasonable and just alternative but to secede from Massachusetts and establish their own government, one more responsive to their needs."

– March 4, 1977

✱ ✱ ✱

The Lady and the Land

INTEREST IN PRESERVATION of the Hornblower land in Gay Head, that historic openness of hills, ponds, marsh and shore, had gone back many years, and more than one syndicate had been formed in the hope of maintaining its natural character with respect for all its qualities and with carefully planned, limited development. The purchase of these 375 acres through a trustee had whetted a natural curiosity as to the identity of the buyer who, it was declared unequivocally, would protect "the moors and dunes, the deer and the birds as they are, undisturbed by development."

Now we know that the purchaser is Jacqueline Kennedy Onassis, and it is not her worldwide fame that makes the transaction important news on Martha's Vineyard, but her new partnership with the native domain. She and the land are the story, the land even more than she herself.

One may say truthfully that this Island is long past bedazzlement by famous figures, so many of whom find sanctuary here and go their chosen ways undisturbed, and although Mrs. Onassis is a personage and symbol of exceptional fame, she too will find the sort of acceptance assured by Vineyard tradition.

No one can help what the voices on the big tourist buses may say, but they will be contained as the buses pass by, and these may yet be excluded from the Island on the score of safety and health. It is the good sense and taste of the Island itself, summer and winter, that will provide honest neighborliness and privacy.

All this was both implicit and expressed in the Gazette report of last Friday, though the name of Jacqueline Kennedy Onassis is bound to leap out whenever it appears in type. We may fairly emphasize that a planned, factual news release would have been the best introduction for this lady and her land; failing that, the news had been bid up week by week, with gossip and speculation, until confirmation of what had become common report was bound to be a sort of explosion.

That's over now, and there are plenty of usual things to occupy gossip and speculation from now until the next northeast storm, or even until the sun crosses the line in September.

– Editorial, August 22, 1978

❦   ❦   ❦

The Big Mac Attack

By William A. Caldwell

WE SHALL NOT FLAG OR FAIL…. We shall defend our Island, whatever the cost may be; we shall fight on the beaches, we shall fight on the landing grounds, we shall fight in the fields and in the streets, we shall fight in the hills; we shall never surrender.

It is said that during a pause for hear-hears after that last peal of "we shall fight" Churchill muttered an aside, "With what? Beer bottles?"

Good question, as apt on one beleaguered little island in January 1979 as it was on another in June 1940.

Thanks to a gutsy board of health in Tisbury, and never have so many owed so much to so few, McDonald's effort to establish a beachhead on Martha's Vineyard has been beaten off. With no especial effort of the imagination it is possible to fancy the gentle surf along Beach Road strewn with the floating bodies of orcs and goblins in Golden Arch T-shirts. It is possible to rejoice in the proved power of public opinion and local government. It is possible even to gloat.

Let's not. This invasion collapsed because it was planned carelessly, so superciliously that a single agency in a single town could repel it with a few old blunderbuss health ordinances. The invaders will be back — if not Big Mac, which has some 500 other irons in the fire, then some other force-feeder of instant crapulence, now that McDonald's market analysts have computed there's a buck to be made on the Vineyard. Next time they'll come prepared with plans that will satisfy all the laws and regulations having to do with sewerage and parking, zoning and pollution and application forms, and we shall fight them in the streets and on the beaches, and with what — beer bottles?

Nobody except maybe that charming promoter from New Bedford who has assured us Martha's Vineyard won't be special long — nobody wants hard-sell hamburgers here. But we can't stave off big business, not to mention paper napkins rustling in the fields and clinging to hedges and picket fences or plastic coffee cups rattling in the streets and bobbing on the ponds, by disapproving such evidences of progress. Before it's too late we'd better decide how to deal with predatory enterprise and write the decisions into enforceable law.

It won't be easy.

How shall we condemn a franchise food hell's architecture as being incompatible with the environment in such a way as to avoid aspersions on the A & P supermarkets, Sears, and the Dairy Queen, not to mention some of the private housing that's trespassing on everybody's skyline?

Considering strictly the, uh, quality of the grub served or bagged to-go in Island-owned beaneries, how do we prove to an appellate court that franchise food is peculiarly unfit for human consumption?

If a Big Mac's generation of traffic and parking problems is an adequate reason for withholding permission to do business, must not the same consideration and the same prohibition apply to Circuit avenue and the two Main streets, the churches and funeral parlors, and the Rev. Steamship Authority?

There's one way of legislating the likes of Big Mac out of our future, and it doesn't mention Big Mac. It is herewith suggested that this is a problem in economics. Sewerage and zoning and nutrition have nothing to do with it. What disturbs us mainly, I think, is the prospect that an off-Island octo — I mean enterprise — would move in and drain out of a notoriously distressed economy money that otherwise would stay here and move about and multiply itself. The Vineyard lives by importing money from the mainland, and any agency that impedes the flow, anything that intercepts the money and turns it about and sends it back to corporate headquarters in Chicago, is bad news.

I am relieved to find that I have discovered a coherent reason for disrelishing off-Islanders.

Well, no fast-turnover cash flow business can make it off year-round people. Its health will depend on trade with preconditioned transients, here for an unforgettable day breathing moped fumes, posing on the Gay Head Cliffs, and — oh, there's a Big Mac, mommy! — relishing the subtleties of the New England cuisine. Keep the transients off the Island, and you'll have kept off the enterprises that live on transients. And there go the mega-buses and the traffic that reduces these narrow streets to steaming parking lots, there go the beer cans on the beach, there go the bicyclists hurling themselves under the wheels of your car.

Why can't it be done? Harry Weiss, the highly savvy ex-bureaucrat who is president of the Vineyard Conservation Society, insists that means now exist in law for limiting what's called growth. Certain it is that the Steamship Authority is the creature of the state and the state is the will of its people and the Authority should and can be forbidden to exploit its control of access to the Islands.

But exploitation — of beaches and appetites, of water and forests and continental shelves — appears to be the name of the game. To be against growth, unless it's a diagnosed form of cancer, just might be un-American. Maybe it's time to haul out those "Secede Now!" bumper stickers and do something serious. Anyway, we shall never surrender.

– Column, January 12, 1979

❧ ❧ ❧

Star Cow from Star Beatle Goes To Nice Islander for $250,000

By Hollis L. Engley

SPRING FARM FOND ROSE is not your average milk cow. In dairy circles there is as much difference between her and the basic black and white Holstein milker as there is between the Chappaquiddick ferry and the Cunard Line. She is simply a superior animal, dairy experts say.

She should be. The five-year-old, pregnant Holstein was auctioned last week at the Syracuse, N.Y. state fairgrounds for

$250,000, a world record for her breed.

Rose's record surpasses the 1976 purchase price of Hanover Hill Barb, who sold in Oakville, Ontario, for $235,000. The average selling price of the 105 cows sold at the June 23 auction was $10,000.

The winning bid came from a representative of Seaside Dairy, the Katama farm now being organized by Stephen W. Potter of Chappaquiddick. Add to the world record the fact that Rose was owned by former Beatle John Lennon and his wife, Yoko Ono, and the cow becomes a celebrity in her own right. It doesn't add to her value, dairy experts said yesterday, but it does give her a certain mystique.

The news that the Lennons' cow brought a record bid alerted newspapers and wire services from New York to Cape Cod, and conveyed celebrity status to Mr. Potter, the shy, 23-year-old farmer who is pulling together the Seaside operation of 145 acres of town-owned conservation land. Most news reports, as well as the public relations department of the Syracuse fairgrounds, said Mr. Potter was the winning bidder and the new owner of Rose.

Mr. Potter said otherwise.

"I am the majority stockholder in Seaside Dairy," he said yesterday, "but Seaside Dairy is acting on behalf of Vineyard Holstein Associates (VHA)."

Vineyard Holstein Associates, he said, is a limited partnership of investors being formed to finance the dairy enterprise. Besides Rose, Seaside Dairy will have to finance the balance of the 150-cow herd, equipment, and renovations to the farm property.

"The value of an animal like this is based at auction on certain genetic and milk characteristics and the ability to transmit those characteristics to her offspring," he said.

Mr. Potter said a cow like Rose might produce 120 pounds of milk a day rather than the 50 of an average registered Holstein. In addition, she has the superior show characteristics that go hand in hand with prime milk production.

"Show business is a big aspect of the Holstein business," he said. "She has the straight back, good color, superior mammary system, leg structure, and body capacity that make her a great animal. These are the same characteristics that lead to superior milk production.

"A cow like this has proven that when she is mated with a proven sire she will produce offspring theoretically as good as or better than either of the two parents.

"The value to a dairy farmer or investors is that they can use this one animal to improve the entire makeup of the herd," Mr. Potter said.

Mr. Potter said that, using a process called embryo transfer and artificial insemination, a superior cow can turn out fertilized eggs which are transferred to other cows to be brought to term. Artificially inseminated by semen from a high quality bull, the prize cow will conceive theoretically superior embryos.

Transferred to healthy, but inferior, surrogate mothers, the embryos should grow to superior heifers and bulls — animals which might bring as much as or more money at auction than either parent.

– July 4, 1980

❧   ❧   ❧

John Belushi — A New Burial

By Richard Reston

THE UNMARKED BUT NOT UNKNOWN GRAVE of comedian John Belushi was moved quietly to a more remote corner of the small hillside cemetery in Chilmark two weeks ago today.

This extraordinary event was undertaken on the gray and rain-soaked morning of Friday, May 27. The time was 10 a.m.

The move grew out of concern from the Belushi family and the town of Chilmark over rising pubic pressure to visit the grave. Both the family and town officials wished to avoid circumstances difficult to control, the kind of public spectacle that often results from too much notoriety.

The decision to shift the grave site of the famed actor from a part of the cemetery in use to a section in isolation passed without fanfare, public notice, or official comment.

It was a decision taken in deference to Mr. Belushi's family, to families with loved ones buried nearby, and to all the comedian's admirers who have turned his Chilmark burial place into a shrine.

Final arrangements to move the grave came after serious deliberations among town officials and direct talks with the family, principally Mr. Belushi's wife Judith Jacklin and her brother who lives in Colorado.

Mrs. Belushi is known to be in complete support of the move and all the sentiments behind it, specifically that the new grave in a different location will allow the immediate family and the town to provide better care for the site which has become a problem at times over the last 15 months. Mr. Belushi was buried in the Chilmark cemetery March 9, 1982.

Family and town officials also believe the change will give Mr. Belushi's public easier access to a site more clearly identified both by location and by new gravestones and inscriptions planned for the burial ground next month.

The Belushi graveside now is immediately to the left of a split rail fence as the visitor first reaches the cemetery along the main drive down the hill to the public parking area.

It is marked for the moment only by a small cairn, a pyramid-shaped monument of Vineyard field and beach stone formed in six layers. Late this week a lovely pink and white fuchsia plant blossomed next to the grave. A single long-stemmed rose, dead now, lay at the foot of the simple memorial.

The grave is bounded on two sides by rail fence with an entry cut to allow public access from the driveway to the cemetery. This entrance is flanked on either side by cedar trees and a few smaller pines. A spreading scrub oak overlooks this corner of the cemetery at the fence line.

The closest graves to Mr. Belushi's are now about 25 yards away, across a sandy dirt road, and some 50 yards from where the comedian was first buried. That old site, now unmarked, is already filled and showing the first signs of new grass.

One of many problems with the old location, it is explained, was that it was in among a normal line of plots along one of the cemetery avenues in the new section opened in 1973.

Constant public traffic to the Belushi grave uprooted all the grass in the area and scattered messy debris everywhere in the vicinity — beer bottles, bottle caps, letters and notes, broken mirrors with messages, roach clips, plants, seashells and stones, St. Christopher medals and money.

There also were reports of mopeds and motorcycles driving across other grave sites and visitors tramping over the graves, sometimes unmarked, of others. Visitors not certain of where the Belushi grave was often wandered throughout the graveyard before finding what they came for.

In the older section of the cemetery gravestones date back to the 1700s and are fragile and in need of protection. This was a serious concern of town officials.

Their responsibility, they felt, was to protect an old and small New England cemetery where often the elderly come to remember and to honor.

During the summer season tour buses now slow or stop to point out the place where John Belushi is buried, much the way they do today in Edgartown when in sight of the tragedy of Chappaquiddick. And that brought notoriety to the Vineyard that the Island community would just as soon forget.

– June 10, 1983

Chappaquiddick and the Press

MARTHA'S VINEYARD is taking a terrible beating in the national press and on television across the country. The trigger for this shameful publicity bashing is of course the 20th anniversary of the tragedy at Chappaquiddick. And to watch the feeding frenzy of the national press on the eve of the anniversary is to believe the incident happened only yesterday, not two decades ago on that dark night of July 18, 1969.

It is tragic enough to recall the agony and the stain of that incident that took the life of Mary Jo Kopechne and the political career of Sen. Edward M. Kennedy to the bottom of Poucha Pond off Dike Bridge. But it is also sad today to observe the national press in its rush to exploit the incident, as if to satisfy some morbid fascination with the Kennedy family name and the tragedy that surrounds it. Perhaps it was all predictable, this chase for a frothy public spectacle, for the fun of a circus that would have played well in the days of Roman amphitheatres. Twenty years, after all, gives the press a nice, even, round number, but then so also did the press chase the anniversary in years seven, eleven and thirteen.

It is no wonder this spectacle of long-distance telephone calls, television cameras, radio talk shows and journalists in pursuit of yellow headlines stirs resentment in the Island community.

Part of the trouble lies in the presumption of the national press that nothing of importance happened on Martha's Vineyard either before or after the tragedy at Chappaquiddick. The other part of this sad spectacle is that the national press is here not to cover the news but to generate it. So Chappaquiddick 20 years later becomes a creature of the press, a creation of journalists who determine this tragedy is news because they wish it to be news, and not because new events demand responsible coverage by newspapers or television.

Accordingly, the Vineyard is portrayed in the mainland press these days as a community preoccupied with the long shadow of Dike Bridge and otherwise only occasionally interesting when celebrities come out to play tennis within shutter shot of the nearest camera. That is the perception of the Island carried in these anniversary days, for example in tabloid television on the program A Current Affair, in the Murdoch headline journalism of the Boston Herald and on the entire front page of the travel section of the Detroit News — under a headline reading Gawkers' Guide to the Vineyard. The Detroit News piece provides a particularly shabby picture of the mainland press treatment accorded the Vineyard at the moment. The newspaper publishes a large color map of the Island with a numbered guide to key places, beginning with Dike Bridge and ending with what the News refers to as "Jackie Country."

The spectacle of the national press groveling at a feeding trough of its own making and at the expense of the Vineyard stands quite apart from other legitimate issues in the Kennedy case. There are still today many doubts and unanswered questions left from the tragedy at Chappaquiddick. And from time to time news stories arise that properly are published and add to a responsible public record on Chappaquiddick. But news manufactured by the press and for the press only distorts and diminishes the public record.

The performance of the national press on this 20th anniversary eve of Chappaquiddick is for the most part a disgrace. And the Vineyard as a community and the national press as an institution deserve better. Much better.

— *Editorial, July 14, 1989*

Not Bad for This Old Black Lab:
Island Dog Worth a Million

By Amy Callahan

OF COURSE YOU HAVE HEARD THE STORIES about Black Dog T-shirts being spotted in faraway places. Well, they're true. And by the looks of things, you'll be hearing more of them. That seemingly obedient black Lab has broken its chain and dashed off into the profitable land of mail order. Black Dog goods are now ordered from every state in the nation by people who have never set foot on the Island, much less bought a cup of coffee in the bakery on Water street in Vineyard Haven.

The business that started in 1971 as a humble waterfront tavern is now a million-dollar enterprise, thanks in part to its thriving mail-order trade.

The Black Dog sends out 20,000 to 30,000 catalogues a year. The 20-plus page books are filled with all sorts of bedogged clothing and other items such as dish towels, beach umbrellas, bicycle water bottles, aprons, granola tins, fanny packs.

Even some items without the dog logo are offered, as are free recipes from the restaurant on how to prepare squid, biscotti and bluefish Genovese.

The mail-order business started less than five years ago when the company sent out about 100 single sheets of paper offering only T-shirts, mugs, cookie tins and posters.

"One of the girls in the bakery and I sent it out," said Elaine Sullivan, who runs the mail-order operation for the Black Dog. "We did it on a typewriter."

Now the catalogues are designed by the Island graphics business Kolodny & Rentschler and are sent out in three editions throughout the year.

The mailing list has ballooned, mostly due to ads placed in Rolling Stone, The New Yorker and Yankee magazines.

Business picked up a little, too, when Rolling Stone proclaimed last year that wearing a Black Dog hat was very hip.

"All hell broke loose," Miss Sullivan said of the Rolling Stone item that included a color photo of three cool women in sunglasses and Black Dog long-billed caps. "We didn't even know it was in there."

Fifty per cent of the mail-order customers have never been to Martha's Vineyard.

"They're not even that interested, but they like the dog," Miss Sullivan said.

For many, this dog has become a symbol of Martha's Vineyard. But what is so appealing about it?

"I don't know," Miss Sullivan said. "They like it."

In last summer's catalogue, on the page that displayed the infamous T-shirts, the company asked folks to send pictures of themselves sporting their dog garb.

A family from Anderson, Ind., obliged by gathering 10 of their clan together to say cheese and wear their Black Dog shirts.

Customers also send clippings whenever the dog sneaks into the news.

People magazine wrote about a man who was sending medical supplies to the former Soviet Union. In the photo, he was kissing his wife and just the top half of his T-shirt was visible. But you could see the unmistakable tail curling up.

"We know that tail," Miss Sullivan laughed.

They also received a letter from John Stone, a U.S. soldier stationed in Germany. He said he saw "an English girl" wearing a Black Dog shirt and tried to bargain for it.

"I couldn't talk her out of it," read Mr. Stone's letter, "so naturally I was thrilled to see your ad in Rolling Stone magazine. I would greatly appreciate one of your catalogues."

The mail-order business is growing every year and shows no signs of slowing down. In fact, Miss Sullivan is always thinking of new products to offer. She said she tries to keep up with trends and tries the prototypes out on the kitchen staff.

The newest products about to be offered are sterling silver Black Dog earrings designed by Island jeweler C.B. Stark and baseball shirts with the year in big numbers on the back.

While the marketing of the Black Dog may be Madison avenue caliber, the offices are not exactly corporate. They are above the tavern where the smells of the kitchen seep up through the worn wood floors. File cabinets are in the hall and everyone seems to share office space.

And the staff is not what you'd call big city slick. The general manager, Joe Hall, keeps a small portrait over his desk of himself cooking lobster.

– May 15, 1992

❧   ❧   ❧

Island White House Leaves Impact

By Amy Callahan

THE PRESIDENT WAS GOING TO BUST in here with a fleet of thousands and tie this place in knots.

But it didn't happen.

Instead, Mr. Clinton arrived on the Island, played a bit of golf, shook a few hands, and changed the spirit of this place with just his presence.

He proved to be an unexpected phenomenon.

People stood for hours on sidewalks, at the airport, at boat docks, waiting for him. They painted welcome signs for him and nailed them to trees or taped them in windows. They invited him to go fishing, and lent him a net to go crabbing.

The people of the Island expressed concern over the President's privacy. They wanted him to get some rest, spend time with his daughter, and enjoy his vacation.

When he appeared in public, they went after him like a rock star. They ran to him, waved to him, noticed what he wore, remembered what he said. They took pictures of him while he stood at the counter and ordered an ice cream.

President Clinton did not bring misfortune to this Island the way the New York newspapers and the Boston television stations predicted he would.

In fact, the only bad thing about his vacation has been those newspapers' and television stations' portrayal of this place as being one big Friday afternoon cocktail party for celebrities.

It seemed everyone, even The New York Times, published a celebrity map of the Vineyard, and declared that Mr. Clinton would be largely unnoticed on this playground for the stars.

Not only did the national media say we felt indifferent toward the President, but it suggested that we didn't even want him to come. "Worse than Rain," they said of his visit.

But the truth of it has been something entirely different. Islanders are glad the President is here. It's not a simple matter of celebrity. Having President Clinton visit Martha's Vineyard is not the same as Billy Joel buying a house in Menemsha. Islanders know that.

"This is the closest I've ever got to any president," said a 68-year-old man who shook Mr. Clinton's hand at the fair.

"He's the President of our country, and we've got to respect that," said a woman who said she was a Republican who voted for George Bush.

Now this is what's interesting. This is the phenomenal impact the President has had on Martha's Vineyard.

From Gay Head to Chappaquiddick, he has united the Island more than anything since the fight against McDonald's fast food.

And for the first time in his presidency, Mr. Clinton has generated true bipartisan support. Or at least he has on Martha's Vineyard.

Usually, it is dangerously easy to change the environment of this fragile Island, while it is nearly impossible to alter the mind-set, the traditions and the opinions of its people.

Mr. Clinton did the opposite. His visit here had a marginal impact on traffic and crowding — even the police admit to this. But his presence had a huge impact on the spirit of the people. Mr. Clinton charmed them as soon as he arrived.

Even people like Victor Oliver were drawn in. Mr. Oliver is a 36-year-old conch fisherman. He was born here and he lives here all year long. He pulls his living up off the ocean floor, and his work is exhausting. So Mr. Oliver is not easily impressed with big names or fancy stuff.

But Saturday afternoon at the agricultual fair, he was leaning up against a horse trailer and keeping an eye on the back gate, just in case the President showed up.

"How many other presidents come here?" was his unapologetic reply to why he was interested. Damn few, was his unspoken, implicit answer.

The First Family's vacation here was expected to strain the Island to its breaking point, during what is already its busiest month of the year. Before the President arrived, there were some complaints about more traffic and rude people invading the Vineyard. Vacationers worried that their own peace would be disturbed or their travel plans ruined.

But aside from a few traffic tie-ups here and there, an occasional crowd, and, of course, the silly nightly television updates about the President's "posh Island getaway," we would really never know he was here.

Police Chief John McCarthy in Vineyard Haven said the annual Tisbury Street Fair was a whole lot worse for traffic than the First Family's trip to Bunch of Grapes.

And the folks at Edgartown's town meeting Wednesday night sat in the Old Whaling Church for a half-hour and missed the President completely as he dashed into Mad Martha's for a cone of mango ice cream. The only indication he had been in town at all was the buzz of excitement on the street after he left.

"Did you see him?" everyone asked.

There have been some out-and-out good things about the President's trip to Martha's Vineyard, namely the economic benefit. On this resort Island where the unemployment rate skyrockets in the off-season, the presidential vacation created a boost in the real estate, retail and accommodations industries. The President also helped raise more than $52,000 for the Martha's Vineyard Hospital.

In addition to the good stuff, this presidential visit has been remarkably absent of the disruptive stuff, such as demonstrators and hecklers who seemed to incessantly hound President George Bush. Two women from the Boston chapter of the Women's Action Coalition (WAC) were on the Island the first weekend the President was, but they decided to leave him be and not stage a protest.

Indeed, there has been no real controversy surrounding the President's vacation, other than the manufactured one about how Martha's Vineyard is an inappropriate place for the populist President to vacation. No matter that the Vineyard has the second-lowest per capita income in the state. Or that generations of African-American families have found acceptance here.

No matter that the Portuguese-American culture is celebrated here, or that we have an active Hebrew center.

No matter that it is a safe place for gays and lesbians to live. Or that our public schools are excellent, or that we have a tribe of Native Americans among us who are valued in the community.

No matter that artists and writers and musicians gather here, or that farmers and fishermen can make a living here, or that women run our government as much as men. No matter that our old folks are cared for, that our water is clean, or that our children are loved.

So perhaps this presidential visit has shown the nation the bedrock American character of Martha's Vineyard.

When President Clinton arrived at the airport a week ago yesterday, he was greeted by a flock of children standing in the VIP waiting area.

"They look like poor kids," someone in the press area commented to another journalist.

Well, they probably were poor kids. But they are treated as important people, and they were happy to see the President arrive. They will be sad to see him go.

— August 27, 1993

❧   ❧   ❧

Princess Diana Vacations in Seclusion On Private Vineyard Estate

By Jason Gay

THE PRINCESS OF WALES is enjoying a private vacation on Martha's Vineyard this week at a secluded, idyllic Island estate surrounded by rolling hills and meadows.

Princess Diana arrived at Martha's Vineyard Airport late Thursday afternoon, and was transported by vehicle to the rented historic manor, located on the Island's north face.

Law enforcement officials protecting the royal guest are sworn to secrecy on her schedule and vacation home, allowing Princess Diana to escape the flashbulbs of the rumor-chasing international press.

Indeed, while the paparazzi and gossip columnists claim to be "in the know," they have learned very little of Princess Diana's vacation, offering only a slew of bogus news stories.

The princess is the guest of the Brazilian ambassador to the United States, Paulo Tarso Flecha de Lima, and his wife, Lucia. Also staying at the manor are two of the de Lima daughters, Isabel and Beatrice, and two grandchildren. The princess' two sons, William and Harry, are vacationing with their father, Prince Charles, in Greece.

In a private talk with the Gazette, Mrs. de Lima said the princess is enjoying her first visit to the Island, and asked the public and press to respect her royal guest's privacy.

"She is very charmed by the Vineyard," Mrs. de Lima said. "She hopes to have a peaceful time here, because it is so beautiful. She knows you are very charming people, and you will be very protective toward her. You will respect her need for some privacy and a vacation."

Mrs. de Lima said Princess Diana decided to visit Martha's Vineyard after observing the private Island vacations of such public figures as President Clinton and the late Jacqueline Kennedy Onassis.

"She came over the Atlantic because she knows it was one of the very few places in the world where she could be surrounded by nice people, and it would be hard to be found by the press," Mrs. de Lima said.

Indeed, it has been impossible for the international press to find, never mind photograph, the royal visitor on the Vineyard. For many locals, the fun of the royal visit is watching so-called inside trackers and paparazzi trip over themselves in an effort to locate the princess.

Many of the weary correspondents are reduced to interviewing uninformed sources, acting on every unfounded tip or rumor they scrounge.

In one hilarious scenario, a troupe of photographers converged outside the Charlotte Inn after hearing the princess would arrive for a Saturday lunch. But the mainlanders were sad to discover the Edgartown inn does not serve lunch — only breakfast and dinner.

But the photographers' instincts were not entirely off course. The Charlotte Inn is owned by Gerret Conover, who hosted the princess on a 90-minute cruise through Edgartown inner harbor late Saturday afternoon.

Princess Diana and members of the de Lima family were guests of Mr. Conover, his wife Paula, and son Gerret Jr. aboard the Miss Asia, a long and graceful motor yacht built in 1923.

The sail went undetected by the international press, however. Precautions were taken to ensure Princess Diana's privacy. After the Conovers boarded the yacht, the princess and the de Limas were picked up at a secret pier in the inner harbor.

After circling around the harbor, Miss Asia headed toward Edgartown Light in the outer harbor. With Gerret Jr. at the helm, the princess and Mr. Conover sat directly behind the wheelhouse, taking in the breezy summer day. The princess, wearing an American flag sweater with white stars and a navy baseball cap, smiled and watched as Mr. Conover pointed across the harbor to Edgartown's historic district.

Miss Asia made a brief swing past the Chappaquiddick Beach Club, and returned to the inner harbor for the remainder of her sail.

The mainland press continues to scramble around the Island, trying to pinpoint the location of the princess' vacation home. Helicopters circle the Island and four-wheelers slog through sandy Vineyard roads, but the off-Islanders have to date found little, stymied by a protective police force and a band of Islanders committed to upholding the royal guest's privacy.

On Sunday morning, the royal estate was quiet, undisturbed by the Fleet Street or mainland American press. Blinds were drawn, and a pair of pesky squirrels bounded across the manicured lawn. An off-road vehicle sat in the driveway.

The 18th-century manor is a restored clapboard home located near water and acres of conservation land. Majestic rolling hills and old meadow land encircle the property, giving way to a distant view of Vineyard Sound.

The stately house, which is more than 200 years old, appears a logical choice for a princess. "It's very beautiful," Mrs. de Lima said. "It's very private."

– August 9, 1994

Vineyard Concert Draws Grateful Fans Of Singers James and Carly

By Yvonne Guzman

FRANCIE SARTAIN DIDN'T HAVE A TICKET, but she came all the way from Bowling Green, Ky., hoping to see James Taylor and Carly Simon sing together. She did.

Ellen Ryan of Boston has never considered herself a big fan, but lately James Taylor's voice brings back high school years for her. So she took the day off and came to Martha's Vineyard Agricultural Society fields Wednesday night.

Islander June Manning knew she was going all along. Holding a $100 ticket she bought at the Gay Head town hall the first hour tickets went on sale, she sat on the ground in front of the first row to see the two people she used to know as regular "summer kids."

"They were like neighbors," Miss Manning said. "They were just normal teenagers, just regular, ordinary people. But we knew they had potential and we knew they would go someplace. They're my two most favorite singers in the world. I love both of them."

The concert "surpassed my expectations. It was undescribable," she said.

These are the people who joined together to blanket the ground outside the agricultural society barn for the most anticipated Vineyard concert in decades, maybe ever.

It was billed as a concert for Islanders, and it lived up to that designation; across the crowd were the singers' friends and family, faces that saw James and Carly perform as kids, and a 14-year-old Tisbury girl, Melissa Carelli, who was "really embarrassed" to bump into Carly a few weeks ago on Main street in Vineyard Haven, almost knocking her over.

"I thought it would be just like going to the boat in the summer, but I'm seeing so many Island people here," said Margaret Stafursky, a teacher at the regional high school. "It's a cross between going to the agricultural fair in the summer and going to the boat. The people in charge were people that you know. Every place I go I see kids that I have taught, that have been in the high school. It just has such an Island flavor."

But the stage reunion of the former husband and wife also brought people from across the country — even though tickets were only sold on-Island and over the phone to people with local mailing addresses. After cajoling Island friends, pounding the pavement and paying scalpers, these people spread their blankets on the agricultural society fields or danced in the lee of the Island's new barn.

Together, they sat on blankets and pillows — a mellow crowd except for the group dancing near speakers set up by the barn. People who remember the No Nukes concert of 1978 described this group as a little yuppier than that one, and to be sure, there were more cell phones and bottles of water. (And yes, they did sneak in a little gin.) But for all its quirks and geographic diversity, this crowd had the most important qualifications: admiration for James and Carly, and respect for the Island. Islanders and off-Islanders shared blankets, reminisced and enjoyed the beautiful Vineyard night that Carly Simon said "just feels right to me."

It felt right to Lorinda Cash, too.

A waitress at the Ritz Cafe in Oak Bluffs and a sign maker, Lorinda loved the music and the sky's sliver of moon — which she pointed out to several people as she danced on the lawn near the speakers.

She grew up listening to James Taylor, she said, and since moving to the Vineyard seven years ago, she describes his talent in a new way.

"He is the feel of the Vineyard," she said. "He says it. He sings it. You can just feel it. I can't help but love him."

She wasn't alone in her enthusiasm. Across the fields, just about everyone had a story about listening to James Taylor or Carly Simon music.

Like Bill Ryan of Falmouth, a bartender at the Lee-side Bar in Woods Hole (where many an Islander has gone for a drink after missing a ferry).

He swayed to the sound of Mr. Taylor's Shower the People, a song that reminds him of one New Year's Eve about 10 years ago, he said.

"It was on the radio," said Mr. Ryan. "I had it on in my car. I was on my way home. When I really listened to that song, it was like a New Year's resolution.

"There was nothing happening in my life. This was just for me, my personal life. I love it. I get really emotional when I hear it."

For Martinzie Richmond, a senior at Boston University, Carly's rich voice brought back the '70s.

"She's got the richest voice I've ever heard in my life," said Mr. Richmond, 21. "When she sang Nobody Does It Better, I almost started crying. I got chills."

A summer police officer in Nantucket, Mr. Richmond came over from Nantucket to do security for the concert.

But it wasn't that easy for many. Francie Sartain, a psychotherapist who lives in Kentucky, quarreled with scalpers and even blew $300 on a ticket scam. But after giving up on the ads in USA Today, she just decided to come to the Vineyard for the week and try to get in.

Luckily, she checked into the Dockside Inn on Tuesday.

It was there that she struck up a conversation with an inn employee who was going home to Ireland. The clerk was depressed, Miss Sartain said, because she didn't have the money to pay a debt before leaving. But she did have something else pretty valuable — a $30 lawn ticket to the concert.

"I said I'd pay her $300 and she started crying and said that was how much she needed," said Miss Sartain, who was happy to pay the high price. "She was young. She needed the money. I needed the ticket."

Miss Sartain enjoyed the concert and the Vineyard, which she saw for the first time this week: "I think it's beautiful. I'm going to come back every year."

George Fisher's tale is the reverse image of Miss Sartain's. An Island native, Mr. Fisher said the concert was special because James and Carly are such a part of the Vineyard. But although he's lived here all his life and always has been a fan, Mr. Fisher had never seen them perform.

"But I'm here now," Mr. Fisher said, "and it's going to help the agricultural society."

And the surprise hit of the night?

That would be Sally, James and Carly's daughter. When the 21-year-old Sally began dancing on stage with her parents — who haven't performed together for 17 years — Islanders were enchanted.

"Can you imagine how powerful it must feel to stand there between your mother and father?" said Charlie Tucker, an Oak Bluffs police officer working at the concert. "Because I'm a father, and I have a daughter, I hope that there will be just one moment, I just hope my daughter feels that power."

"It was really nice to see their little daughter Sally," added Miss Manning.

"You couldn't have asked for a better concert. It was fantastic. It was just great. They should do it every year."

– September 1, 1995

❧   ❧   ❧

The Place to Be

Tabloid stars and heads of state
Haunt the Vineyard, as of late.
If Christ or Elvis reappear,
Rest assured they'll do it here.

D.A.W.

Jacqueline Kennedy Onassis
Leaves Legacy of Grace

By Amy Callahan

JACQUELINE BOUVIER KENNEDY ONASSIS, the Vineyard's most celebrated and elusive resident, died a week ago yesterday, on May 19, in New York city at the age of 64. She suffered from lymphatic cancer.

Her unexpected passing was mourned by longtime Vineyard friends as well as by Islanders who knew Mrs. Onassis only by her incredible fame and her quiet bicycle rides around Gay Head.

As the widow of the 35th President of the United States, John F. Kennedy, she was remembered by the nation this week as a historic woman of grace, style and strength.

As an Islander, she was remembered on the Vineyard as a woman with an adventurous spirit, an understated elegance, and a devotion to the natural world.

While the nation knew her as glamorous "Jackie O," no one but Vineyarders knew Mrs. Onassis as a gutsy outdoorswoman who cut across Squibnocket Pond in her kayak. No one else knew her as the proprietor of the roadside spring that she left running for anyone to use as needed.

Not many others saw her out and about with her grandchildren — laughing and eating ice cream. No one else could imagine her spending the day barefoot or monitoring her osprey pole or walking and boating around Menemsha, offering demure hellos, without a single person snapping a photograph.

And no one else but the people of Gay Head knew her as the pleasant neighbor who pedaled past on her bicycle, waving on a summer afternoon.

On the Vineyard, Mrs. Onassis was free to be alone, or she was free to be part of a community, if she chose.

Unlike Manhattan where crowds filled the sidewalks below

her apartment, on the Vineyard the only public display of grief was the collection of flowers tied to her driveway gate with string and bits of cloth. Some bouquets were tagged with handwritten notes, some were brought from the florist and some were obviously plucked from the wilds of up-Island. There were lilacs and roses and even a small pink geranium in a dark green flower pot.

"Love from a neighbor," read one note. "May you rest in peace. Thank you for being in Gay Head and helping us protect our land."

Mrs. Onassis began her life on Martha's Vineyard in 1978, with a privacy and understatement that would set the tone for her next 16 summers on the Island. She secretly purchased a 375-acre tract of undeveloped land in Gay Head, leaving the Island worrying for months about the fate of the pristine territory of woodland, meadows, parts of Squibnocket Pond and stretches of beach on the Atlantic Ocean.

Soon, though, the Island's fears were soothed, as Mrs. Onassis emerged as the owner and announced that she had no intention of developing the land, beyond building a private home for herself and her family.

She kept the land's native vegetation, and built her house the way the rest of the Island did: with shingles and white trim and gardens all around.

In the days since her death, praise for Mrs. Onassis has come from across the Vineyard, from fishermen and selectmen, conservationists and summer people. She was, simply, adored.

"She really had a profound effect on my life," said Gus Ben David, director of the Audubon sanctuary at Felix Neck. "She personified everything good. The whole Island should be very thankful that she owned that estate and preserved it."

Mr. Ben David said Mrs. Onassis regularly visited Felix Neck, arriving in a Jeep and bringing along her grandchildren and her omnipresent caretaker, Albert O. Fischer 3rd, whom she called "Bert."

They all would go out onto the lawn with Mr. Ben David's collection of live snakes, turtles and eagles, and Mrs. Onassis was just as fascinated as the children.

"Mrs. O would touch the snakes and get such a kick and excitement out of everything," he said.

Shortly after each visit, Mr. Ben David said, he would receive a handwritten thank-you note from Mrs. Onassis. He received the last one in September, on light blue stationery.

She wrote, "Dear Gus, You gave the children and me such an unforgettable afternoon. I think it will affect their lives and thinking forever."

Ann Nelson, owner of Bunch of Grapes Bookstore where Mrs. Onassis shopped, said: "The thing that impressed me most about Jackie is that she never sought any preferential treatment. She stood in line like any private citizen would. She truly exhibited and exemplified all the graces of a true lady."

Even her young riding instructor at Arrowhead Farm was touched by Mrs. Onassis last summer.

"She spent most of the ride asking me questions about myself, which I found extraordinary for a public person," said 18-year-old Rosi Kerr, a seasonal resident of Tisbury. "I didn't think she'd be interested in me, but she was great."

More intimate memories were shared by Rose Styron this week, who, with her husband William, was friendly with Mrs. Onassis for many years.

Just as Mrs. Onassis would have done, Mrs. Styron recently arrived on the Vineyard for the season. She wrote her thoughts from her home in Vineyard Haven.

"My memories of Jackie are sentimental: a boat trip on the sun-blessed Sound with her and Maurice; a quiet lunch on her terrace, like last July's for her old pal George Plimpton and his mother, where Jackie gave me the recipe for her grand dessert called summer pudding; laughing later when I inflicted my unsuccessful version of it on my guests: 'But Rose, you can't get good red currants here — you should know that!'

"Jackie in our kitchen sneaking a piece of fried chicken before appearing for dinner; Jackie in our kids' bedroom the summer after President Kennedy's death (she came to stay with Caroline and John-John; he lost their rabbit down the hole in the floorboards between the beds, and Jackie was on her hands and knees trying to pull it back out); Jackie with her big bare feet propped on the dining table…. Winters we met even more sporadically, but Jackie's warm smile lit up the room for me in welcome on each occasion."

Mrs. Styron continued: "Each time I had the luck to encounter Jackie it was like coming upon a fine favorite poem, one which in its spareness would never quite reveal itself, but whose gift of a splendid word, a spirited insight, would reveal the listener's self to him or her, anew.

"Original in her choice of gifts — to me, to us, to the nation — somehow Jackie always got it right."

– May 27, 1994

ISLAND

❧

SMALL TOWNS ARE PLACES that people normally leave.
History is an idea they mostly ignore. The wilderness
is a world they often abuse. But neighborliness, a sense
of the hard working past, the nearness of the ocean and
the open spaces — these are the salient virtues of Island life,
the attachments everyone speaks of when they talk about preserving the quality of Martha's Vineyard.

Why is it different here?

The stories that follow suggest that people believe in things
just a bit more deeply on the Vineyard. They believe more deeply
because the Vineyard is separated enough and small enough that
in every undertaking a few can make the difference. There is

something fortifying about crossing that strip of water, something that encourages the individual to make a leap of faith, to dare to commit to a cause.

Here you will meet young men and women who give their hearts to something as simple and old-fashioned as a town band. They are rewarded by crowds who seek them out wherever they play on starry evenings by the sea. Here an older woman volunteers to clean and polish all 1,008 prisms in the Fresnel lens of the old Gay Head Light, satisfying a dream she had since childhood in Kansas to serve as keeper of a lighthouse.

Here you find the conviction and the toil of the men and women who preserve and put to use Island inheritances of all sorts — the Flying Horses, Cedar Tree Neck, the seaport at Menemsha — that otherwise might lie abandoned and die, leaving the citizenry longing for what has been lost.

This is part of the difference of Island life. There is room for faith, the faith of as few as one or two who believe that something can be brought back, or made better, or created from practically nothing. That sort of faith is wanted, needed and celebrated. It matters. Vineyarders and visitors seem to sense that when they've contributed to the conservation or enrichment of even one facet of Island life, they've contributed to the whole. Something of what they love in a place is reclaimed, preserved or improved by the work of their hands, hearts and minds.

That's the larger meaning of Island life — that your work will affect people you may never know, that a definable world gains from what you give, that what you contribute will live on and give pleasure after you are gone.

This is what holds the Vineyarder and the visitor to the sort of small town life that people elsewhere usually leave. This is what connects them to the land, the sea and the sky, and what makes so many care so deeply about what came before and what will come after. The quality of Island life often rests on the idea of service — not so much what a person draws from the character of the place, but on what he or she contributes to it.

The secret is that the giving is also the reward — a reward of abiding satisfaction, of place, of connection, of knowing one's own worth.

"Where is the journalism of the future which will continue to recognize the individual, his initiative, his dignity, his tastes, his separateness, instead of contriving to skim off that part of him that can be generalized into a convenient mass?" asked Henry Beetle Hough in the first Vineyard Gazette Reader, published at the end of the 1960s.

That journalism is here. The individual and what he contributes to Martha's Vineyard remain the principal concern of the Vineyard Gazette, in heart and mind a journal of Island life.

– T.D.

❧ ❧ ❧

Through a Lighted Window

GO OUT AT DAY'S END, in the evening about dusk, and wander the streets and lanes of Island towns and villages. Stay out in the gathering darkness, a little beyond the hour of dinner if possible. The way winds past the white and gray-shingled houses of the Vineyard, past open doors and windows cracked just enough to let a spring breeze blow. The time is twilight, when the Island lies early in shadow, when lights twinkle on and the evening stirs just before nightfall.

Listen. The sounds in these Island lanes come from behind those doors ajar, from behind the rustle of curtains, from inside, where evening lights now shine warm and mellow. Listen. An unanswered phone rings in the distance. Clatter on the porch. Conversation from a kitchen window. Choir practice somewhere in the neighborhood. A screen door banging. Calls to dinner. Scurrying children protesting the unfinished work of the day's play. Laughter. A barking dog, someone's pet. Talk in the streets. People homeward bound.

Life on the Vineyard is changing, shifting with the season. Yesterday to spring; tomorrow toward summer. It is the evening light in the windows of Island homes that best tells the tale of a community awakening. Only a few days ago, it seems, these same houses were dark and shuttered. So also was there a stillness at dusk. And in village streets the sounds of silence.

But look to the days ahead. May is the Vineyard's beckoning month, a signal to seasonal friends from afar, an alert to year-round citizens here. This month reminds us all of where the calendar stands. Winter is over; summer approaches. The lights of the Vineyard are on and the Island stirs, as does the countryside, in the song of cardinals and whippoorwills, in the colors of tulips and daffodils. This is when the Vineyard extends to all her invitation to return.

The migration begins. Already old friends arrive and chance meetings form new acquaintances. Strangers come for a first visit and probably not the last. License plates read like a diplomatic list of foreign nations — Texas, Colorado, California, Florida, New York and all points west of the Vineyard, west of this Island outpost of land in the sea beyond the land.

– Editorial, May 12, 1989

❧ ❧ ❧

Off-Island Driving

The Vineyard driver breaks and swerves,
Then overcomes his case of nerves
And quickly gets it through his head
To stop when traffic lights turn red.

D.A.W.

Bound for Home Aboard the Islander, Queen of Steamship Authority Fleet

By Amy Callahan

SHE CASTS A HUGE SHADOW off the starboard side, onto the green sun streaked water in Woods Hole harbor. The sun has been up for a few hours and glares through the haze above Nobska Light. As she has done for more than 40 years, the Islander chugs across the horizon, bound for the Vineyard.

It has been a year since she pushed through these waters, and despite the new engines and paint, she is still the slow, big-boned vessel that will make a fool of any captain who thinks he has mastered her. She is hard to steer, unpredictable in the tide, and could back up if only she had a rear view. She has run aground, almost sunk, and even once collided with another boat.

But since 1950 when she arrived from the Maryland Drydock Company — heralded as a modern super ferry — the Islander has been the most reliable vessel in the Steamship Authority fleet.

And, as far as Vineyarders are concerned, she is the most beloved.

"We know we're going to Vineyard Haven and back. We've always gotten there with this one," says Capt. Thomas Manley, who has captained Steamship Authority boats since 1980 and Woods Hole Oceanographic research boats before that. He will spend this summer and the rest of the year on the Islander.

He knows she is a favorite. The reasons, he says, are both sentimental and practical. Some people have grown up riding to the Vineyard on the Islander and regard it as the quintessential ferryboat. Some people just appreciate being able to open their car doors more easily than on the Nantucket. For the crew, she is a challenge.

About 15 people run the Islander at a time. When on their

24-hour shifts, the crew eats and sleeps on the boat. With the officers' quarters above deck and a good cook in the galley, she's known as good living.

But not just anybody can run this boat. She is different, for sure. And she always has been. Ever since Eads Johnson designed her with two sets of doors, and she arrived on the scene as the largest passenger ferry in New England, the Islander has been unique. From the propellers positioned on both ends, to the portable log book carried across the deck between the two bridges, the Islander is a vessel of secrets and surprises. For all her blunt appearances, she is subtle and mysterious. And for all her comforting familiarity to Vineyarders, she is a massive puzzle of steel to those who navigate her. She is a two-faced lady in the Sound. She goes back and forth, but she doesn't turn around.

"She's as old as I am and is running better than I am," says William Walsh, who's taking tickets on the ramp.

"And she's prettier," adds Capt. James Lodge, who has run the Islander on and off for the past five years. This curly-haired father of two who lives on the Vineyard is one of three captains who will run the Islander this summer. He came up through the ranks on this boat and remembers trips when the Islander was so tossed by the sea that the captain's strategy turned into deciding which object in the harbor was safest to hit.

Captain Lodge says he has heard stories of new captains quitting after one trip on the Islander.

How are they to know that the best way to make sure she's lined up correctly in the Woods Hole slip is to take a peek out the small window at the back of the wheelhouse and look for Mr. Mellon's chimney?

That's what Captain Manley does every time. When the black railing on the deck is in line with the chimney on Mr. Mellon's Penzance Point boathouse, then he knows the bow has a tight fit against the ramp.

The tide is tricky, too. And getting the Islander into a slip is a one-shot deal.

If there is a flood tide in Woods Hole, the pilot has a few seconds to make the turn and guide her in or the boat will be pushed off course. Captain Manley says this tide from the east is so strong here that you hear it hit the boat. Passengers may think it's an engine kicking in or a door opening on the freight deck, but it is in fact a wall of water against which the Islander, with its propellers lined up one before the other, is defenseless. The Islander doesn't go sideways.

"I don't really feel an outsider could walk on this boat and learn it," Captain Manley says. Just when you think you know all her tricks, he says, "She'll turn around and get you. You've bounced off every piece of wood in the slip."

It is dusk now in Woods Hole and the Islander is approaching the dock. Captain Manley is on duty. The sky is washed in streaks of pink and gray. After unloading here, the Islander will make one last trip back to Martha's Vineyard where she will sleep tucked in behind the breakwater, in between the tar pilings in Vineyard Haven harbor. As pilot Al Brox steers the Islander into the slip, passengers are gathering up their bags and heading to the stairwells. Tonight, it's an ebb tide, but docking is still not easy. Mr. Brox is at the wheel, which, since the Islander came back from its $1 million in-house repair work, is turned only a few inches when steering. It used to be that the big steel wheel was spun round and round to turn this boat.

It used to be, too, that the rudder on the stern was locked with a pin which after each trip was carried the length of the freight deck and inserted in the other end. And down in the engine room things are different. Not only is everything shining like it just came from a factory, but the two 10-cylinder Fairbanks-Morse engines are gone. The engineers keep snapshots of the old engines in the drawer. Now there are two eight-cylinder electromotive diesel engines made by General Motors.

In the galley, there are new refrigerators and table tops complete with raised edges so coffee cups won't slide off in rough weather. And most everyone by now has noticed the new decks, which are treacherously slippery when wet. Another nuance on the Islander.

In many ways, this is a new vessel passing between our harbor and theirs. In most ways, though, the Islander is what she always has been: our link to America, and our passage home.

– June 12, 1992

❧ ❧ ❧

Underwater Economy Takes Deep Dive; Coin Catchers Blame Time and Tide

By Mark Alan Lovewell

THE ISLAND COIN DIVERS, who have their fingers on the pulse of the tourist economy, have seen a dramatic drop in the money tossed off the Oak Bluffs Steamship Authority wharf.

For generations, young swimmers have gathered just off the wharf, calling out, "How 'bout a coin? How 'bout a coin?" to the Island visitors coming and going.

Usually, without much urging, these Vineyard visitors will toss quarters, nickels and dimes into the water and watch as the swimmers gather them.

Pennies? Don't even think of it.

Money collected this year is less than last year, the divers complain.

Money earned from diving helps these young men get through a summer of rising expenses. The cost for movies, candy and other important things is up, the divers report, while the business of collecting chucked coins hasn't kept pace.

After a half-hour of diving Tuesday afternoon, the swimmers got together to compare notes and figures about the season now winding down. Dripping wet, and with towels wrapped around them, they spoke of the summer economy. "People are throwing more dollar bills than last year but the money just doesn't add up to last year. Last year was great," said Connor Tierney, 11, of Phoenix, Ariz.

In preparation for a 10-day visit to the Vineyard this summer, Mr. Tierney said he practiced diving for coins in his swimming pool at home in Arizona. The practice was worth it because with less coins being pitched into the water, his ability to recover all the coins pitched has improved.

"Money is down about a half," Mr. Tierney said.

In five days of diving, Mr. Tierney said, he has earned $94. He plans to save the money to buy a stereo. If this were last summer, he believes he would have collected much more.

Of course it is not all due to the economics of the Island. Two weeks worth of coin diving was interrupted when the Oak Bluffs Steamship Authority wharf was closed for repairs. Add to that bad weather. For that costly vacation, Mr. Tierney said there were only five days he was able to go diving.

All things considered, it pretty much comes back to this: Vacationers just aren't throwing as much money into the ocean as they did last year.

Jon Cleasby, 12, of Cranston, R.I., thinks the economic slowdown is due to "the 1986 Tax Reform Act now taking effect on the economy. It is a lot slower. Last year I got $34 a day. This year I get $24. People don't have as much change to spend."

Mr. Cleasby is a second generation coin diver. His father, Robert Cleasby, who is president of the Friends of Nobska, used to dive for coins off the Authority wharf when he was a kid.

Mr. Cleasby's older brother Andrew, 17, used to coin dive, as well as his sister Meredith, now 18. The young Mr. Cleasby said that when he talked of his hardships with his siblings, he got no sympathy.

Jeremy Requena, 11, of Oak Bluffs has had a good summer. This is his first summer as a coin diver.

"I was trying to find a job I could do all summer, so I thought

I would try this," he remarked. Apparently, he does not mind that he went into this summer without on-the-job experience.

So far his pocketed earnings have helped pay for frequent trips to the movies. He has seen Batman, Lethal Weapon, Turner & Hooch and other films. "I usually save my money. I saved $70 in quarters but then I spent half of it," he said.

When Mr. Requena began diving for coins at the start of this summer he got only $2 and $3 a ferry. Now he sometimes doubles that. Between diving, he rises to put his quarters in a plastic container that hangs from his neck.

"Last year people had plenty of change and they would try and get rid of it," said Chris Giacalone, 12, of Beverly. "Last year a friend and I earned $400. We met almost every boat that came each day," he said.

With the money shortage, Mr. Giacalone said he has noticed divers haven't been as courteous as in years past.

"There is more competition. They push each other. We are more greedy for the money," he said.

After meeting three ferries, Mr. Giacalone said he has collected $10. "I'm saving the money so when I go home I can buy gifts for my parents. And yeah, maybe some school clothes or something like that," he said.

At the entrance to the Steamship Authority dock, Peter Duart, Authority agent, stands checking traffic. Whenever he sees the young divers ("We call them wharf rats," he says), he gets a little chuckle.

Mr. Duart, 41, says that as a kid he used to dive for coins too. "In those days there was a whole bunch of us. We would work the boats in both towns. We'd work the boat in Vineyard Haven, then jump on our bikes and ride to Oak Bluffs to meet that boat."

The money was important back then. "We'd spend it on the Flying Horses. And I used to turn my money in to the bank for silver dollars. I wish I had them now," he says.

– August 25, 1989

Music of the Rings: Some Carousel Customers Have Sticky Fingers

By Jason Gay

The thing with kids is, if they want to grab for the gold ring, you have to let them do it, and not say anything. If they fall off, they fall off, but it's bad if you say anything to them.
– Holden Caulfield in J.D. Salinger's The Catcher in the Rye

IF HOLDEN CAULFIELD had watched Jamie Meader snatch five rings with her index finger and one with her pinky, he probably would have scrapped his whole soliloquy about golden rings and talked about her instead. If he just saw the 17-year-old extend her arm from a chariot and grab six — *six* — steel rings in quick-handed succession, defying both laws of gravity and balance, he might have even jumped on the carousel and given it a whirl himself.

This is a story about rings — old, grimy carousel rings rolling from creaky metal chutes at the oldest platform carousel in the United States, the Flying Horses in Oak Bluffs. Historians speak fondly of the amusement ride's antique horses crafted more than a century ago by Brooklyn woodcarver Charles W.F. Dare, or the hand painted folk art panels that adorn its sides, but aficionados know the Flying Horses experience concerns rings. It is one of the last places in America — in the world — offering people a chance at a brass ring and a free ride.

It's not much of a chance, however. A Flying Horses ride spews out hundreds of steel rings but offers only two cracks at the precious band of brass — once from the old chute hanging from the balcony steps, another from a new arm at the carousel's center. Luck remains more important than skill. The brass ring that is announced and dropped in the final moments of the four-minute tour always results in a frantic grabbing session by passengers; still, the winner is often plumb surprised when he or she pulls down the magic circle.

Brett Leighton, 14, of Oak Bluffs owns what he labels the "coolest job on the Island" — dropping rings into the outside Flying Horses chute. Although he's had the glamour gig for less than a summer, Brett works the chute like a seasoned professional, gathering clumps of the gray rings and dropping them into the swinging arm. Today, the temperature in his stairwell perch eclipses 90 degrees and sweat soaks the brim of his back-turned baseball cap, but Brett retains a toothy smile.

"This is nothing today," he says, judging a midmorning crowd composed mostly of yuppies and small children who muster only one or two rings each pass. "When you have someone good aboard, you have to work a lot faster."

What is considered good at the Flying Horses? Brett tells of a fortyish woman from town who has been riding "since she was, like, four" and can strip eight rings in one turn. "She's unreal," confirms carousel supervisor Georgie White. "She doesn't miss. I call her queen of the rings."

The king of the rings, most agree, is Jamie Meader's brother Jared, now 20, who in his heyday could twist nine rings from the outside arm. Like most of the great ring-grabbers, Jared preferred to stand alongside a chariot, where he could hold a support pole with one arm and attack the ring chute with the other — bang-bang style. Nine rings, we are told again. Legally.

But you see, ring-grabbing is a family business in these parts. Jared's and Jamie's mother is Robin Meader, otherwise known as the Flying Horses manager. An affable, even-tempered woman — excellent personality traits during rainy days when customer lines often swell out the carousel doors — Mrs. Meader swears she can *hear* a brass ring trickle down the chute. Steel rings make a tinny clang when dropped in the arm, she says, but brass makes a more solid, steadier sound. "Hear it?" she asks, and Brett and Georgie nod in agreement.

Despite her family's talents, Mrs. Meader says there is trouble with the beloved rings at the Flying Horses: They are disappearing, and fast. "We are having our biggest ring problem ever," she says. "We are losing them by the thousands. I got about 80 brass ones left, and we lost one last night."

To the mostly teenaged Flying Horses staff, Mrs. Meader's lost brass ring announcement is kind of like Santa Claus telling the elves that the sleigh is missing on Christmas Eve. "Really?" Brett asks, horrified. "How?"

"How is the easy question," Mrs. Meader explains. Rings are stolen in pockets, backpacks, purses, bras, socks and shoes, stuffed sometimes by the dozen. Steel or brass are equal targets, and the major culprits are teenagers and — yup — adults. "The funniest thing is in the evening, when you can go outside on the steps and hear people walking out with their pants jingling," Mrs. Meader says.

The Flying Horses staff is not afraid to chase down the lowly ring scofflaws, as was the case a few weeks ago when they followed a group of kids up the street, only to have the thieves toss their booty into the ocean. But Mrs. Meader had a more successful confrontation last year.

"We saw this guy take a brass ring and get off the carousel, so I went up to him and asked him about it, and he said he threw it back," she recalls. "I went back and checked, and it wasn't there.

"So I went next door into this store where the guy was, and I asked him about it. He said he didn't take it — and said I was a liar. I asked him again and he said, 'Oh, you have plenty, you have millions,' and he started to call me a few choice names. Finally, he pulled out the brass ring and threw it at me. I didn't care; I got my ring back."

Such stories aren't very amusing to Chris Scott, executive director of the Martha's Vineyard Preservation Trust, owners of the Flying Horses carousel. Mr. Scott estimates that stolen rings cost his organization more than $1,500 per year.

"It seems innocuous if you've picked off 10 rings in a ride and you think, 'What's the big deal about taking one ring?' " he says.

"But when we do 250,000 rides a year, and one of those rings costs 16 cents, it starts to add up."

As a result, Mrs. Meader's Flying Horses crew has stepped up its ring enforcement. Staffers are positioned along the circumference of the carousel, and if the day's count gets low, they take the accumulated rings from passengers during the middle of a ride — a process called "recycling." The brass ring is watched even more closely; when it is pulled, a crew member descends on the lucky winner and snaps it up before it can be hidden.

The changes have irked some longtime customers, but Mr. Scott insists that the tighter patrol is necessary. "But we're not at the point where we are going to use metal detectors," he jokes.

Neither Mr. Scott nor Robin Meader believes a day will come when no Flying Horses rings are stolen. Rings continue to turn up as jewelry, toys and even on the diplomas of graduates from the Oak Bluffs School (they pay for them). Robin even reports having seen teenagers hanging rings from the back of adjustable baseball caps. It seems that many people don't mind breaking the law for a little loop of Americana, no matter what the consequences are.

"I mentioned the problem at a board meeting, and one of our trustees said, 'Oh, one of these?' and pulled out a steel one attached to his key ring," Mr. Scott sighs. "But this man has done as much as anyone to restore the carousel, so I think he's entitled to one — one."

– July 28, 1995

❧   ❧   ❧

Chicken on the Beach

The water's cold; the waves look rough
— My feet are wet, and that's enough.
D.A.W.

A Grand Vineyard Tradition: Town Band Plays On

By Paula Delbonis

"THERE'S SOMETHING ABOUT SITTING on the bandstand in Oak Bluffs on a Sunday night, looking over the park and seeing thousands of people and looking out at the sea," says John Schilling. "It's absolutely priceless."

Since Mr. Schilling was 13 years old, he has been enthusiastically bringing his brass trumpet to two of the Vineyard's most beautiful bandstands, playing the marches by John Philip Sousa and loving every minute of it.

It's been 21 years, and Mr. Schilling is still playing his heart out, every Sunday night of every Island summer — in Oak Bluffs in Ocean Park and in Vineyard Haven at the seaside bandstand in Owen Park — with the Vineyard Haven Band.

Families and friends are drawn to the growing glow of the bandstands as the sun sets, like summer's moths. Families with blankets and lawn chairs gather as the uneven sounds of tuning begin, even before the band bursts forth with the first melody at 8 p.m.

This town band has been playing for 121 years. The band was 18 members strong when it gave that first public performance at the West Tisbury agricultural fair in 1868, according to Thomas Bardwell, president of the band from 1969 to 1979.

As in the diversity of the instruments played, the band shows a cross section of Vineyard life. There are children and grandparents, summer residents and year-round Islanders. Anyone who can play an instrument and read the music is welcome.

According to Mr. Bardwell, a renowned band historian, the Vineyard Haven Band is one of the oldest town bands in the state and the oldest organization of public music on the Vineyard.

Originally there were no women in the band, but that changed long ago. Eleven-year-old Robin Carliss, who has played the drums in the Oak Bluffs School for three years, is the newest addition to the Vineyard Haven Band. Her proud father Glenn has been playing trumpet with the band on and off for 15 years.

"A large part of the whole thing is tradition," Mr. Schilling says of the band. "It's family."

In the true spirit of town band tradition, 29-year-old Chris Allen took over as conductor and director of the band with the first concert of the season last month. Now a new, upbeat attitude can be detected among the band members.

Mr. Allen began playing clarinet with the band when he was 10 years old and a student at the Tisbury School. He began composing music when he was 15, and now he has returned from a career and education in music to conduct the Vineyard Haven Band.

"He's a perfectionist," says Frank Dunkl, band president. "And that's good for us as a band."

"I enjoy playing for a challenging director," says Mr. Schilling, who fondly remembers Chris Allen from his early years playing in the band. "It makes me pay attention and it gives us a needed, fresh perspective on a lot of the music."

The aging sheaves of classic bandstand melodies are as much a part of the tradition as the music itself. Many of the worn and yellowed pieces of sheet music have been with the band since the 1800s. A grant five years ago allowed the band to begin preserving the collection, which is stored away in the basement of the Old Stone Church in Tisbury.

Every Monday night the 30 or 40 members of the band gather in the church to practice tunes for the Sunday night concerts.

But Chris Allen, and others in the band, modestly claim little credit for keeping the band going during good times and bad. In the course of 121 years, it seems the tradition has taken on a life of its own.

"It keeps itself going," the young director says, attributing the longevity to the beauty of the event itself. "I guess everybody likes a parade and the sound of a parade."

Mr. Allen admits there's nothing quite like the sound of Stars and Stripes Forever played with gusto from a bandstand.

How true! A crowd gathered in Owen Park found it impossible to listen to the rousing rendition without clapping hands and stomping feet.

The enthusiasm bubbled from the silver sea to the reclining audience. The kids from Camp Jabberwocky, the Island's cerebral palsy camp, clapped along from their wheelchairs and blankets sprawled across the lawn, and the entire crowd joined in.

In Oak Bluffs, every other week, strings of young children skip wildly around the bandstand to the fast-paced tunes, lending enthusiasm to the band members.

"Vineyard Haven is a bit better suited for listening on a quiet level," says Mr. Allen.

But enthusiasm has been building for the band, both on the lawns and in the bandstand.

On the Fourth of July, as the band played from the Memorial Wharf in Edgartown, the audience wouldn't let the band skip away.

"They literally insisted on two encores," Mr. Allen says. "It was a fun concert."

Mr. Allen, as the new director, sees his roll essentially as a motivational one.

"You are dealing with people of all ages, all levels of ability and all levels of confidence in their playing," Mr. Allen says. "It's not so much a job of keeping time for them. A lot of it is spur of the moment, whipping them up. But when everybody gets going, there's such an intensity there."

Before the first concert of the season on June 25, Mr. Allen had seven intense rehearsals. "They can do it," Mr. Allen says. "I knew they could. I knew it was a good band that just needed some tender loving care and some musical discipline. On the whole we have a younger band than we've ever had before."

About half of the band members are young students — ranging from third grade through high school and college.

And when it comes to marches....

"I love them," Mr. Allen says. "They are truly some of the great slices of American music."

Along with the world-renowned John Philip Sousa, the band has been playing many tunes by R.B. Hall, whom Mr. Allen calls "a lesser known but one of the greatest and most innovative composers."

The R.B. Hall selections are, by far, Mr. Schilling's favorites.

And Jack Simmons, who lives in the Camp Ground in Oak Bluffs, says he could never pick a favorite from all the wonderful melodies the band has played over the years.

"I love them all," he says, exuding enthusiasm. "I'll play anything."

"Except rock," adds his wife from the background.

"That's right," Mr. Simmons chuckles. "I'll die before I play rock and roll."

Not much has changed in the past 121 years. The two bandstands, the atmosphere and the music have remained constant.

The only noticeable change has been the uniforms.

Mr. Simmons, who has been playing the trumpet since he was nine years old, has the distinction of being the Vineyard Haven Band's longest playing participant. This year he has taken a few Sunday nights off because of a bad back, but he hopes to be back in full force by Illumination Night.

Mr. Simmons has been playing the Vineyard bandstands for 36 years, ever since Thomas Bardwell's father approached him on the street and asked him to join the band. Mr. Simmons was the conductor when current director Chris Allen was a boy in the band.

Mr. Allen went on to study clarinet at Boston University and composition at Marlboro College in Vermont. During the day he works for Jimmy B Hauling Service, and on Sundays he directs the church choir at the Old Stone Church in Vineyard Haven.

At 67, Mr. Simmons has fond memories of his years in the band and of the other members, including Chris Allen.

"I feel like a father to a lot of them," he says sentimentally. "I've seen them grow up and do a lot with their love of music.

"I remember the first time Martha Mosher, now Martha Childs, came to practice as a little tyke, carrying her flute."

Martha's father was also a longtime band member, and Martha still plays with the Vineyard Haven Band.

"Everyone comes for the love of playing," he says, "or to learn."

When Illumination Night comes later this month, band director Chris Allen will sit on the sidelines while his proteges perform the highlight of the evening — Stars and Stripes Forever. Last year, as a fund-raiser for Martha's Vineyard Community Services, the chance to direct this Sousa march was auctioned off to the highest bidder — for $2,000.

If you've missed the band this season, you know where to find it. Sunday night they will play in Ocean Park beginning at 8 p.m. and the following Sunday in Owen Park, Vineyard Haven. They'll be at Illumination Night, of course, and the agricultural fair.

As veteran band member Mr. Schilling says, "It's priceless."

– August 4, 1989

❧ ❧ ❧

Campers Through the Looking Glass

IN LEWIS CARROLL'S CLASSIC STORY, a girl named Alice falls down a rabbit hole and into a world where all the rules of everyday life are turned upside down. Something like that happens to a lucky group of three dozen campers each July, and to another, younger group each August when they travel from all across the United States to gather for a month of fun at Camp Jabberwocky.

The camp's nominal base is in Tisbury, but everybody who understands the spirit of Camp Jabberwocky knows that its real campus is the whole Vineyard. And the true magic of Camp Jabberwocky is the way it takes the campers through the looking glass — from the hard realities of life with cerebral palsy and other disorders, to an experience of joy and community that some of the supposedly ablest people among us will never know.

The campers of Jabberwocky shared that joy and showed their amazing strength of spirit with a show and sale of art last week, and again with two weekend performances of Alice Through the Looking Glass as even the prodigious imagination of Mr. Carroll could never have pictured it. The art show featured pottery made by the feet of campers who cannot control their hands, and essays written one eloquent character at a time by Paul Remy, who uses a head-pointer to communicate his thoughts to the world. At the performances of Camp Jabberwocky's theatre, those campers who could not walk joined the dance anyway, careening in the wonderful wheelchair choreography that has become a happy camp trademark.

"Sentence first — verdict afterwards!" shouts the mad queen in Lewis Carroll's story. And indeed the campers of Jabberwocky might seem to be people who have had a heavy sentence handed down before their lives were fairly begun. But the gift of Camp Jabberwocky is in its way of reaching past the sometimes faltering body to tap the awesome potential of the human spirit. When we hear its message, Camp Jabberwocky is a gift not only to a small corps of happy campers each summer, but to every member of this Island community. Its gift is love, and its invitation is to the dance of life.

– Editorial, July 25, 1995

A Caretaker's View: Fragile Expanses Of a North Shore Sanctuary

By Amy Callahan

IT'S HARD TO CONFESS YOU LOVE SOMETHING so wind-swept and vulnerable. So it isn't until he leaves the woods and reaches the top of the grassy bluff that Dick Johnson finally puts it into words, as if the wind has come up and blown it out of him. "I feel very protective of this place," he says. "It just hurts because I love this place so much." Mr. Johnson is the care-taker of Cedar Tree Neck Sanctuary. He is a big, quiet, bearded man who for the past two years has walked this land on the north-west shore of the Island nearly every morning. His hurt comes in small doses from finding litter or destruction along the trails. But the real ache, the one that is lodged in the chest of all peo-ple who care about the environment, is from our way of life that physically and spiritually removes us from nature.

On Martha's Vineyard, where nature's beauty is almost in-escapable, it may be a little different. Or maybe not. All across the Island conservation land is little used and virtually hidden. And there is some discussion in land management circles about whether this is a good or a bad thing.

Dick Johnson is unsure.

The trails at Cedar Tree Neck are not wide enough for two people to walk side by side. They wind through woods where oak and sassafras are thinner than a man's leg and younger than many Island houses. Beach trees grow twisted and squat, wildly pruned by sea winds.

In some spots, low-growing flowers spill out across the path, apparently safe from tramping feet. On the beach, the only foot-prints are from deer.

The brochure for Sheriff's Meadow Foundation, which owns the sanctuary, states: "Wherever you are on Martha's Vineyard, land owned or protected by Sheriff's Meadow Foundation is nearby."

Nearby perhaps, but not necessarily known. The names of the preserves are not household names. They are not popular destinations. Ask a longtime Vineyard visitor or even an Islander where Caroline Tuthill Preserve is. Or Roth Woodlands.

Even in the height of summer, when the Island is seething with traffic and vacationers, there will be no more than 15 cars parked at Cedar Tree Neck.

This is because one does not just happen upon the pristine 200-acre sanctuary. It requires a drive down an unmarked dead-end road in West Tisbury, and a sharp right turn onto an unpaved way. It is at this turn that the first sign for Cedar Tree Neck is posted. The sanctuary parking lot is another 10 minutes down the dirt road.

This is the way they want it.

"We're not as people oriented. We're more wildlife oriented," Mr. Johnson explains. "I feel our first obligation is to protect the values of the land."

With this in mind, the sanctuary is trying to strike a balance between protecting the land and opening it up so people will know about it, and care about it.

That means at Cedar Tree Neck there is no running, swimming, picnicking, camping or biking. Pets are not allowed.

Rather, it is a place for walking and watching birds. Or sitting silently by a still pond.

"We're out for a more contemplative experience," the caretaker says while standing in front of the posted rules at the edge of the parking area. He almost apologizes for the sign's restrictive tone.

But rules like these need to be spelled out. While most of the visitors to the sanctuary are not destructive, there is a mind-set, Mr. Johnson says, that he and other land managers are dealing with.

"It says the world is ours to use. For humans to exploit. To use for our own purposes. That we are somehow, as humans, separate from nature. Somehow above nature. It is becoming clear to people right now that this just doesn't work."

Mr. Johnson worries that while more environmental crises surface, the split between humans and nature widens. Some charge that environmentalists care more about birds and bugs than they do about people.

But Mr. Johnson says it is because he cares about people that he wants to protect the environment.

As he sees it, the bugs will survive. It is humans who are endangered.

"We're not going to wipe out life on earth. When we make the world unfit for ourselves, life will go on, and off in different directions. The world will survive, short of actually blowing the place up. But it'll be just cockroaches and starlings."

While saying this, he is having a cup of tea in the small wood house at the entrance to the sanctuary. Books about birds are piled on a shelf. Raincoats and parkas hang on the back of the door.

He and his partner live here year-round, and they are expecting a baby in September.

Each time we lose a species, he says, we are chipping away at an ecosystem crucial to sustaining human life: "We have to protect the world and things in it if we're going to survive."

But aside from whatever benefits humans get from plants and animals, humans have an obligation to respect and protect all life, he says.

"Whether valuable to humans or not valuable to humans, they have the right to exist."

This figures even in his decision to repair a footbridge out on the trail.

The old bridge was a rustic, mossy board laid across the stream. The new bridge is painted and put together with neatly sawed lumber and nails.

"Is it worth it to make this place a little more pristine and have someone twist an ankle?" Mr. Johnson asks.

Still, the wildlife is winning here, as proven by such things as the Canada mayflower. This flower, which is also known as wild lily of the valley, will only grow in mature woodlands 80 to 100 years old.

Ospreys fish here. Cranefly orchids grow here. But the truest sign of the sanctuary's protection, however, might be the song of a shy brown bird.

Mr. Johnson listens for the wood thrush in the morning. He has heard it this spring and feels reassured the land is safe.

"To me, it's really important to hear them."

– May 12, 1992

❧   ❧   ❧

Staunch Supporters Seek to Defend Good Name of Richard III

By Tom Dunlop

THE ADVERTISEMENT IS ARRESTING because it is simple and stark, bordered in black, and with nothing to sell. If the design doesn't catch the eye, the words "In Memoriam" usually do.

"In Memoriam," it read in the Gazette of August 21, 1979. "Richard Plantagenet Killed on Bosworth Field by Troops of Traitorous Henry Tudor."

Most years since then — on the Tuesday or Friday nearest August 22 — the ad has said nearly the same thing. But the designs have become bolder. The first year, the small outline of a boar stood at the bottom of the box. More recently the ads have become larger, the print blacker, and the words more forceful:

"In Memoriam: Richard III, King of England, Slain at the Battle of Bosworth Field August 22, 1485."

The ads are unsigned. Yet through this small, yearly message, the Island of Martha's Vineyard has become a resting place for the embattled, maligned memory of Britain's most notorious king.

Richard III, the White Boar, the last Plantagenet, the final son of the House of York, died 500 years ago this week on a field near Market Bosworth, England.

Richard III, falsely described as a hunchback, mythically accused as the murderer of Henry VI and his son, the Prince of Wales. And despite modern historical thinking, still wrongly remembered as the assassin of his brother's children, the child king Edward V and his younger brother, Richard of York.

The sponsors of the Gazette announcements have asked for anonymity. Last week, only days before the 500th anniversary of the death of Richard III, the request for an interview was gently turned down.

So this week the ad will reappear, simply reminding us that someone on the Vineyard has not accepted the party line about Richard. Someone, somewhere has looked beyond the Tudor propaganda, the Shakespeare play, the delicious horror of the popular story, to seek the truth about the man.

These remembrances come on an Island 3,000 miles from London, 500 years after the event, concerning a man who ruled 100 years before the first Englishman set foot on the future county of Dukes County.

It says a little about life on Martha's Vineyard, about the special things some of us care about, and even about the way we deal with people. True enough, a few other Americans will find a way to honor Richard III, whose name to the unquestioning is synonymous with regicide and child murder. There is even an American branch of the Richard III Society, created to reassess the king's brief life and two-year reign.

But there is no chapter here. Just an individual or two or three who believe a man was spectacularly wronged, who read and research a bit in their spare time, and spend a few dollars a year in the Gazette to say that Richard, the last Plantagenet, was betrayed and killed in the heart of England.

Martha's Vineyard seems to nurture loyalists like these. Our best institutions — The Nathan Mayhew Seminars, Felix Neck — grew because the Vineyard encourages faith and belief. Little things have a place alongside the big. Most important, there is time to let the mind range, to dwell on what's important to the soul. If the King Richard effort on the Vineyard never gains another compatriot, there will always be room for the few who already are. Quorums are not required here.

We can't know what compels them. Certainly not zeal; the ad, after all, doesn't take up a page. There will be no public demonstration, no reenactment of the last battle on the football field at the high school. Until they decide to speak, we can only put them down as people who endorse and support the memory of Richard III as any good friend does another in time of trouble. The way neighbors do in small towns like ours where one knows one's neighbors.

Richard's reign from 1483 to 1485 was perhaps the briefest and most turbulent in English history. His biography has been written and rewritten, first by partisans of his usurpers, among them the Tudor court dramatist William Shakespeare, and finally by more objective historians. Even in the 1980s a pendulum swings between accusation and exoneration. Did he kill his nephews, the small princes in the Tower? Or was he a loyal member of the family York, who revered and protected his older brother King Edward IV and later assumed the throne in an effort to save England from civil war and disintegration?

The Martha's Vineyard sanctuary for Richard III has never clamored for attention, and quietly attending to one's own business is another Island trait. The ad is there for anyone to see, once a year, but it does not demand that you call, or write, or clip or buy. It's an idea cast on the waters, unsponsored and unforced, the kind of idea that provokes thought and action on

Martha's Vineyard. Who else has spotted the ad on a Sunday evening and asked how the leering creature Laurence Olivier created on film could possibly have been "betrayed"?

How many have gone on to read a biography, or even reread the play?

Josephine Tey, in the best introduction to Richard III revisionism, creates a hospitalized detective and an American student who use their idle hours to find the truth about Richard and his alleged crimes. Her book has this exchange about the king after the pair solve the archaic mysteries:

"I know one thing he was spared."

"What?"

"The knowledge that his name was to be a hissing and a by-word down the centuries."

On Martha's Vineyard, for one week out of the year, this son of York has his place in the sun.

– August 20, 1985

❧   ❧   ❧

Town of Chilmark Fights to Preserve Fishing Village of Menemsha

By Amy Callahan

MENEMSHA SITS LIKE A BRIGADOON in the up-Island fog, beneath a canopy of rusted ship rigging. It is a washed-up cluster of shacks and docks, strung with buoys and driftwood signs. It looks like it floats in and out with the tide.

Menemsha has a timelessness and a reality that is hard to find in any other village on Martha's Vineyard. But the place is not magic. It's no Brigadoon. What is unusual about Menemsha is not that it has escaped change, but that it has hid it well. The topic is talked about sometimes, but never very loudly.

Up in town hall, selectman Jonathan Mayhew may mention it in passing. He says people don't realize what's happening in Menemsha, that the fishing industry can no longer support the fleet. He wonders how long the big fishing boats, some of them owned by his family, will remain in the harbor.

Pamela Goff, another selectman in town, nods and mentions that she sees the scene around the harbor changing, too, especially at night in summer when the people come to watch the sunset, or listen to the drums, and their cars fill the parking lot.

Now, in September, the pink and white tour buses still lumber down the hill and out to Dutcher Dock. But the tourists who climb out of them will not see boatloads of fluke unloaded in Menemsha. Instead, they'll see some mackerel pulled in on a hook by sport fishermen standing on the dock. Those fish will not be sold at market. They'll be used for bait in the derby.

Not too long ago, things were quite different.

"We had a big fleet of boats fishing out of here," says Everett Poole of Poole's Fish market. "Now, it's a whole different ball game."

As recently as a decade ago, a lot more people were making a living off the fish they hauled from the waters around Martha's Vineyard. Now, only a handful of fishermen — by some estimates fewer than a dozen — make their living by fishing full time out of Menemsha. This is compared to the scores of down-Island commercial fishermen.

With the fluke fishery closed, the codfish all but gone, the swordfish fishery opened for only a few days of the year, it is no wonder why. These days, the big fishing ships sit idle, victims of state regulations and a depleted resource, and the only ships working the water with any regularity are lobster boats and charter fishing boats.

Yet Menemsha still looks very much like a busy fishing port. The boats and barrels along the docks do not reflect the dramatic change that swept in here as inevitably as the tide. And that is because the image of Menemsha is protected. It's on its way to becoming a salty veneer that is less a result of a healthy fishing industry and more a product of purposeful regulation by the town.

"We would like to see it remain the way it is," says Philip Smith, a Chilmark Planning Board member. "I don't think Menemsha will change a lot."

On a drizzling weekday morning, Mr. Smith scans the harbor. He points out how the dock areas are segregated to create space for fishermen in a harbor that otherwise would be very quickly swallowed up by sailboats and yachts. In summer, visiting boats are turned away daily from Menemsha, and even Mr. Smith admits he has had his schooner on a waiting list for a slip since 1968.

"I could see this place getting filled up with yachts," he says, and points out that fishing boats have already been squeezed out in Oak Bluffs and even in Edgartown. "Unfortunately, the character of Menemsha would go with it."

According to the existing rules in Menemsha, the fishing boats have priority. The big commercial boats like the Mayhews' blue-hulled Quitsa Strider II and Unicorn are given space along squid row, on the northeast side of the harbor where Larsen's and Poole's fish markets are located.

Christopher Murphy keeps his boat, Theresa M., back with the rest of the small commercial boats. He basically fishes for whatever is in season and for whatever he can pull aboard the Theresa M. in the Sound or aboard a skiff in the ponds: scallops, scup, quahaugs, oysters.

When he was building his big boat back in the early 1980s, that was not his intention.

"I wanted to go codfishing, but by the time I finished building it, there wasn't any codfish in Vineyard Sound," he says.

Mr. Murphy, who is also on the town planning board, is one of the few who try to make a living fishing out of Menemsha. There's Jimmy Morgan, Greg and Jonathan Mayhew, Dennis

Jason, and the handful of lobstermen. There's Robert Flanders, who still goes out nearly every day, and who, as much as any of the picturesque village scenery, helps maintain the image and the spirit of Menemsha. He is approached by tourists regularly, with questions about fishing or where to get something to eat.

"Menemsha is the picture of the fishing port," Mr. Murphy admits, but adds, "Edgartown is the reality."

But if reality were allowed to grab hold of Menemsha, all the old fishing shacks might turn into summer cabanas and the place could be a hideaway only for the rich. With the town keeping change like that in check, the village has a chance of holding on until the industry regains strength.

"I think the neat thing about Menemsha is the hope for the future," Mr. Murphy says. "The town is committed to keeping a viable fishing port."

– September 28, 1993

🍂 🍂 🍂

Generations of Flynn Family Gather at Pohogonot

By Edith Blake

THIS WEEKEND THE FLYNN FAMILY, all 75 strong, will be gathering out at Pohogonot for their 100th anniversary on the farm.

Yet this is not the story of a family. It is the story of an Island capable of bringing back, year after year, second cousins to romp with first cousins, sons in law to hunt and fish with fathers in law and grandsons. Also to bring new brides and grooms to meet their new relations and become friends.

Many families through the generations tend to grow, as this

one has, but they fragment hither and yon, some members never to be seen again. But the charm of Martha's Vineyard's wildness and remoteness has brought the generations back to grow and play together so that they all know each other.

It all started in 1903 when George Daniel Flynn was in a train accident and his doctor told him he needed a rest from the turmoil of Fall River. The perfect spot seemed to be Crane House on the Love Smith shooting land at Pohogonot.

Much of the land out on the plains was then used for sheep farming with little houses built well behind the dunes to be used as shooting boxes. Mr. Flynn repeated his visits and soon bought land and built other little houses for his family. One burned in 1911 but this did not deter him and in 1920 a long guest house similar to a motel was built, which is still there, and will be much in use this weekend, when most of the family will be staying on the farm.

Mr. Flynn's son, George Jr., loved the land and did much to improve it, buying more and adding other houses for his children, or gazebos and bridges to make it a wonderful and hospitable place. Eventually it became one of the sites on the Island to visit, so it has had many famous visitors, such as Robert Montgomery, James Cagney, Ed Wynn, his son Keenan Wynn, Ralph Bellamy and Ed Vincent, the raconteur of Island history. Senator Butler, builder of the building on the wharf now owned by the Edgartown Reading Room and resident of the Daniel Fisher House, went to Pohogonot many times.

Governor Walsh appeared on the Island, as reported by the Gazette in 1914, and was welcomed with all the fuss the Island could give him. He was entertained at the Home Club and while everyone stayed and sang he was driven out to Pohogonot.

Golf was often played on the expanse of field and lawn and planes were landed on the same fields.

At one point the government placed telegraph poles along the shore, but there were no telephones at the farm until after World War II.

Entertaining at Pohogonot seemed to have been constant, and each year Henry Beetle Hough remembered through his boyhood the planning of long trips by horse and wagon which would take him and his family for a day of play and lemonade. The trips were always reciprocated that same summer with the Flynn family going from Pohogonot to Fish Hook on Indian Hill. Naturally these were events looked forward to all summer, if not all year, and since the roads were dirt and in poor condition, it was a dawn to dusk operation. How the plans were made is a mystery since neither family had a telephone.

Giant Sunday picnics were started in 1940 and went on for 40 years, with friends and family all bringing their own lunches, and something to pass around. It seemed half the Island would be involved.

There will be a clambake tonight, with games of all sorts planned for the weekend when everyone will be divided into two teams, the POHOS and GONOTS. The big traditional Sunday picnic on the beach will probably have some surprises.

Five generations will be on the farm for the weekend. Mrs. George D. Flynn Jr., the former Dorothy Jopp, and called Aunt Dot by all, is the oldest, having been born in 1902; the youngest is Jeffrey Young Flynn Jr., who is four months old.

There were so few girls in the family that the name of Flynn is mixed or welded with Thurlow, Chaffee, Keeler, Fuller, Woodland, MacKenty, Bigelow, Peters, Coward and Lamborn, to name just a few.

When the Island does her job this weekend she will be drawing the families from Maine, Boston, Philadelphia, New Jersey, New Hampshire, Florida, Colorado, California, Connecticut, Maryland and Vermont. They will be coming because the Island is the one place which has enough continuity and has created enough happiness to keep a family this large together through the generations.

– August 20, 1993

Devoted Hands Cleanse Facets
Of Historic Lighthouse Lens

By Elaine Lembo

E LEANOR OLSEN OF EDGARTOWN once let slip just how much she admires lighthouses. In early spring, she demonstrates the depth of her reverence when she wipes and cleans and cuts her fingers on the 1,008 prisms of the Fresnel lens from the old Gay Head Light.

There were no lighthouses where Mrs. Olsen grew up. As a child, she lived on a farm in Kansas, and every Saturday morning her mother took her to the library. She discovered lighthouses there and never abandoned the daydreams they gave her.

"I read all the lighthouse stories I could find. I wanted to go to faraway places," the thin, tall woman explains.

She got to the faraway places. She moved to Boston after college, and after that, she went to New York city. Later she traveled the world with her husband Niels, a commercial sea captain.

She found her lighthouse in Edgartown. This lens first achieved fame at the Paris Exhibition of Industry in 1855, when a gold medal was awarded its creator, Henry Lepaute, and designer Augustin Fresnel. The lens, which was installed in the Gay Head Lighthouse in 1856, was a featured attraction for the thousands of tourists who made the excursion by ox-cart "taxis".

Since 1981 the Olsens have lived in Edgartown. From her bedroom window Mrs. Olsen can see the lens, which is cared for by the Dukes County Historical Society at Cooke and School streets. It was placed there in 1952, when the introduction of the high-intensity electrical beacon rendered the lens unnecessary.

"I'm a self-appointed keeper. I can see whether it's on from my bedroom window. If it's not, I walk over and turn it on," she says.

Gallons of sperm oil in a large lamp once burned to throw a signal to seafarers up to 20 miles away from Gay Head. Now a 135-watt bulb casts its beam through the glass onto the neighborhood of Edgartown. On Sunday evenings, the Fresnel lens revolves.

Mrs. Olsen says she always admired the lens when she took her dog Henry on walks through town. "I was in awe of it," she says.

Four years ago she attended the annual meeting of the Dukes County Historical Society, and heard Arthur Railton, who was president, make a plea for someone to help clean the lighthouse. It hadn't been cleaned for about 20 years, she says.

"My cousin was with me at the meeting. We went home and she said, 'Eleanor, I bet we could clean that lens.' So I volunteered. My cousin went home and left me; Arthur Railton supplied me with a ladder and encouragement," she says.

That was four years ago. For Mrs. Olsen the spring cleaning of the lens has become a ritual.

"It gets easier every time," she says.

Approaching the lens in its truncated lighthouse on the historical society lawn, much less cleaning it, is not easy. Narrow, thin, curving stairs lead up to the area. The lens, which is supported at the base, is also partially carried by iron rods bolted to the ceiling of the small red brick building.

Mrs. Olsen and Henry walk over to the lighthouse before 7 a.m. The cleaning must be done in the early spring because of the heat inside the lens, which can quickly climb to an intolerable 99 degrees before 8 a.m. Alone, it takes Mrs. Olsen about two weeks of early mornings to complete the job.

Mrs. Olsen describes her work:

"I go through bottles of Windex and at least one roll of paper towels. One time I had the paper towels on the lamp. All at once I smelled smoke. A little light beam, no bigger than a pinpoint, had burned a hole down to the tube. It was ready to burst into flames. The beams can focus and get on the roof, so they installed curtains in the windows.

"All these edges have got to be cleaned. I can never do it without getting any cuts. It is dizzying work, so we do it one section at a time. When the Windex drips, you can't tell which lens it has dropped on. The most fragile parts are the red reflector panels," she continues.

The prisms are contained in 16 panels. Six red glass reflector panels are mounted over them. They were added after 1873, so that each horizontal flash from Gay Head had a sequence of three white flashes followed by one red flash, to distinguish it from the white flash of other lighthouses.

She holds in her outstretched hand a tiny fragment of red glass that has fallen from a panel. "I grieve about anything like that. I'll ask the museum director to see if any of them can be put back," she says.

"I always look at it and admire it and think it's my lighthouse. There is a couple who comes here to take care of the turning mechanism. There is a man who comes to polish the brass. Arthur Railton changes the light bulbs. But I always think of it as my lighthouse."

– May 23, 1986

❧   ❧   ❧

Whither Shall I Wander?

AFTER 31 YEARS ON THE VINEYARD, Oak Bluffs selectman Linda Marinelli will make her first visit ever to neighboring Nantucket in December. More surprisingly, Mrs. Marinelli lived on the Island for 28 years before she made the 20-mile journey up-Island to see the Gay Head Cliffs.

– November 20, 1987

Annual Reports of Vineyard Towns Offer Snapshots of Community

By Amy Callahan

SOME PEOPLE DESCRIBE OUR ISLAND as chic and fancy, or think of it as a seaside playground for the rich and famous. And it may be just that at various times, especially during the summer season when there are cocktail parties and so forth. But the heart of the Vineyard is so much more than that. And so unlike that.

What this place all comes down to, really, is six little towns. Budgets, ballots, boards of selectmen. And the key to finding out what's really going on around here emerges every spring in the pages of the annual town reports.

They are, in all their deceiving blandness, the true insider's guide to Martha's Vineyard.

How else could you find out how many fence viewers are in Chilmark? (Three.) Or how many permits were issued by West Tisbury's milk inspector? (Four.)

When it's all pared down, typed up and bound together in a booklet, life here seems as universal as anywhere. Our dogs get loose. Our houses catch on fire. People go to the library and check out books. Taxes are collected. Babies are born. Couples get married. Old folks die.

But, as the town reports on Martha's Vineyard reveal, there is ever so much more to it.

Unlike many communities, the towns on the Vineyard keep track of significant things, such as how many deer-car collisions there are, and how many moped accidents happen. And the towns are small enough here so that we can be specific about it. For example, of the scores of alarms sounded in West Tisbury, you can read in the annual report that three were for house fires, three were for "smoke in house" and one was for "man in tree."

Last year in Gay Head, police dealt with 42 alarms, two annoying phone calls, six arrests, and "one dog bite against assisting officer."

The animal control officer in Tisbury responded to "many calls on a wandering flock of turkeys," a turtle slowing traffic on State Road, 12 loose Hereford cattle, a muskrat in a windowsill, a mallard with a broken bill, a sea gull caught in a dumpster, a sparrow inside Rainy Day, a cat asleep in a bank, a skunk entangled in a volleyball net, and two loose oxen.

In 1992, there were 38 babies born to Oak Bluffs parents, 21 to Edgartown parents, 18 to West Tisbury parents, four to Chilmark parents, and one baby girl, Lydia Alison Fischer, was born to parents in Gay Head. For some unexplained reason, the Tisbury town report does not include the 1992 births. But that's okay, because the Oak Bluffs report doesn't have a table of contents. And Gay Head listed Valorie Colebrook, while Tisbury calls her Valorie Goldenbrook. But we all know who they're talking about anyway.

Often, the annual town reports on the Vineyard are personalized by the town officials who put them together. John Alley, for example, turns the West Tisbury town report into something of a historic scrapbook. There are old advertisements for such things as carriage painting and confectionaries throughout. At the bottom of page 26, just below the report of the registrars of deeds, there is an ad from 1922: "Custom Hatching and Day-Old Chicks For Sale. Edward Lee Luce. Phone 35-14."

The West Tisbury annual report also features a number of black and white photos, from present day (John Alley and Nelia Decker doing what looks like the jitterbug at the centennial ball) and from days gone by (Antone Alley and Johnson Whiting shearing sheep in 1925).

In the Chilmark report there is a bit more humor than in those from the other towns. Even in the cemetery report.

Basil Welch, cemetery superintendent, writes: "To the citizens of Chilmark: Once again, it's time for the annual report of the cemetery department. Things are quiet at Abel's Hill. The grass, trees and bushes continue to grow and to get cut back. New lots are being measured and bounded and also occupied. Visitors are numerous. Some to look at the old stones, some to visit family or friends, and many to visit John and leave their beer cans with him. That's about all I can say except to 'come on down.' To visit, that is."

The planning board members in Chilmark also used some sarcastic humor to get their point across:

"Boston, as you probably have heard, is in the process of constructing a nine-mile pipe out into Cape Cod Bay for the purpose of spreading their sewage around New England. We all appreciate their attitude toward sharing, but feel that they are being a little too generous."

And the Chilmark Fire Department included this item in its list of fire calls in 1992: "one nighttime pyrotechnic demonstration (for grandchildren)."

In the Edgartown report, between the listings of "surveyors of lumber" and "town accountant," appeared a little-known office: "Measurers of Wood and Bark and Weighers of Coal." It is generally agreed that this is not a position of great consequence to the town, yet the dutiful selectmen continue to appoint people to it. Martha Look was nominated earlier this year while she was on vacation in Florida. At the time, this was lauded as a smart move by selectmen, who avoided any protests from the nominee.

Some town reports are like custom-made almanacs. Edgartown and Tisbury, for example, print census information and historic tidbits on the inside cover. Tisbury has 2,795 residents according to the 1992 census. Edgartown has 3,062 according to the 1990 census. Edgartown, which includes Chappaquiddick, covers 21 square miles; Tisbury covers 7.5 square miles. The tax rate in Tisbury is $14, while it's under $7 in Edgartown.

In 1992, Edgartown was the site of 61 marriages, with couples coming from New York, Denver, Taiwan and Paris. Gregory Drake and Eve Domont even came all the way from West Tisbury to tie the knot.

The annual town report is also a place to memorialize the former community servants who passed on. Gay Head memorialized every resident who died in 1992. There were six: Wenonah Silva, James Gentry, Geraldine Arens, Albert Hydeman, Lucille Vanderhoop and Rose Hawley. Oak Bluffs had a dedication page in addition to its memorial page. The 1992 Oak Bluffs annual report was dedicated to Anna L. Oliver Andrews, who served the town for 38 years.

Town reports are humble publications. Their no-gloss packaging offers nary a clue to the bounty of interesting stories that lies inside. They are nothing like the supermarket checkout line tabloids. They do not scream at you about all their fascinating facts and figures. A town report won't just appear in front of your nose, on your doorstep, or in your mailbox. You usually have to be in town hall for one reason or another — buying a dump sticker or applying for a building permit or something. They'll be stacked usually in a cardboard box under a table. Or maybe someone actually has put them out on the table. Often the cover is a neutral color, with black lettering saying "Annual Town Report," with some illustration or photo, and then the town seal stuck somewhere.

Once you have picked up your town report, you have to spend some time with it, get to know it. You have to sit down with it, work the stiff binding, read the table of contents.

Then, tucked in amongst the school budget and personnel board's report, you can find the dirt. Such as the suspicious item in the Gay Head expense budget: "Chilmark Chocolates, $42.50."

Or this interesting purchase by the Chilmark Police Department: $3.77 at Alley's General Store. Was it a new roll of Scotch tape, a pack of batteries, a squirt gun?

For the nosiest among us, the town reports also tell you how much everybody makes for a living. And if you compare a few, it is interesting to see that the town clerk in Oak Bluffs is paid almost exactly $30,000 more a year than the town clerk in West Tisbury.

Or, if you spend some time reading the town report, you may find that there isn't so much going on here after all.

"There's not much to report about from this department," writes the Gay Head highway surveyor. "The usual mowing and trimming of brush was carried out and potholes patched here and there. A little more erosion took place along Lobsterville Beach but not as severe as the previous year. We plan to resurface the rest of Lighthouse Road this spring. There are some really bad spots on this road."

Not much else to say. End of report.

— June 11, 1993